Language, Discourse, Society

Series Editors: **Stephen Heath**, **Colin MacCabe** and **Denise Riley**

Selected published titles:

Rob White
FREUD'S MEMORY
Psychoanalysis, Mourning and the Foreign Body

Teresa de Lauretis
FREUD'S DRIVE
Psychoanalysis, Literature and Film

Mark Nash
SCREEN THEORY CULTURE

Richard Robinson
NARRATIVES OF THE EUROPEAN BORDER
A History of Nowhere

Lyndsey Stonebridge
THE WRITING OF ANXIETY
Imaging Wartime in Mid-Century British Culture

Ashley Tauchert
ROMANCING JANE AUSTEN
Narrative, Realism and the Possibility of a Happy Ending

Reena Dube
SATYAJIT RAY'S *THE CHESS PLAYERS* AND POSTCOLONIAL THEORY
Culture, Labour and the Value of Alterity

John Anthony Tercier
THE CONTEMPORARY DEATHBED
The Ultimate Rush

Erica Sheen and Lorna Hutson
LITERATURE, POLITICS AND LAW IN RENAISSANCE ENGLAND

Jean-Jacques Lecercle and Denise Riley
THE FORCE OF LANGUAGE

Geoff Gilbert
BEFORE MODERNISM WAS
Modern History and the Constituency of Writing

Stephen Heath, Colin MacCabe and Denise Riley (*editors*)
THE LANGUAGE, DISCOURSE, SOCIETY READER

Michael O'Pray
FILM, FORM AND PHANTASY
Adrian Stokes and Film Aesthetics

James A. Snead, edited by Kara Keeling, Colin MacCabe and Cornel West
RACIST TRACES AND OTHER WRITINGS
European Pedigrees/African Contagions

Patrizia Lombardo
CITIES, WORDS AND IMAGES

Colin MacCabe
JAMES JOYCE AND THE REVOLUTION OF THE WORD
Second edition

Moustapha Safouan
SPEECH OR DEATH?
Language as Social Order: a Psychoanalytic Study

Jean-Jacques Lecercle
DELEUZE AND LANGUAGE

Piers Gray, edited by Colin MacCabe and Victoria Rothschild
STALIN ON LINGUISTICS AND OTHER ESSAYS

Geoffrey Ward
STATUTES OF LIBERTY
The New York School of Poets

Moustapha Safouan
JACQUES LACAN AND THE QUESTION OF PSYCHOANALYTIC TRAINING
(*Translated and introduced by Jacqueline Rose*)

Stanley Shostak
THE DEATH OF LIFE
The Legacy of Molecular Biology

Elizabeth Cowie
REPRESENTING THE WOMAN
Cinema and Psychoanalysis

Raymond Tallis
NOT SAUSSURE
A Critique of Post-Saussurean Literary Theory

Laura Mulvey
VISUAL AND OTHER PLEASURES

Ian Hunter
CULTURE AND GOVERNMENT
The Emergence of Literary Education

Language, Discourse, Society
Series Standing Order ISBN 0–333–71482–2
(*outside North America only*)

You can receive future titles in this series as they are published by placing a standing order. Please contact your bookseller or, in case of difficulty, write to us at the address below with your name and address, the title of the series and the ISBN quoted above.

Customer Services Department, Macmillan Distribution Ltd, Houndmills, Basingstoke, Hampshire RG21 6XS, England

---

Freud's Memory

Psychoanalysis, Mourning and the Foreign Body

Rob White

palgrave
macmillan

First published 2008 by
PALGRAVE MACMILLAN

Palgrave Macmillan in the UK is an imprint of Macmillan Publishers Limited, registered in England, company number 785998, of Houndmills, Basingstoke, Hampshire RG21 6XS.

Palgrave Macmillan in the US is a division of St Martin's Press LLC, 175 Fifth Avenue, New York, NY 10010.

Palgrave Macmillan is the global academic imprint of the above companies and has companies and representatives throughout the world.

Palgrave® and Macmillan® are registered trademarks in the United States, the United Kingdom, Europe and other countries.

ISBN-13: 978–0–230–00264–7 hardback
ISBN-10: 0–230–00264–1 hardback

This book is printed on paper suitable for recycling and made from fully managed and sustained forest sources. Logging, pulping and manufacturing processes are expected to conform to the environmental regulations of the country of origin.

A catalogue record for this book is available from the British Library.

A catalog record for this book is available from the Library of Congress.

10 9 8 7 6 5 4 3 2 1
17 16 15 14 13 12 11 10 09 08

Printed and bound in Great Britain by
CPI Antony Rowe, Chippenham and Eastbourne

Contents

Acknowledgements

I am grateful to Maud Ellmann, Andy Gallacher, Jeanne Gamble, Pelagia Goulimari, Gerard Greenaway, Franck Guyon, Stephen Heath, Vidhya Jayaprakash and her team in Newgen Imaging Systems Pvt Ltd., Jill Lake, Colin MacCabe, Forbes Morlock, Denise Riley, Christabel Scaife, Roy Sellars, Robert Smith, Caroline Jane Williams, Sarah Wood.

In memory of Malcolm Bowie (1943–2007).

Introduction: the Psychoanalytic Labyrinth

Intervening in contemporary debates about psychoanalysis, this book emerges from the post-structuralist account of Freud, especially as it was undertaken by Jacques Derrida – but not without some scepticism towards that account, especially its celebration of apparent failures of meaning that are, rather paradoxically, presented as a sort of hedonistic melancholy. Having particular value as a practice of close reading (though one which tends to be amplified philosophically), the post-structuralist account has shown above all how internally complex Freud's writings are. To quote Leo Bersani: 'philosophers, psychoanalysts, and literary critics have convincingly made it seem very naive to take what might be termed the official Freud literally.'[1] Rather than being a quasi-scientific explanation of general psychological functioning – or at least in addition to that – it becomes possible to redescribe Freud's work as an especially intricate and labyrinthine series of writings whose patterns of rhetoric and argument put into question their own concepts and conclusions. As Tom Conley puts it, Freud's writing 'works through a gnostic rationale by the myriad ways that it rides along the paradoxes its expression puts forward as emblems, conundrums, or other shapes of wit.'[2] The readings of Freud in this book constitute a wide-ranging attempt to explore some of these emblems and conundrums.

My focus therefore is Freud's language, which I approach using literary-critical methods. What is the relationship between my own critical language and Freud's own? The post-structuralist approach to Freud has been assiduous in posing versions of this question, as with a recent formulation by Samuel Weber:

> [C]an psychoanalytic thinking itself escape the effects of what it endeavors to think? Can the distortions of unconscious processes be

> simply recognized, theoretically, as an object, or must they not leave their imprint on the process of theoretical objectification itself? Must not psychoanalytical thinking itself partake of – repeat – the dislocations it seeks to describe?[3]

Despite Freud's claims to classify psychological processes and components, the manner of his doing so always seems to yield complexity rather than unitary explanation. Weber suggests that such self-complication is inescapable: psychoanalytic theorizing cannot help but be tangled up in the processes it ventures to define. There is therefore repetition; objects do not remain static – instead they cease to be knowable as stable entities; dislocations occur; 'theoretical objectification' begins to seem like an impossibility because theory cannot achieve proper disentanglement. And so it begins to be possible to imagine an endlessly self-implying process whereby theory confounds itself and so fails ever to exit the maze of its peregrinations.

Close to Freud

In one of his later interpretations of Freud, to be found in the book *Archive Fever,* Derrida poses his own set of questions:

> Must one apply to what will have been predefined as the Freudian or psychoanalytic archive in general schemas of reading, of interpretation, of classification which have been received and reflected out of this corpus whose unity is thus presupposed? Or rather, has one on the contrary the right to treat the said psychoanalytico-Freudian archive according to a logic or a hermeneutic independent of Freudian psychoanalysis, indeed anterior even to the very name of Freud, while presupposing in another manner the closure and the identity of this corpus?[4]

These remarks are in certain respects typical of the deconstructionist approach. One may note the use of complicated tenses ('will have been predefined') which sometimes take on a quasi-prophetic air, Derrida a reader of auguries; the insistent self-qualifications ('a logic or a hermeneutic') that seem to be designed to pre-empt through the listing of alternatives any possible suggestion of terminological imprecision; the invocation of portentous ethical considerations ('the right to treat') framing the work of interpretation. This is, in its way, powerful writing and the business of its rhetoric is to refute conventional interpretative claims of dispassionate scrutiny whose viewpoint is extraneous to what is being studied. Post-structuralism has often forcefully and successfully critiqued such claims: the interpreter, it is argued, is always already implicated in the material being interpreted. One cannot stand quizzically back, be separate and then look squarely at, for example, a writer's work as if it were some classifiable, delimited object. Deconstruction often therefore arrives at some version or other of an idea of interpretative inescapability and then *affirms* the idea as the necessarily inconclusive end-point of its critique, as if nothing were so good as to be caught in a hall of mirrors.

Derrida has taken this argument beyond argument into quasi-literary experiments that enact a drama – it is something more emotionally serious than a game – of inextricability based on what I would call conceits of intimacy. In one text this goes as far as prosopopeia, Derrida speaking not on behalf of Freud but (in the terms of the rhetorical conceit) as if he were Freud:[5]

> You have always taken me, like Fliess, for a 'mind reader'. Contempt. You are waiting holding your breath. You are waiting on the telephone, I imagine you and speak to you on the telephone, or the teleprinter seeing that I've prepared a lecture which I will never give.... Well, you are wrong, for once, you will discover nothing from me as regards the 'enigma of telepathy'. In particular, I will preserve this at all costs, you will not be able to know 'whether or not I believe in the existence of a telepathy.' This opening could still allow one to think that I know, myself, whether or not I believe, and that, for one reason or another, I am anxious to keep it secret, in particular to produce such and such a transferential effect (not necessarily on you or on you, but on this public within myself which does not let go of me)....I pretend...to admit that I do not myself know. I know nothing about it. I apologize: if I have given the impression of having secretly 'taken sides' with the reality of telepathy in the occult sense.[6]

There is a certain winning jokiness in this essay, which is to some extent a skit on the idea of telepathy (see also Chapter 5) and a writing-exercise that plays out rather than simply asserting the proposition that interpretation is necessarily implicated in its object. In Derrida's later work, the playfulness is increasingly replaced by tones of grave seriousness: the idea of interimplication is reinforced to the extent of becoming the basis of an ethical theory of indissoluble interpersonal bonds (see

Chapter 3). Some of that seriousness, a sense of pathos, is evident here: 'I will preserve at all costs... I am anxious to keep it secret.' Derrida adopts the conceit of intimacy to such an extent as to use the first person, but this is consistent with the emphasis on inescapability.

In the deconstructionist account, one cannot penetrate the labyrinth of Freud's writing and then simply pass through it. The process is thus like getting caught in a trap. But it may also start to seem, as in Derrida's telepathy-simulation exercise, rather like taking a part in a melodrama. Emotional considerations come into play. An argument about epistemology develops a psychological dimension: it becomes *personal*. It is as if the questioning of concepts were a pretext not simply for biographical speculation but for some more transcendent communion between persons, as if theory were transforming into prayer. I find it odd, to say the least, that those who are concerned with psychoanalytic theory should think it appropriate, desirable or even feasible to imagine some intimate affinity with Freud; it seems to me that it is overfamiliar. Arguably such overfamiliarity may be justified when it is part of a writing-experiment, yet the trait is not confined to Derrida. Another conceit of intimacy is to be found in a book on Freud by an otherwise more traditional cultural historian, Yosef Hayim Yerushalmi, in which he uses the device not of prosopopeia but of apostrophe, in the form of a 'Monologue with Freud':

> Professor Freud, at this point I find it futile to ask whether, genetically or structurally, psychoanalysis is really a Jewish science; that we shall know, if it is at all knowable, only when much future work has been done. Much will depend, of course, on how the very terms *Jewish* and *science* are to be defined. Right now, leaving the semantic and epistemological questions aside, I want only to know whether you ultimately came to believe it to be so.
>
> In fact, I will limit myself even further and be content if you answer only one question. When your daughter conveyed those words to the congress in Jerusalem, *was she speaking in your name*?
>
> Please tell me, Professor. I promise I won't reveal your answer to anyone.[7]

In this curious passage, the author seems to be asserting a kinship with Freud or privileged access to his ideas. It is moreover an assertion that Derrida discusses in *Archive Fever* and the claim of intimacy is compounded by further remarks he makes in the context of Freud's book on Wilhelm Jensen's novel, *Gradiva*. Derrida refers to a passage in that book (a passage I will quote fully in Chapter 1) in which Freud recalls something that once happened to him, having initially suggested that what is described in fact happened to someone else. Derrida glosses his paraphrase of Freud's remarks in this way:

> Here is the *coup de théâtre,* the dramatic twist. Freud pretended to speak of someone else, of a colleague. (If I were to be immodest to such a point, doubly immodest, I would say that he did what I am doing in speaking of a colleague, Yerushalmi, while I am speaking of myself).[8]

The claims to intimacy here become serial and replicative. Derrida claims to draw together himself, Yerushalmi and Freud into a confraternity. Again individual personalities have come to the forefront in these imaginary conjunctions; again argument has given way to a psychodrama.

A remark from a practising analyst about the nature of professional psychoanalytic debate exemplifies the problem of overfamiliarity in another way. Patrick Mahony writes:

> [R]eading Freud as opposed to reading other colleagues is an especially complicated matter, given the transferences we may have to him, to the human subjects of his writings, to his fictively created interlocutors, and to the psychoanalytic institution. Time willing, diverse readings of Freud will be classified by century and nation, much as has happened with the Bible and Shakespeare (the Spanish Shakespeare, eighteenth-century Shakespeare, and so on). Perhaps the embittered rivalry seen between the interpretations of the 'French Freud' and the 'Anglo-American Freud' will serve for future reflection on the possible psychopathologies of reading Freud in order to distinguish among hysterical, obsessional, narcissistic, fetishistic, and other kinds of readings. Such possibilities notwithstanding, we should conceive of a reading alliance according to which we as agents participate and observe ourselves in our reading of Freud.[9]

Freud is one colleague among many. Though reading Freud is 'especially complicated', according to Mahony, it is not different in kind from other professional relationships; the protocols of professional debate apply, though added care is needed. Once it had become a profession worthy of the designation, Freud occasionally made comments about professional psychoanalysts, as in 'Analysis Terminable and Interminable' (1937, an essay I will discuss in greater detail in Chapter 5): 'we often hear [analysts] say, when they are deploring or excusing the recognized imperfections of some fellow-mortal: "His analysis was not finished" or "he was never analysed to the end"' (**23: 219**).[10] Being a lay commentator, I will avoid discussion of psychotherapy as a practice and a branch of medicine; I am interested in Freud's writing. But it is appropriate to note here the existence of significant and often credible accounts of a disreputable professional culture pertaining to psychoanalysis.[11] Freud's remark conjures up for a moment a rather poisonous, bickering atmosphere, with analysts gossiping about each other's shortcomings. No doubt in such an atmosphere, psychoanalytic labels would be flung about in the manner of Mahony's inventory of pathological interpretations: 'hysterical', 'narcissistic' and so forth. Mahony's project of classification looks to me rather like a scheme for the codification of insults. Presented in the plain language of peer-to-peer professionalism rather than the differing but equally quasi-literary styles of Derrida or Yerushalmi, the personalizing approach seems to me no less problematic.[12]

Mahony claims that psychoanalytic concepts can categorize and explain any difficulties that might arise in the scrutinization of Freud's insights. Mahony's weird idea of a taxonomy of 'psychopathologies of reading Freud' is both indicative of complete assurance in psychoanalytic explanations and a self-valorizing account of professional competence: the psychoanalyst can stand apart, self-supervisorily, even in the act of participating in a 'reading alliance'. For Mahony, it seems, psychoanalysis is a paradigm and a set of diagnostic categories that may be applied functionally; their application, however, needs to be understood psychoanalytically – so that any 'psychopathological' elements or trends in it may be recognized in psychoanalytic terms. Mahony's idea of 'reading alliance' as a kind of self-observed participation claims that there can always be an external vantage point. But in another sense there is no such position: the vantage point is still psychoanalytic. Mahony envisages the psychoanalysis of psychoanalyses of psychoanalysis.

On the outside

I approach Freud in a fundamentally different way, resisting wherever possible implication in psychoanalysis. This may be my own conceit – one of distance rather than intimacy – but it seems to me to be necessary to draw attention to it, especially in respect to the terminological decision that is a premise of this book. I have avoided all psychoanalytic terms (including common words such as 'unconscious', 'repression', 'symptom', 'fantasy', 'ego') except, with great care, when I am paraphrasing particular formulations by Freud.

I have entirely avoided one term in particular, 'trauma.' Given what I have to say about transgression, mourning and even anguish and brutalization, this decision may seem perverse and it is therefore worth offering some brief explanation, showing in so doing some examples of my avoidance of psychoanalytic terms. As is well known, the psychoanalytic theory of trauma is complex. 'Trauma' may refer either to an event (and especially sexual abuse) or to something imagined or wished-for. The traumatic incident, whether real or not, has this particular specific elusiveness in psychoanalysis: it causes psychological damage only after a while. According to psychoanalytic theory, the mind cannot originally cope with the incident – it is too much shocked by it – and so it sets it to one side, hides it, denies it or in some other way keeps it at bay. But it may return – in a powerfully damaging but necessarily distorted, partly unintelligible guise, prompting illness and distress. Psychoanalysis aims, through therapy as well as theory, to undisguise the incident as best it can, which is never so well since it is always a matter of inference. The complexity at stake is therefore considerable: traumas, according to psychoanalytic theory, are radically elusive by virtue of both their variable reality-status and the malformations ensuing in the course of delay. The instigating incident becomes meaningful only in its eventual disguised or substituted form; it is hard therefore to speak of a trauma even as an incident (let alone an event). Its belated shapeshifting involves an erasure of its notional existence as a distinct intelligible entity. 'Trauma' in psychoanalytic theory is both labyrinth and minotaur, a concept once more involving interimplication.[13] In a psychoanalytic context, 'trauma' is moreover almost always used metaphorically, the literal and original meaning having to do with wounding, with injury done to the body. The usage in Freud's writing begs especially vexed questions about ideas of harm, given that much of his work was directed at proposing psychological theories of conditions that had been explained in physiological terms; I shall have plenty to say about these questions and to use 'trauma' (as opposed, at least in some instances, to 'pain' – see especially Chapter 4) in my own commentary would beg the very question about the status of figurative language (concerning especially metaphors of wounding) that I am seeking to address.

That argument involves the contention that Freud is often deceptively confident about his explanatory achievements: he declares that he has managed to understand something but when one stops to consider the terms of this declaration, they tell another story, a sadder and more troubled story. (That is not to say that Freud is dissembling or duplicitous. I am not seeking to add to the voluminous Freud-as-fraud literature. I refer rather, as I explain in Chapter 1, to the idea that Freud's figurative language has 'countersense': concepts are, as I put it, 'smuggled' like contraband into psychoanalysis – contrapuntal concepts, which are to do with unintelligibility rather than effective explanation.)

Methodologically, therefore, I seek to interpret Freud without the help of specifically psychoanalytic terminology. In so doing I claim, for the sake of argument, a position outside psychoanalysis.

1
Figures of Freudian Theory

How significant are apparently incidental or subsidiary features of Freud's writing to his larger theoretical enterprise? How seriously should one take asides, disclaimers, interruptions, digressions, counterintuitive points of textual organization or essayistic structure and, in particular, metaphors and other devices – what, in rhetoric and literary criticism, are called figures or tropes, turns of phrase and thought that somehow shift the meaning of words or ideas? Is it important, for instance, that Freud's *psycho*analysis is often preoccupied by thoughts of *physical* injury, or that its rational, scientific approach permits the discussion of ghosts and other apparently preternatural phenomena?

Let me take a small local example. In *The Interpretation of Dreams* (1900), Freud remarks: 'Children know nothing of the horrors of corruption, of freezing in the ice-cold grave, of the terrors of eternal nothingness – ideas which grown-up people find it so hard to tolerate, as is proved by all the myths of a future life' (**4: 254**, 4: 354). This statement, with its emphasis on childish ignorance framed in terms of an implicit ethics of reality-directed rationality, is conventional in a psychoanalytic context, and yet we may notice its unexpected (though perhaps sophomoric) intensity, its quasi-poetic interest in imagining a cold, lonely, terrible death, or even, given the concern for the sensation of freezing, in being buried alive.

This melancholy flourish reminds me of Lionel Trilling's comment that Freud's work exhibits a 'quality of grim poetry'.[1] There is in the passage a broad negativity. Horror, fear, the agony of freezing – these concerns seem palpable. If they are also to be found elsewhere in Freud's work, then this aside may be read as more widely significant than its local context would initially allow. I am interested precisely in problems of negativity and pain in Freud's work. I believe these problems are fundamental and I want to demonstrate through a reading of Freud's texts in what ways this is so. My contention is that scattered but recurrent figures in his work have more than incidental or illustrative significance for psychoanalytic theory: they amount to a kind of dispersed argument which it is possible to reassemble. I want to undertake some of that reassembling in this book and in this first chapter I will set out both my method and some of the themes and questions that will emerge in the chapters that follow.

Theory's sense of itself

The turn of phrase or argument at stake is often of a conspicuously self-referential kind: Freud changes his subject in order to say something about himself, his method, an incident in his life or in the history to that point of psychoanalysis. A good example of this tendency, and one which resonates with the remarks quoted a moment ago, is to be found in *Delusions and Dreams in Jensen's* Gradiva (1907 [1906]):

> It must be remembered ... that the belief in spirits and ghosts and the return of the dead [*Geister und Gespenster und wiederkehrende Seelen*], which finds so much support in the religions to which we have all been attached, at least in our childhood, is far from having disappeared among educated people, and that many who are sensible in other respects find it possible to combine spiritualism with reason. A man who has grown rational and sceptical, even, may be ashamed to discover how easily he may for a moment return to a belief in spirits under the combined impact of strong emotion and perplexity. I know of a doctor who had once lost one of his woman patients suffering from Graves' disease, and who could not get rid of a faint suspicion that he might have contributed to the unhappy outcome by a thoughtless prescription. One day, several years later, a girl entered his consulting-room, who, in spite of all his efforts, he could not help recognizing as the dead one. He could frame only a single thought: 'So after all it's true that the dead can come back to life.' His dread did not give way to shame till the girl introduced herself as the sister of the one who had died of the same disease as she was suffering from. The victims of Graves' disease, as has often been observed, have a marked facial resemblance to one another; and in this case this typical likeness was reinforced by a family one. The doctor to whom this occurred was, however, none other than myself[.] (**9: 71–2**, 14: 95, *7: 98–9*)

Freud begins in a way that is familiar to any reader of psychoanalysis, anecdotally – as he frequently does when he illustrates a point with reference to a patient he has treated or when he makes an observation about a member of his family. Just as is often the case in those kinds of asides and exemplifications, Freud is concerned with a disordered thought process – a delusion, say, that defaces reality so that it looks more like it is wished it could look. Insofar as this passage is conventional, one expects the disordered thought process to be interpreted by Freud so that its desiring misrepresentation is exposed for what it is, restoring reason's authority over delirious imagining.

Freud insistently denounces and calls for the most widespread possible renunciation of any such superstition – whether it takes the form of prayer or ritual or any other belief that refuses to accept that death is, as Freud puts it in *The Interpretation of Dreams*, 'eternal nothingness' and there is no return from it. So although Freud does the job of rebutting an occult explanation by explaining that the patient was the sister of the sufferer from Graves' disease, he has seemed strangely taken with the thought of a *revenant* ghost. And the expected rebuttal in terms of psychoanalytic theory is replaced here with the dramatic twist of self-disclosure. Freud gives us more of himself (including his readiness to believe in ghosts) than we expect and more than is needed for the purposes of making the point. There is an element of orchestrated surprise in the passage which foregrounds the potential of Freud's writing at any point to take an autobiographical turn, but we may sense also that this is not just game-playing. The doctor's dread is related to his sense of guilt, to his 'faint suspicion that he might have contributed to the unhappy outcome by a thoughtless prescription'. That the problem of malpractice or negligence – and the problem will be evident again in Chapter 5 – is the focus of what we take to be a needless worry (though there is nothing here to say that there was no medical error) suggests that however much there is here a joke-like structure with an unforeseen punchline, there is also something more pressing, as if the joke were also serving the purpose of self-exonerating confession.

Confession, however, is not the kind of self-awareness that particularly interests me. I am interested rather in what Malcolm Bowie has called 'Freud's dreams of knowledge' and their 'multifarious secret life'[2] – in the turns his theorizing takes not to get away from itself but to get, whether advertently or not, another view or a sense of itself. Throughout this book, I will be interested to notice moments in Freud's work when he reflects on his own methods, describes his own processes of deduction and interpretation, or summarizes his insights. Quite often, these moments are rather abstract; or, when they are not so abstract (as with the self-disclosure quoted a moment ago), I will tend to treat them in terms of their relevance to abstract problems of theoretical organization or methodology. In so doing, I want both to draw attention to a feature of Freud's writing and also seek to describe and interpret it in terms that are only minimally psychological. One needs an idea of self-awareness and self-reflexivity in order to deal with this aspect of Freud's writing, but my premise is that there is benefit in elaborating this as much as possible in non-psychological terms, even if that means one must make do with such ideas as Freud's work's 'sense of itself' as much as Freud's 'dreams of knowledge'.

I will use two terms, 'figure of theory' and 'countersense', in this book in trying to explore this form of reflexivity. They need some introduction, which can usefully be made with reference to Bowie's reading. He focuses on a range of rhetorical devices with which Freud seeks both to expound and to defend his interpretative method – especially Freud's comparison of himself and his works with those of military conquerors, archaeologists and geologists. In so doing, Bowie discusses the 'wishful substratum' of psychoanalysis,[3] including the mode of theorizing which is ambitious (to the extent of being presented by Freud as heroic) and whose motivation may be said to be desirous rather than dispassionate – desiring ordered and expansive knowledge not only of psychological phenomena but also their near and distant causes. Bowie writes:

> The desire-laden phantasies that I have been discussing are the fertile psychical soil from which Freud's working fictions and conceptual models sprang. What sort of inferential procedure brings them forth, however? We might imagine an orderly process, occurring in the mind of a representative scientist, in the course of which, by successive acts of filtration and refinement, phantasies yielded models, models theories and theories, if suitably tested Truth; by patient coaxing, Dionysus would become Apollo. But Freud does not observe any such sequence. His epistemological phantasies are insistent and reiterative. They interrupt and deflect the construction of theories. They compromise the 'scientific outlook' and offer divergent paths for the pursuit of truth. The extraordinary intellectual authority that Freud's work still possesses come in part, of course, from his willingness to divulge and discuss the unruly dreams of knowledge among which his formal contributions to knowledge were born. But that authority comes too from his inadvertences, from the multifarious secret life that science leads within his texts.

> As a theorist Freud was, in his own terms, both an adhesive and a mobile libidinal type.... In Freud's writing a legitimate despair makes itself felt: what if theories of mind were indefinitely mutable, and what if such credibility as any one of them might command were based upon the simple reiteration of the theorist's verbal formulae? What sort of claim to be science could theories make if they were creatures merely of a self-corroborating text? And the palliative to this despair – the exit from 'theory' and 'text' alike – was forcibly imagined by Freud as antiquity, bedrock, the first cause.[4]

Bowie compellingly describes the drama of interpretative self-awareness, self-justification and self-satisfaction that is evident in so many of Freud's texts. Freud often gives a commentary on his work of explanation, a commentary which is also often an historical polemic concerned to defend the legitimacy and value of psychoanalysis as a therapy and a form of scientific knowledge. Bowie specifies some of the factors which make Freud's commentary such a complex phenomenon – its iterativeness, its tendency to 'interrupt and deflect' the purposeful momentum of an argument. Bowie finds these factors to be evidence of desire – alternatively 'adhesive' and 'mobile' – and also of despair, the despair of expending great interpretative energy only to end up with a 'self-corroborating text' without strong foundations.

Desire in the sense of some kind of concupiscent discursive mobility or libidinal *bricolage* is not something I will emphasize in my account of Freud. But I will note both loss and longing, less happy correlatives of desire. In this regard, I will say a great deal about Freud's interest in 'antiquity, bedrock, the first cause' and what kind of interpretative interest it is – especially its relation to a transgressive crisis of identity and understanding. This crisis has an affinity with despair and anguish and I will on various occasions deal with these states – especially as, or so I argue, elements of a theorizing that gets itself into trouble.

Initially, I want to zero in on some recurrent themes. Freud's writing reveals a tendency to dwell, as with that ice-cold grave, on morbid subjects, and to do so in partly autobiographical terms. Likewise, as I shall discuss in the last section of this chapter, Freud may be found preoccupied by scenarios in which a loved one is absent or distant or even a threat. That very preoccupation, especially when it is expressed in autobiographical terms, or when it is the pretext for an allusive or figural digression, suggests that Freud's work has a certain melancholic quality. And indeed it does. Having said that though, I need to emphasize that my focus is not psychobiographical. As this book progresses, I will repeatedly propose ways in which Freud's rhetoric might be argued to exemplify a strictly argumentative distress. In Chapter 3, for example, I will consider an idea of mourning as stalled or deceptive explanation. I am especially interested in how assertions of explanatory success in Freud's work fail, on closer inspection, to seem very successful or entire. In the last chapter, I will pay special attention to the metaphor of the 'foreign body' as one crucial image that may be interpreted as doing service both as an apparent emblem of psychoanalytic understanding and therapy, and as a figure of an inconclusive theorizing that can be understood both as transgression and, as such, anguish.

Elucidation, involution, countersense

As I conceive the idea, countersense is not necessarily something that is hidden or implicit; nor is it an idea of meaning in crisis or suspension. It is a matter rather of images, concepts and expressions which convey an additional sense that may subvert the nominal argument being made. We might look at another reference to ghosts in *The Interpretation of Dreams*. In the book's theoretical chapter, Freud writes:

> They [unconscious wishes] share this character of indestructibility with all other mental acts which are truly unconscious ... These are paths which have been laid down once and for all, which never fall into disuse and which, whenever an unconscious excitation re-cathects them, are always ready to conduct the excitatory process to discharge. If I may use a simile, they are only capable of annihilation in the same sense as the ghosts [*Schatten*] in the underworld of the Odyssey – ghosts which awoke to new life as soon as they tasted blood. (**5: 553n**, 4: 704–5n, *2/3: 558n*)

Freud's emphasis in this passage is on 'indestructibility' and that emphasis is supported by the allusive reference to ghosts that are continually capable of being woken 'to new life'; the figure makes sense – the citation of Homer illustrating the question of wishes that do not permit being annihilated or extirpated from the mind. But, all the same, a problem of general psychology in individuals is being described in terms both of classical literature (which is a kind of counterpoint to the quasi-electrical circuitry of pathways being laid down forever) and of especially ancient supernatural entities. This passage therefore reminds one of Freud's erudition: he was an antiquarian and lover of classical civilization who was also a modern scientist, and the way in which he combines the two branches of research is a persistently interesting feature of his writing.

But there is more to it than that. Elsewhere in his work, as I shall discuss extensively in the next chapter, Freud also theorizes the way in which modern individual minds are to some degree always lost in an ancient past, subject to what is asserted to be phylogenetically acquired memory. So the conjunction of a metaphor drawn from electrical engineering and a simile drawn from Homer in fact suggests in a pre-emptive way (since the theory is not specifically formulated at this point) the psycho-Lamarckian theory that Freud develops in the 1900s about transgenerational 'memory-traces'. That theory is at odds with some fundamental premises of psychoanalysis – especially its account, however complicated that account may sometimes be, of personal identity (however multilayered or subdivided) and of the grounding function of experience (however enlarged that idea may be so as to include purely imaginative experience, for example). The countersense is that one is somehow inhabited – 'haunted', one might say – by others' memories.

These issues are pertinent also to Freud's comparisons between archaeological and psychoanalytic reconstruction, such as the one in the 'Dora' case history, 'Fragment of an Analysis of a Case of Hysteria' (1905 [1901]), which is also discussed by Bowie:

> In face of the incompleteness of my analytic results, I had no choice but to follow the example of those discoverers whose good fortune it is to bring to the light of day after their long burial the priceless though mutilated relics of antiquity. I have restored what is missing, taking the best models known to me from other analyses; but, like a conscientious archaeologist, I have not omitted to mention in each case where the authentic parts end and my constructions begin. (7: 12, 8: 241)

As well as being understood in psychological terms as a 'dream of knowledge', this passage also provides what I want to call a figure of Freudian theory – a scene of the interpretative or explanatory work Freud sets out to do. It is, as it happens, a scene in which a person appears: there is specifically an individual, the 'conscientious archaeologist', doing work that is both physical and intellectual, digging, sifting, then attempting to make simulacra out of the debris of fragmented objects. Bowie is surely right to propose that the comparison shows how Freud imagined psychoanalytic reconstructive understanding in terms of 'a dream of unitary and unidirectional knowledge', which moves 'back towards the lost wholeness of each fragmentary thing' so that the 'objects of mental science are thus rescued from the perils of multiple causation'.[5] And the rescuing in Freud's comparison has a certain scrupulousness also, a self-qualifying rigour (as it is presented) which claims certainly to retrieve 'what is missing' but not without indicating 'where the authentic parts end'. The ambition and confidence of this figure of theory is supported by the emphasis on its constructedness – that emphasis being in its way rhetorical, the idea of carefully self-appraised presentation of research findings.

Actually I will be less concerned with figures of theory that involve a personified agent of explanation than with figures that are, in particular, spatial, geographical or paradoxically material. But such figures are akin to the ones Bowie discusses, further elements in the complex self-commentary of Freud's writing – and it will remain to be seen to what degree they are 'self-corroborating' or 'palliative'. The figure of theory is ambitious, assertive, confident, but it is also, as I read it, preoccupied in a certain way. And its preoccupation is not hidden or disguised: the distant past, interred ruins, 'mutilated relics', lost cultures, structures and images reduced to rubble or fragments. To be sure, the emphasis is on reconstruction but the material which is to be pieced together is, quite simply, extremely ancient and incomplete. An especially far-reaching kind of retrospective investigation is therefore required. There is, on the one hand, the sense of unifying explanation; but there is also, on the other hand, a countersense of fragmentation and antiquity. I am interested in the extent to which the latter concern is more powerfully at work in Freud's writing than is often allowed. If the analogy with the archaeological excavation in the Dora case history is, to whatever extent, 'a dream of unitary and unidirectional knowledge', it may perhaps be said also to convey a sense of the intensely disunified evidence that is left from the past. There is no absolute contradiction here, just a question of degree and emphasis that I would like to extrapolate with reference to a literary text.

Bowie also quotes another reference to burial in *The Interpretation of Dreams* when Freud recalls – 'I had already been in a grave once, but it was an excavated Etruscan grave near Orvieto, a narrow chamber with two stone benches along its walls, on which the skeletons of two grown-up men were lying' (5: **454**, 4: 588).[6] Freud's aside puts me in mind of some lines in the eighth of Rilke's *Duino Elegies* (1923):

Und doch ist in dem wachsam warmen Tier
Gewicht und Sorge einer Groß Schwermut.

Denn ihm auch haftet immer an, was uns
oft überwältigt, – die Erinnerung,
als sei schon einmal das, wonach man drängt,
näher gewesen, treuer und sein Anschluß
unendlich zärtlich. Hier ist alles Abstand,
und dort wars Atem. Nach der ersten Heimat
ist ihm die zweite zwitterig und windig.
O Seligkeit der kleinen *Kreatur,*
die immer bleibt *im Scooße, der sie austrug;*
o Glück der Mücke, die noch innen *hüpft,*
selbst wenn sie Hochzeit hat: den Schooß ist Alles.
Und sieh die halbe Sicherheit des Vogels,
der beinah beides weiß aus seinum Ursprung,
als wär eine Seele der Etrusker,
aus einem Toten, den ein Raum empfing,
dich mit der ruhenden Figur als Deckel.

And yet the weight and care of one great sadness
lies on this warm and watching creature.
Because what often overwhelms us
also clings to him – the memory
that what we so strive for now may have been
nearer, truer, and its attachment to us
infinitely tender, once. Here all is distance,
there it was breath. After that first home,
the second seems drafty and a hybrid.
Oh, blessed are the tiny creatures
who stay in the womb that bore them forever;
oh the joy of the gnat that can still leap *within*,
even on its wedding day; for the womb is all!
And look at the half-certainty of the bird
almost aware of both from birth,
like one of the Etruscan souls rising
from the dead man enclosed inside the space
for which his reclining figure forms a lid.[7]

Rilke's Etruscan tomb, with its lid-forming 'reclining figure', is perhaps more elaborate and difficult to visualize than Freud's, but the 'one great sadness' – a sadness of loss, exile, dispossession and regret – seems to me to have relevance to Freud's work. The relevance is specific (as I will show a little later in this chapter) but also to do with the larger problem of retrospection. Freud's archaeological analogy implies a broad kind of claim to an understanding of the original state of the historical past: the past can be reconstructed. But it is arguable that such a claim alternatively implies an anguished relationship to the past – the claim to knowledge perhaps suggesting an 'overwhelm[ing]' preoccupation with the traces of the past that are inscrutable and fragmentary now, spectral and shadowy and therefore not available to be recaptured in an 'infinitely tender' kind of intimate knowledge, because it is too late for that. A concern with the ancient past may, to put this another way, be a pretext for a particularly ambitious claim to understanding; but it may equally suggest in an acute way a sense of the extent to which meaning is felt to have been lost in the past.

Ghosts, graves, relics, ruins, underworlds: these are often passing concerns or allusions and they can be dismissed in specific contexts as marginal or illustrative. But we may begin to see that they are all the same recurrent themes in Freud's writing and, moreover, that they have an affinity with his interest in what persists in modern life and in individual modern minds of the distantly ancient past. Freud looks to the past for meaning and it is often not a very happy kind of looking-back. It finds terrifying things in the past and it understands these terrifying things to hold sway still, however obscurely, over the present. In the next chapter, I will explore the patricidal narrative that Freud believed was the key to the history of religion and social organization, and the key moreover to formative disturbances in the individual mind. When Freud speculates about human history, it is to unfold a saga of bloodthirsty rebellion, murder, retaliation and guilt. In terms of content, Freud's saga is thus not immediately similar to the pastoral phantasmagoria of Rilke's poem. However, as in the passage from the *Duino Elegies*, Freud's writing discloses a *fascination* with history. Retrospection is the dominant hermeneutic habit of psychoanalysis. Freud is concerned most often with the nearer history of childhood, but he cross-refers that to a farther anthropological history. In both these realms, he finds warring emotions or actual violent conflict, the one echoing or prefiguring the other; in both he repeatedly claims to have found specific determinants that, now isolated, explain what comes afterwards.

The search for origins, the idea of history as the gravitational force to which understanding necessarily plunges – the idea of what one might term, echoing Rilke, *once-trueness* – is dominant in Freud's work. The problem, as I shall discuss, is that Freud's search for meaning in the past starts to seem compulsive; its very extensiveness – especially the way it *alternates* between contemplating pasts that are far or near, more or less partially inconspicuous or unintelligible pasts – leads to uncertainty, obscurity, to serial rather than definitive meanings. There is a paradox in Rilke's lines: the idyll of truth and proximity, warmth and union, is a vision of consolation. But this consolation has disappeared. It is lost. The striving plea of the poem is futile and the chilliness of its sad recall is only the more evident for the emphasis on a vanished scenario of womb-like comfort. The registers are of course different, but the paradox has, I think, valence in a study of Freud's writing, whose retrospective enthusiasms also disclose a sense of loss.

The cunning, complex self-disclosure in the *Gradiva* book is an especially conspicuous instance of self-referentiality in Freud's writing, conspicuous notably by its autobiographical personification (which it shares with Freud's comparisons between psychoanalysis and archaeology). But there is also, as I have suggested, a more abstract kind of self-awareness, involving more abstract figures of theory. And these figures of understanding are also subject to overturning or undermining. Two examples may serve as illustration.

There is, firstly, the question of explanation and elucidation as such, the psychoanalytic *Aufklärung*. Freud repeatedly asserts that psychoanalysis has developed unprecedented insights into various problems. His statements in this respect are often unequivocal. There is, for example, a twofold claim in 'A Short Account of Psycho-Analysis' (1924 [1923]) regarding the psychoanalysis of culture: 'the researches of psycho-analysts have in fact thrown a flood of light on the fields of mythology, the science of literature, and the psychology of artists' and 'psycho-analysis is in a position to speak the decisive word in all questions that touch upon the imaginative life of man' (**19: 207–8**, 15: 180). Freud does not, of course, always set psychoanalysis so directly against art, but here he is a kind of patriot of science, a demystifier, an unsentimental champion of rational understanding. The two figures – enlightenment and quasi-forensic declamation – here are conventional: the science sheds light on obscure problems and aspires effectively to give right names to unclassified or wrongly classified phenomena.

It is the idea of naming that interests me in particular. Freud's writings on art repeatedly draw attention to the elements of disguise and elision in artistic techniques – works of art dissemble, withholding their true subjects. Discussing Ibsen's *Rosmersholm* in 'Some Character-Types Met with In Psycho-Analytic Work' (1916), Freud observes how its 'deeper motive could not be explicitly enunciated' (**14: 329**, 14: 314). Of concealed meaning in *Hamlet*, Freud comments in 'Psychopathic Characters on the Stage' (1942 [1905–6]): 'the impulse that is struggling into consciousness, however clearly it is recognizable, is never given a definite name' (**7: 309**, 14: 126). Indeed, Freud asserts, such is the artfulness of the play's techniques of concealment that 'it was left to me to unearth' (**310**, 126) the true nature of its underlying psychological conflict.

The work of unearthing that Freud imagines here, which has a certain poignancy in the wake of that frightening ice-cold grave, is congruent with his archaeological analogies. The idea of name-giving is less elaborately put forward as a model of psychoanalytic understanding, a figure of theory, but it is not the less an indication of Freud's explanatory confidence and ambitiousness. Right-naming would stand alongside elucidation ('flood of light') and irrefutable summing-up ('decisive word') and all their numerous cognates – a major one is riddle-solving – as types of confident self-assertion concerned with truth-telling and the scientificity of psychoanalysis. When Freud is most concerned with advertising the explanatory achievements of psychoanalysis as well as its reputability as a scientific discipline, he tends to speak in these terms.

What, then, is one to make of this version of the same idea of right-naming, to be found in 'The Future Prospects of Psycho-Analytic Therapy' (1910)?

> [T]he psychoneuroses are substitutive satisfactions of some instinct the presence of which one is obliged to deny to oneself and to others. Their capacity to exist depends on this distortion and lack of recognition. When the riddle they present is solved and the solution is accepted by the patients these diseases cease to be able to exist. There is hardly anything like this in medicine, though in fairy tales you hear of evil spirits [*bösen Geistern*] whose power is broken as soon as you can tell them their name – the name which they have kept secret. (**11: 148**, *8: 112*)

Here is, once more, the counterintuitive talk of spirits alongside terms that are often to be found as watchwords of psychoanalytic rational explanation: 'recognition' is often used by Freud as the epitome of the cognitive work done by psychoanalysis, whether therapeutically or theoretically. And what is recognized and robbed of its mystery or ambiguity by psychoanalysis is frequently called a riddle or something, especially, that has been subjected to purposeful disguise and 'distortion'.[8] I do not want to make too much of this passage – its hyperbole and polemical self-justification account well enough for this surprising comparison between Freud's method and magical declamation; it is enough to show how one can, following a term or phrase's recurrence, read across from text to text to find an arresting reimagining or juxtaposition, whose sense is, if not necessarily at odds with the rhetoric of explanation and elucidation and recognition, then at any rate dissonant.

And, secondly, there is, more specifically, the idea of understanding as an undoing of complexity, which Freud elsewhere figures conversely as a kind of tangle (see Chapter 2). The idea in this case follows on from the idea of psychoneurotic illness disappearing as a result of right-naming. In *Jokes and their Relation to the Unconscious* (1905), Freud asserts that 'it remains an uncontradicted fact that if we undo the technique of a joke [*mit der Rückbildung der Technik der Witz*] it disappears' (**8: 73**, 6: 113, *6: 79*). Like enlightening, the undoing here is a conventional metaphor for explanation and understanding. What I find to be interesting, however, is the recurrence of the specific word – *Rückbildung* – in a rather different, less conventional context, in *Beyond the Pleasure Principle* (1920): 'biology teaches us that higher development in one respect is very frequently balanced or outweighed by involution [*Rückbildung*] in another' (**18: 41**, 11: 314, *13: 42–3*). Whereas the psychoanalysis of jokes involves an undoing that is claimed to be, so to speak, progressive, an undoing that does the work of scientific elaboration, here the figure is one that is purely regressive, tending not towards anything elaborate but only to stasis or inertia. Involution is the kind of process that Freud, in fact, ascribes (having at last arrived at that concept in *Beyond the Pleasure Principle*) to the death drive, whose work is, as Freud puts it in *An Outline of Psycho-Analysis* (1940 [1938]), 'to undo connections and so to destroy things...to lead what is living into an inorganic state' (**23: 248–9**, 15: 379–80).[9]

As one reads across from one passage to another, one can observe an uncanny rejoinder to an initially confident and seemingly straightforward assertion. The scientist's right-naming is reprised in terms of incantation or exorcism; his disentangling method is counterpointed and a chill, eerie tone, or rather a deathly lull, can as a result perhaps be heard in it. The second context for the trope of undoing or involution undercuts the first. By bringing the two occurrences together, it is possible to begin to infer a sort of secret sense, a countersense, which emerges out of the conjunction, a sense whose connotations are dark and negative. There is, one might intuit (though this is not really my focus), something violent and destructive in the vainglorious self-promotion of Freudian explanation, with its large claims to understanding. It is as if there were some deep underlying awareness of death in Freud's writing, the nightmare of frozen entombing being – in combination with the ghosts and, less flagrantly, the concern for the biological trend of involution – both indicative of it and in dissonant relationship to the rational explanatory project of psychoanalysis.

Unexpected returns

Deathly involutionary explanation can bring us back once more to ghosts. Such is Freud's surprise when he misrecognizes the sister of his dead patient that his response is superstitious: 'So after all it's true that the dead can come back to life [*es sei doch wahr, daß die Toten wiederkommen können*]' (*7: 98*). That disarming surprise makes an appropriate reappearance in 'The "Uncanny"' (1919):

> Let us take the uncanny associated with the omnipotence of thoughts, with the prompt fulfilment of wishes, with secret injurious powers and with the return of the dead. The condition under which the feeling of uncanniness arises here is unmistakable. We – or our primitive forefathers – once believed that these possibilities were realities, and were convinced that they actually happened. Nowadays we no longer believe in them, we have *surmounted* these modes of thought; but we do not feel quite sure of our new beliefs, and the old ones still exist within us ready to seize upon any confirmation. As soon as something *actually happens* in our lives which seems to confirm the old, discarded beliefs we get a feeling of the uncanny; it as though we were making a judgement something like this: 'So, after all, it is *true* that one can kill a person by a mere wish!' or, 'So the dead *do* live on and appear on the scene of their former activities!' [*Also ist es doch wahr... daß die Toten weiterleben*], and so on. Conversely, anyone who has completely and finally rid himself of animistic beliefs will be insensible to this type of the uncanny. The most remarkable coincidences of wish and fulfilment, the most mysterious repetition of similar experiences in a particular place or on a particular date, the most deceptive sights and suspicious noises – none of these things will disconcert him or raise the kind of fear which can be described as 'a fear of something uncanny'. The whole thing is purely an affair of 'reality-testing', a question of the material reality of the phenomena. (**17: 247–8**, 14: 370–1, *12: 262*)

Freud is staying fairly neutral here, confining himself to the mind's work of knowing reality rather than wider questions of cultural belief. It is interesting, given that he has reported himself as making the very assessment – in some of the very words – that the dead can return, that his point is that those who have divested themselves of quasi-animistic beliefs will be in fact unable even to frame such a thought. But Freud was, after all, vehement in his atheism and his fierce rationalist critique of religion and superstition, especially in *The Future of an Illusion* (1927):

> [R]eligious ideas ... which are given out as teachings are not precipitates of experience or end-results of thinking: they are illusions, fulfilments of the oldest, strongest and most urgent wishes of mankind. The secret of their strength lies in the strength of those wishes. As we already know, the terrifying impression of helplessness in childhood aroused the need for protection – for protection through love – which was provided by the father; and the recognition that this helplessness lasts throughout life made it necessary to cling to the existence of a father, but this time a more powerful one. Thus the benevolent rule of a divine Providence allays our fear of the dangers of life; the establishment of a moral world-order ensures the fulfilment of the demands of justice, which have so often remained unfulfilled in human civilization; and the prolongation of earthly existence in a future life provides the local and temporal framework in which these wish-fulfilments shall take place. Answers to the riddles that tempt the curiosity of man, such as how the universe began or what the relation is between body and mind, are developed in conformity with the underlying assumptions of this system. It is an enormous relief to the individual psyche if the conflicts of its childhood arising from the father-complex – conflicts which it has never wholly overcome – are removed from it and brought to a solution which is universally accepted. (**21: 30**, 12: 212)

There are various major Freudian themes here as well as the outright pessimism that also characterizes *Civilization and its Discontents* (1929 [1930]). The talk of love is soon displaced not just by a child's helplessness, but by 'helplessness ... throughout life' and 'the dangers of life'. Freud's rhetoric is stoical but rooted also in the values of rational inquiry, that ethic and practice of explanatory method that we have already encountered and which is conspicuous in the reference to riddles.

Freud's anti-religious rationalism would seem to preclude the very superstition that he admits, albeit in an especially artful and self-aware way, to entertaining in the book on *Gradiva*. I want to try to work along the faultline of this paradox a little and to do so without resorting to facile ideas of clumsy inconsistency, let alone hypocrisy. The paradox is more interesting than such ideas would permit and in my view it deserves to be taken seriously so that we may see what, if any, sense – or rather countersense – it has. It is worth stressing that my premise here and elsewhere is that when Freud resorts to ostensibly inappropriate ideas, and especially occultist ideas, this is not evidence of just that vestigial superstition that he delights in tracking down in apparently more mature belief systems.[10] I read these references as being a form of reflexiveness, as when I correlate the references to ghosts with Freud's insistent retrospection.

It is perhaps worth entering a caveat here. One has to allow for a writer's rhetoric. In the reading of *Gradiva*, for example, there is a certain leisureliness – applying psychoanalysis to this archaeology-themed novel is a pleasant diversion for Freud and so we may choose to read his admission of superstition as to some extent playful or ironic, no matter the seriousness of the question of negligence. And, in looking at figurative language more widely, one needs to take care to concede that figures of speech are in the business of shifting meanings around, turning them in some direction or other, calling one thing by another's name. But, all the same, there are certain figures which are especially inappropriate in a psychoanalytic context, or which one may think of as being appropriate to use only with special caution. So, talk of ghosts and evil spirits and *revenants* is made problematic in this context because of the severity of Freud's polemic against superstition.

There is another figure that is especially troublesome and seemingly paradoxical in the context of psychoanalysis: the description of psychological states in physical terms – and, especially, in terms of physical injury. Freud was a physician and therefore such an analogy might occur to him quite naturally. So, for example, in the *Studies on Hysteria* (1893–95), co-written with Joseph Breuer, there is this simile:

> [T]he causal relation between the determining psychical trauma and the hysterical phenomenon is not a of a kind implying that the trauma merely acts like an *agent provocateur* in releasing the symptom, which thereafter leads an independent existence. We must presume rather that the psychical trauma – or more precisely the memory of the trauma – acts like a foreign body which long after its entry must continue to be regarded as an agent that is still at work; and we find the evidence for this in a highly remarkable phenomenon which at the same time lends an important practical interest to our findings.

> For we found, to our great surprise at first, that each individual hysterical symptom immediately and permanently disappeared when we had succeeded in bringing clearly to light the memory of the event by which it was provoked and in arousing its accompanying affect, and when the patient had described that event in the greatest possible detail and had put the affect into words. [**2: 6**, 3: 56–7, emphases suppressed]

Or, in 'Mourning and Melancholia' (1917 [1915]), which I will discuss in greater detail in Chapter 3: 'The conflict in the ego ... must act like a painful wound' (**14: 258**, 11: 267).

In the *Studies on Hysteria*, the foundations of psychoanalysis are being put in place: the idea, especially, of shock being something that is often only belatedly, 'long after its entry' as a problem for the mind, transformed (if it is) into illness, and moreover the technique of enabling a patient to recall a shocking incident by finally talking about it, putting it into words. The matter of finding the right words is at stake here where Freud and Breuer use, albeit only in the form of a simile (as with the use of 'wound' later), terms that describe physical injury – specifically the injury done to a body by an intrusive extraneous element (shrapnel, for example) – when what is crucial to their argument, without which there would be nothing startling in it, is that mental illness is not caused by injury but by a failure of remembering. A text from the period in which Freud consolidated his preliminary theories, 'Psychical (or Mental) Treatment' (1905), makes the point clearly:

> [M]edicine ... has shown that the organism is built up from microscopically small elements (the cells), it has learnt to understand the physics and chemistry of the various vital processes (functions), it has distinguished the visible and observable modifications which are brought about in the bodily organs by different morbid processes, and has discovered, on the other hand, the signs that reveal the operation of deep-lying morbid processes in the living body; moreover it has identified a great number of the micro-organisms which cause illness and, with the help of its newly acquired knowledge, it has reduced to a quite extraordinary degree the dangers arising from severe surgical operations. All of these advances and discoveries were related to the *physical* side of man, and it followed, as a result of an incorrect though easily understandable trend of thought, that physicians came to restrict their interest to the physical

> side of things and were glad to leave the mental field to be dealt with by the philosophers whom they despised.
>
> Modern medicine, it is true, had reason enough for studying the indisputable connection between the body and the mind; but it never ceased to represent mental events as determined by physical ones and dependent on them. (**7: 283–4**)

Freud's innovation in the treatment of illness and distress was to posit mental causes for what he observed and tried to treat. There was not, he claimed, any toxic or physical explanation for neurosis. And it was no good therefore treating the condition on the basis of that explanation. What was needed instead was an understanding of the mind's ability, almost always in childhood, to block out – to eradicate from consciousness or easy recall the details of something shocking or unintelligible – but, in some cases, to block out only incompletely and temporarily such that what has been eradicated may later find a disguised form of re-expression. The harmful returning memory could not be medicated, electrocuted or cut away in surgery, though it could be made accessible or even annihilated through hypnosis; what was needed instead was structured conversation in which a patient could find the means to discuss and disclose the trouble and so remember it and be rid of it.

These are relatively early writings, but Freud continued in the same vein throughout his career, arguing for psychological explanations of certain forms of illness and psychotherapeutic treatments of them. The 1905 paper is, for example, echoed in 'The Resistances to Psycho-Analysis' (1925 [1924]):

> The symptoms of hysterical neuroses were looked upon as shamming and the phenomena of hypnotism as a hoax. Even the psychiatrists, upon whose attention the most unusual and astonishing mental phenomena were constantly being forced, showed no inclination to examine their details or inquire into their connections. They were content to classify the variegated array of symptoms and trace them back, so far as they could manage, to somatic, anatomical or chemical aetiological disturbances. During this materialistic or, rather, mechanistic period, medicine made tremendous advances, but it also showed a short-sighted misunderstanding of the most important and most difficult among the problems of life. (**19: 215–16**, 15: 266)

As in the earlier paper, Freud's polemic is connected to the distinctiveness of psychoanalytic explanation (and psychotherapy): the breakthrough

Freud claims for his work is to see that certain illnesses are not to be understood (or cured) physiologically – they must rather be explained and treated as mental phenomena. These illnesses, in other words, are a matter not of wounding or intoxication or poisoning but of thought processes that have become impaired.

My point is to underscore the extent to which Freud insists on distinguishing psychoanalysis from medicine just as he distinguishes mental activity from the functioning of the body. But his account of this subject has various additional nuances which are worth acknowledging here not only because I will explore them further in later chapters but also because they have to do once more with ghosts. So, firstly, Freud has some exemplary remarks to make in 'A Difficulty in the Path of Psycho-Analysis' (1917) about mental disorders:

> Psychiatry... denies that such things mean the intrusion into the mind of evil spirits from without; beyond this, however, it can only say with a shrug: 'Degeneracy, hereditary disposition, constitutional inferiority!' Psycho-analysis sets out to explain these uncanny disorders; it engages in careful and laborious investigations, devises hypotheses and scientific constructions, until at length it can speak thus to the ego: – 'Nothing has entered into you from without; a part of the activity of your own mind has been withdrawn from your knowledge and from the command of your will. That, too, is why you are so weak in your defence; you are using one part of your force to fight the other part and you cannot concentrate the whole of your force as you would against an external enemy.['] (**17: 142**)

What is of note here, in addition to the dismissal of the 'evil spirits' explanation (which all the same brings ghosts back into the discussion), is the way Freud introduces a military metaphor. I will return to a more important such figure in Chapter 5.

In Freud's staged recollection of his patient who died, the illness she succumbed to was Graves' disease. Freud has that affliction in mind again in 'The Resistances' and in discussing it he modifies his account of the sphere of psychoanalytic expertise in a crucial respect:

> From a clinical standpoint the neuroses must necessarily be put alongside the intoxications and such disorders as Graves' disease. There are conditions arising from an excess or a relative lack of certain highly active substances, whether produced inside the body

> or introduced into it from outside – in short, they are disturbances of the chemistry of the body, toxic conditions. If someone succeeded in isolating and demonstrating the hypothetical substance or substances concerned in neuroses, he would have no need to worry about opposition from the medical profession. (**19: 214–15**, 15: 265)

Although Freud's polemic about the distinctiveness of psychoanalytic explanation and the specificity of the causes of certain illnesses relies on a refusal of non-psychological theories, that refusal may be only provisional. (I will return to this question in Chapter 4.) And so, overarchingly, there is an apparent paradox in the use of terms from, precisely, the vocabulary of conventional medicine concerned with physical injury. Such a vocabulary, however natural to a doctor, is at odds with Freud's basic premises. One might add here that it is not as if conventional medicine in the early days of psychoanalysis was welcoming to Freud's theories. It is a subject that Freud cannot write about with much equanimity. In 'The Future Prospects', for example, he declares:

> I must not let myself be led into describing my agreeable [*sic*] experiences during the period when I alone represented psycho-analysis. I can only say that when I assured my patients that I knew how to relieve them permanently of their sufferings they looked around my modest abode, reflected on my lack of fame and title, and regarded me like the possessor of an infallible system at a gambling-resort, of whom people say that if he could do what he professes he would look very different himself. Nor was it really pleasant to carry out a psychical operation while the colleagues whose duty it should have been to assist took particular pleasure in spitting into the field of operation, and while at the first signs of blood or restlessness in the patient his relatives began threatening the operating surgeon. (**11: 146**)

In these strident remarks, Freud uses the medical metaphor against the profession, figuring the reception of psychoanalysis among doctors in terms of the grossest kind of malpractice but, in so doing, he once more confuses the issue somewhat with the reference to a 'psychical operation'.

The vividness and forcefulness of Freud's rhetoric in this context are reprised a few years later in the *Introductory Lectures on Psycho-Analysis*

(1916–17 [1915–17]), in reference to the career prospects of a doctor choosing to practice psychoanalysis:

> As things stand at present, such a choice of profession would ruin any chance he might have of success at a University, and, if he started in life as a practising physician, he would find himself in a society which did not understand his efforts, which regarded him with distrust and hostility, and unleashed upon him all the evil spirits [*lauernden Geister*] lurking within it. And the phenomena accompanying the war that is now raging in Europe will perhaps give you some notion of what legions of these evil spirits there may be. (**15: 16**, 1: 40, *11: 8*)

Once more ghosts have been unleashed, this time in a dispute about the border between allegedly distinct areas of professional expertise, that expertise turning on different accounts of the autonomy of the mind in being able to bring about its own suffering. It is not necessarily easy to reconcile what begins to seem like a serial preoccupation on Freud's part with ghosts with his scientific rationalism. It would have seemed to make more sense, finally, whatever allowances one makes for familiar points of reference, if Freud had not spoken about ghosts and evil spirits, given the stridency of his opinions about religion and superstition; and had not used the analogy of physical injury, given his overriding concern with disorders of mental functioning insusceptible (at the time of writing anyway) to surgical or pharmaceutical treatment.

We are left therefore with a paradox contained in a scattered assortment of remarks. It may not seem very significant. The argument I want to make in this book, however, culminating especially in Chapter 5, is not only that the paradox is significant but also that it is, in fact, not a paradox. The references to ghosts and wounds, that is to say, make sense or, rather, a countersense.

And not only that, I claim that the ghosts and wounds are in fact different versions of the same arguments about the weight of the past and its penetration of the present. Moreover, lastly, the dissident 'argument' of the figures eventually emerges explicitly. It will be as if the countersense of the figurative language finally overruns psychoanalytic theory.

I will turn in a more detailed way in the next chapter to the problem of Freud's psycho-Lamarckian theory of inherited memory but first I want to look at another illuminating series of figures in Freud's writing – images of modern technology and especially the telephone – although this series is, as we shall see, interrelated with the ones discussed so far.

Telephone trouble

There are modern types of pain – or, at any rate, specifically modern causes of pain and injury and death. With the modern mechanization of war, for example, bodies could be newly torn apart, exploded, flung, broken or disfigured, just as minds could be ruined in unprecedented ways – as in what were called 'war neuroses', which Freud addressed in a posthumously published 'Memorandum on the Electrical Treatment of War Neurotics' (1955 [1920]). There Freud recommends psychotherapy as a benign alternative to electroshock treatment, arguing that the distress of the patients in question is psychologically caused, not the result of damage to the nervous system. It is clear, though, that he is disturbed and moved by thoughts of the overwhelming force, velocity and destructive power of martial machinery and ordnance. That earlier horror of being entombed stirs again when he writes of 'such a gross impact as that produced by the concussion due to the explosion of a shell near by or to being buried by a fall of earth', incidents that would indeed likely lead to 'gross mechanical effects' on the body and its organs (**17: 212**). These thoughts and observations resurface in *Beyond the Pleasure Principle*, where Freud – again in the context of disclaiming the physical aetiology of neurotic illnesses – refers to 'severe mechanical concussions, railway disasters and other accidents involving a risk to life' and 'organic lesions of the nervous system brought about by mechanical force' (**18: 12**, 11: 281).

Freud seems to have had an aversion to modern technology and machinery. It is the railway disaster that comes to his mind rather than, say, the opportunities for travel afforded by motor vehicles. It is worth mentioning in this context another self-reflexively autobiographical moment, comparable to the one in the *Gradiva* book but contemporaneous with his war-shadowed remarks, in 'The "Uncanny"':

> I was sitting alone in my *wagon-lit* compartment when a more than usually violent jolt of the train swung back the door of the adjoining washing-cabinet, and an elderly gentleman in a dressing-gown and a travelling cap came in. I assumed that in leaving the washing-cabinet, which lay between the two compartments, he had taken the wrong direction and come into my compartment by mistake. Jumping up with the intention of putting him right, I at once realized to my dismay that the intruder was nothing but my own reflection in the looking-glass on the open door. (**17: 248n**, 14: 371n)

As with the other passage the problem is one of misrecognition that is the cause of alarm, apprehension, distress. Freud describes how his perception and understanding correct themselves – as they did when he realized that the woman in his consulting room was not his former patient but her sister – and things therefore finally seem to be made right. Freud refamiliarizes himself with himself, reasserting his own knowledge. But there has been a crisis of recognition, the 'dismay' it causes here only a little less a perturbation than the 'dread' (and 'shame') Freud reports he felt when he was confronted by his former patient's sister. Therefore, as with the archaeological analogy in the Dora case history, the final emphasis of Freud's remarks has to do with reconstructed knowledge that in this case fixes Freud's sense of himself, dispelling dismay with restored meaning. But Freud has made a point of giving a self-referential account of a peculiarly acute state of failed understanding and one may suggest, as with the Dora passage, that the reassertion of ordered and accurate perception does not fully bring resolution to the sense of dismay – that the report of restored knowledge draws attention as much to the crisis of knowledge and its distressing emotional impact as to the restoration itself. Freud is at a confusing distance from himself.

Dislocation, distance, dismay, persons misrecognized as familiar when they are not or unfamiliar when they are indeed familiar, one's own self a confusing flickering apparition: this passage and its counterparts are personalized anecdotes that present in a stark and vivid way a crisis that I will argue is much more widespread in Freud's work, expressed in impersonal and abstract terms. Pending further substantiation of that claim, I propose that the autobiographical passages I have quoted can be read not as illustrative asides or autobiographical digressions that somehow pause the business of theorizing, but as themselves figures of theory. Psychoanalysis, after all, deals with kinds of internal and interpersonal recognition and misrecognition. But for all Freud's emphasis on various readjustments and reassertions of knowledge and familiarity, he insistently dwells on the extent of the gaps and partitions and shadows in the way, as if (recalling Rilke again), theirs is the truer reality, theirs the compelling evidence for a lost understanding:

> the memory
> that what we so strive for now may have been
> nearer, truer, and its attachment to us
> infinitely tender, once. Here all is distance,
> there it was breath.

Consider in this respect, bearing Rilke's rueful words in mind, some further remarks prompted by modern technology, such as a comment Freud makes in *Civilization and its Discontents*:

> If there had been no railway, my child would never have left his native town and I should need no telephone to hear his voice; if travelling across the ocean by ship had not been introduced, my friend would not have embarked on his sea-voyage and I should not need a cable to relieve my anxiety about him. (**21: 88**, 12: 276–7)

Here are further notes of sadness, even grief, entering into Freud's writing. It is initially worth registering just this tone or mood, although one can then proceed to indicate the recurrence of an association between modern technology and physical or emotional distress, on the one hand, and, on the other, a plainly but complexly stated kind of self-disclosure that occurs only after a moment of self-veiling or self-misrecognition. There is a doubling-up of hurt and anxiety in the way Freud writes about modern machines in another passage, which is in part famous, from *Civilization and its Discontents*:

> With every tool man is perfecting his own organs, whether motor or sensory, or is removing the limits to their functioning. Motor power places gigantic forces at his disposal, which, like his muscles, he can employ in any direction; thanks to ships and aircraft neither water nor air can hinder his movements; by means of spectacles he corrects defects in the lens of his own eye; by means of the telescope he sees into the far distance; and by means of the microscope he overcomes the limits of visibility set by the structure of his retina. In the photographic camera he has created an instrument which retains the fleeting visual impressions, just as a gramophone disc retains the equally fleeting auditory ones; both are at bottom materializations of the power he possesses of recollection, his memory. With the help of the telephone he can hear at distances which would be regarded as unattainable even in a fairy tale. Writing was in its origin the voice of an absent person; and the dwelling-house was a substitute for the mother's womb, the first lodging, for which in all likelihood man still longs, and in which he was safe and felt at ease. (**21: 90–1**, 12: 279)

And he goes on: 'Man has, as it were, become a kind of prosthetic God. When he puts on all his auxiliary organs he is truly magnificent; but these organs have not grown on to him [*nicht mit ihm verwachsen*] and they still give him much trouble at times' (**91–2**, 280, *14: 151*). The doubling-up that I am interested in here occurs with the idea of a prosthesis growing – or, rather specifically, failing to grow – on to a body. Freud's metaphor is medical and physiological; the mechanical 'auxiliary organs' are, for all their empowering qualities, described as doing bodily injury that requires healing-over, as of a wound. (Freud's figure here is thus comparable to what he calls technological 'materializations ... of memory'.) It is not enough for Freud to describe the sadness of departure and distance; he adds to the descriptions of those states a figure of wounding – or, to be quite specific, of post-surgical non-healing around a prosthesis.

What is most profoundly at issue in this section of Freud's book is not motorization or telecommunication or the expediency of scientific instruments, but, at its simplest, loneliness. The lost and longed-for womb, the missing child, an absent friend far away – these poignant thoughts chime tonally and emotionally with the solitary confusion of an old man in a railway carriage and also, by implication at least, with the underlying terror caused by the prospect of the ineffable loneliness of being laid in a frozen tomb. This acute sense of isolation is unmistakeable here and I want both to draw attention to it in itself and notice how its expression reaches a culminating point in the metaphor of incomplete healing. This 'materialization' does make a figurative sense, but one does need to observe again that that figurative sense – loneliness imagined as physical damage and pain – is problematic in a psychoanalytic context. The problem arises, as it does incidentally in the comments about 'war neurotics', because the figurative preoccupation with the physicality of burial or concussion is at odds with the argument about the non-physiological cause of the medical conditions being discussed.

There are a few further references to telephones in Freud's writing and each of them has to do with the problems of love and loneliness that also surface in *Civilization and its Discontents*. The first of these mentions comes very early, in the 'Project for a Scientific Psychology' (1950 [1887–1902]):

> it happened to me during the agitation caused by a great anxiety that I forgot to make use of the telephone, which had been introduced into my house a short time before. The recent pathway succumbed in the affective state: *facilitation* – that is, what was *old-established* – gained the upper hand'. (**1: 357**)

Again here is an explicit mention of Freud's own gloomy mood and the casual reference to the new communication tool strangely anticipates the mention many years later: in his agitation, the phone is no good to Freud – it cannot, because of his agitation, in which he loses some possession of himself, be of assistance to him. As in *Civilization and its Discontents,* the technology really cannot much alleviate a problem of isolation and disconcertedness. One might discern here the beginnings of a rough morphology of psychoanalytic accounts of interpersonal crises; first of all, as with the primitive dwelling, the 'first lodging', there is the problem of dismaying separateness and isolation, where the structures that are built or the tools that are available for use are necessary but insufficient compensation for the fact of a lonely independence which can be jeopardized in moments of alarm such that available assistance is forgotten.[11]

But in addition to the fundamental problems of isolation and panic, there is also the obverse danger of overdependence or misplaced, self-damaging loving – a danger that is one of the most distinctively and elaborately described states in Freud's work. In the *Introductory Lectures,* he describes an occurrence in his treatment of a patient: 'I had forbidden him to telephone to the girl he was in love with, and then, when he meant to telephone to me, he asked for the wrong number "by mistake" or "while he was thinking of something else" and suddenly found himself connected to the girl's number' (**15: 78**, 1: 106). On this occasion, as on many others that Freud describes, the problem is not distance nor absence but rather a corrosive intimacy and one that persists in spite of absence. Loneliness is better in such a case than love because the love in question causes harm. Whereas the telephone Freud forgets to use is there so that, if he were but to remember, he could call out for help, this other telephone is a licentious instrument that enables precisely what it did not in Freud's case: access to a longstanding, 'old-established' source of comfort – but a comfort, we must suppose by virtue of Freud's prohibition, that is in fact debilitating. Absence and separateness here are essential to well-being.

In the face of all the havoc in modernity, all the destruction and momentum and undeflectable, wound-inflicting mechanical force, Freud looks to the bonds between people for consolation. 'Here all is distance / there it was breath' is Rilke's formulation, imagining a palpable physical presence as a lost state that a present loneliness cannot get back to – and whose recollection only compounds a sense of isolation. Freud also has a sense of such an intimate presence and familiarity, as with his remarks about family and friendship in *Civilization and its*

Discontents. More interestingly still, though, is the distinctively psychoanalytic idea of interpersonal connection, which Freud of course calls 'transference', in psychotherapy – a radical breaking-down, as Freud imagines it, of the partitions between persons. As Freud writes in the technical paper, 'Recommendations to Physicians Practising Psycho-Analysis' (1912):

> Just as the patient must relate everything that his self-observation can detect, and keep back all logical and affective objections that seek to induce him to make a selection from among them, so the doctor must put himself in a position to make use of everything he is told for the purposes of interpretation and of recognizing the concealed unconscious material without substituting a censorship of his own for the selection that the patient has forgone. To put it in a formula: he must turn his own unconscious like a receptive organ towards the transmitting unconscious of the patient. He must adjust himself to the patient as a telephone receiver is adjusted to the transmitting microphone. Just as the receiver converts back into soundwaves the electric oscillations in the telephone line which were set up by sound waves, so the doctor's unconscious is able, from the derivatives of the unconscious which are communicated to him, to reconstruct that unconscious, which has determined the patient's free associations. (**12: 115–6**)

Given the context of loneliness and the absence of loved ones, this miraculous telephone interconnects persons so that there is no impediment to their blending together, with no obstruction to the transmission of information, knowledge, emotion. It is like the breathing presence Rilke imagines. And, especially in its emphasis on how the psychoanalyst may 'reconstruct that unconscious' which is laid so bare in this telecommunication, this passage is a figure of Freud's theory that directly corresponds with the remarks about archaeology in the Dora case history, the imagined telephone being an analogue of the full understanding to which Freud often lays claim.

And there is no conspicuous sense here of ruined and fragmentary evidence, no countersense like that. Yet we may note that the boundaries of selves are disappearing in this passage and that disappearance is troubling in the context of psychological theory. So indeed trouble and countersense may not be far away – and trouble of a recognizable kind. One may note another description of the transference, to be found in *The Question of Lay Analysis: Conversations with an Impartial Person* (1926):

> It would be folly to attempt to evade ... difficulties by suppressing or neglecting the transference; whatever else has been done in the treatment, it would not deserve the name of an analysis. To send the patient away as soon as the inconveniences of his transference neurosis make their appearance would be no more sensible, and would moreover be cowardly. It would be as though one had conjured up spirits [*Geister*] and run away from them as soon as they appeared. Sometimes, it is true, nothing else is possible. There are cases in which one cannot master the unleashed transference and the analysis has to be broken off; but one must at least have struggled with the evil spirits [*bösen Geistern*] to the best of one's strength. (**20: 227**, 15: 328–9, *14: 258–9*)

In this final quotation, Freud explicitly uses the vocabulary of supernaturalism in order to discuss problems of psychoanalytic theory. The ghosts here are not spectral apparitions on some windswept rampart; they are rather figures of endangered understanding and, in this case, of therapeutic crisis. In the context of psychoanalytic treatment, and especially the notional blending together of patient and doctor, the crisis extends also to the integrity and identity of individual minds and it is to other manifestations of that crisis that I shall now turn.

2
Others' Memories

In the first part (1992) of *Angels in America*, Tony Kushner has Harper, the saddened wife of a secretly homosexual husband, make a statement that, in isolation, would seem plainly self-evident:

> If I didn't ever see you before and I don't think I did, then I don't think you should be here, in this hallucination, because in my experience the mind, which is where hallucinations come from, shouldn't be able to make up anything that wasn't there to start with, that didn't enter it from experience, from the real world. Imagination can't create anything new, can it? It only recycles bits and pieces from the world and reassembles them into visions.[1]

And this is surely uncontentious – this is how the mind works. It is a matter of common sense. One sees something, feels, learns and through those processes one accumulates sensory information (including information about mental internality) which, in the form of memory, is the ground of thought and perception and knowledge. If one has not seen someone, one cannot recognize them; if one has not witnessed something, one cannot remember it. It would seem unreasonable or mystical to suggest otherwise.

But fiction, for a start, complicates this empiricist good sense. In this scene, Harper is addressing Prior – recently diagnosed with HIV, subsequently abandoned by his lover and soon to experience visions of ancestors and angels – whom she has never met. The stagecraft problematizes the self-evidence of Harper's remark. Harper '*is having a pill-induced hallucination*', but the scene is in fact a '*Mutual dream scene*'.[2] Each character dreams, Harper in a narcotic delirium, and in these dreams, or rather this shared dream, when the scene is performed (or filmed),[3] they meet and speak; the reality of the performance frames this hallucinatory encounter made possible by an impossible shared dreaming, a fantasia.

Impossible? A passage in another work in the tradition of American visionary fiction proposes something every bit as strange. In *Moby-Dick* (1851), Melville dwells on the involuntary primal terror caused by the dreadful white whale – a terror that seems deeper than conscious understanding and which he elaborates in relation to the behaviour of a young, wild horse:

> Tell me, why this strong young colt, foaled in some peaceful valley of Vermont, far from all beasts of prey – why is it that upon the sunniest day, if you but shake a fresh buffalo robe behind him, so that he cannot even see it, but only smells its wild animal muskiness – why will he start, snort, and with bursting eyes paw the ground in phrensies of affright? There is no remembrance in him of any gorings of wild creatures in his green northern home, so that the strange muskiness he smells cannot recall to him anything associated with the experience of former perils; for what knows he, this New England colt, of the black bisons of distant Oregon?
>
> No: but here thou beholdest even in a dumb brute, the instinct of the knowledge of the demonism in the world.[4]

With its own wild frenzies and bursts, this passage is no observant treatise on equine behaviour, nor yet, at all, a philosophical argument; it defies rationalism in favour of some other, quasi-mystical modality of apprehension.

The reasonable account of experience and real-world observation informing perception and understanding cannot make room for 'the instinct of the knowledge of the demonism in the world' – for knowledge cannot, in rational terms, be instinctual; it is a perceptual acquisition stored as memory. Melville acknowledges this: the colt has 'no remembrance' of what terrifies him – the dense, rich smell of the buffalo 'cannot recall to him anything associated... with experience'. And yet, says Melville, both the colt and Ishmael have such knowledge of some sort, as he himself does. '[N]either knows where lie the nameless things of which the mystic sign gives forth such hints; yet with me, as with the colt, somewhere these things exist'.[5] These passages from literature are fascinatingly congruent with Freud's work when it comes to the problem of the supposedly logical relationship between perception, experience, knowledge and memory – and, further, the notional relationship between persons that would preclude as impossible such a phenomenon as a 'mutual dream'. In his early work, Freud echoes Harper's experience-based assumptions about knowledge. He writes in the 'Project' that:

> The aim and end of all thought-processes is thus to bring about a *state of identity*... *Cognitive* or *judging* thought seeks an identity with a bodily cathexis, *reproductive* thought seeks it with a psychical cathexis of one's own (an experience of one's own) [*mit einer psychischen Besetzung (eigenes Erlebnis)*]. Judging thought operates in advance of reproductive thought by furnishing it with ready-made facilitations for further associative travelling. If after the conclusion of the act of thought the indication of reality reaches the perception, then a *judgement of reality, belief*, has been achieved and the aim of the whole activity attained. (**1: 332–3**)[6]

But later he grows convinced – increasingly so, in fact – that another kind of so-called knowledge might exist in the mind. An inherited forgotten knowledge which travels across history and between minds, a knowledge without a basis in personal experience, a stranger to it. Near the end of his life, despite all protests and objections, Freud definitively insists on his longstanding belief that, as he puts it in *Moses and Monotheism: Three Essays* (1939 [1937–9]), 'the archaic heritage of human beings comprises not only dispositions but also subject-matter – memory-traces of the experience of earlier generations' (**23: 99**, 13: 345). Freud, in fact, like Melville, makes a direct analogy in the 'Wolf Man' case history, 'From the History of an Infantile Neurosis' (1918 [1914]), to the '*instinctive* knowledge of animals' (**17: 120**, 9: 364)[7] – the knowledge itself having a certain 'demonism': 'men have always known (in this special way) that they once possessed a primal father and killed him' (**23: 101**, 13: 246), as Freud puts it in *Moses and Monotheism*.

A country outside identity

Freud's psycho-Lamarckian convictions – his belief in the inheritance of acquired characteristics as a species evolves and, more specifically, the transgenerational survival of unrecalled memories – are among the most controversial ideas in his work. They are so controversial that, as I shall discuss, they are often simply dismissed as aberrant and irrelevant. And indeed they defy not only science but also rationality:[8] what is supposedly acquired has the status of knowledge, though knowledge that may generally be inaccessible to conscious understanding, which is not a by-product of cognition, not having derived from perception or reason or even imagination. It is vestigial and quasi-instinctual.

The difficulty involved here has been precisely outlined by Cathy Caruth in terms of what the psycho-Lamarckian theory means in relation to the psychology of an individual: 'How can there be, at the origin, already a memory?'[9] Freud's inherited-memory theory is at odds with the idea that the mind of an individual is self-constituted on the basis of experience and cognition. Instead it is proposed, insistently so, that the individual mind is at its inception not its own: others' memories are there already, the memory of others' experiences exist at the outset. The different accounts of relationships between persons that were mentioned in the last chapter all assumed a sense of what an individual is such that both loneliness and destructive interdependence emerge as problems. The inherited-memory theory shakes that fundamental concept, suggesting instead that, as Mikkel Borch-Jacobsen puts it in a discussion of dreaming, 'the ego blends its characteristics with those of an outsider.'[10] There is a radical problem of non-identity, non-selfsameness, Freud's comments in the 'Project' notwithstanding, caused by the theory of inherited memory.

Not everything that is considered and explored in the 'Project' comes to fruition in Freud's canonical and published works. But much does re-emerge. That thought is expeditionary but instrumental, purposeful in its work of unifying or bringing together, and is an idea that carries through from the 'Project' into, for example, *The Interpretation of Dreams*: 'All thinking is no more than a circuitous path from the memory of a satisfaction (a memory which has been adopted as a purposive idea) to an identical cathexis of the same memory which it is hoped to attain once more through an intermediate stage of motor experiences' (**5: 602**, 4: 762). This is abstract but it is also essential: a very definition of the thinking process.

Thinking is a process and a journey by this account; but it is a journey down the road of remembering. The 'circuitous path' of thought may be circuitous, but it is still a path. Thinking is expeditionary, travelling, but a way is already made for it, and the destination is familiar: it has been visited before and the work of thought is to find it again, 'to attain once more' the place that has been made by an experience or the memory of that experience. So thinking has a purpose that is achievable because its journey is already prepared for, mapped. The difficulty presented by the theory of inherited memory is that it removes one crucial basis, one's own experience, for the intelligibility of such an account of thinking; it shakes fundamental ideas of identity, self-sameness, ownership.

These are disturbingly counterintuitive ideas. What sense can we make of them, if any at all? In order to approach some answers to this question, it is worth exploring in some more detail the radical overturning of theoretical assumptions that found psychoanalysis – the shift, that is, away from identity-based psychology – which occurs as a result of Freud's psycho-Lamarckism.

How does Freud get to the inherited-memory theory and then consolidate it? There are two precipitating theoretical developments that pave the way for the consolidation of the inherited-memory theory, both of which are well known and may for my purposes be summarized. The first of these occurs in the mid-1890s, when Freud gives up his belief that abuse or molestation necessarily cause neurotic illness. Freud posits instead that the illness should in many cases be traced back to fantasy. The second decisive development occurs definitively with the publication of *Totem and Taboo: Some Points of Agreement between the Mental Lives of Savages and Neurotics* (1912–13), with its elaborate account of the prehistoric murder of a primal patriarch by his rebellious sons. That extraordinary anthropological hypothesis is not by itself decisively significant, however fascinating and daring it may be; what matters is Freud's further assertion, which he never gives up, that the fact of the murder is stored from generation to generation in the form of unconscious memories.

So, Freud writes in *Totem and Taboo*, anticipating his unequivocal acceptance of psycho-Lamarckism:

> Unless psychical processes were continued from one generation to another, if each generation were obliged to acquire its attitude to life anew, there would be…next to no development. This gives rise to two further questions: how much can we attribute to psychical continuity in the sequence of generations? and what are the ways and means employed by one generation in order to hand on its mental states to the next one? I shall not pretend that these problems are sufficiently explained or that direct communication and tradition – which are the first things that occur to one – are enough to account for the process. Social psychology shows very little interest, on the whole, in the manner in which the required continuity in the mental life of successive generations is established. A part of the problem seems to be met by the inheritance of psychical dispositions which,

> however, need to be given some sort of impetus in the life of the individual before they can be aroused into actual operation.... The problem would seem even more difficult if we had to admit that mental impulses could be so completely suppressed as to leave no trace whatever behind them. But this is not the case. Even the most ruthless suppression must leave room for distorted surrogate impulses and for reactions resulting from them. (**13: 158–9**, 13: 220–1)

Freud's qualification of the basic idea of 'the inheritance of psychical dispositions' – that they require to be given individual 'impetus' – is important and, later, it will allow him to rebut the suggestion that he is formulating a version of Jungian theories (see Chapter 3). One can sense here a certain struggle on Freud's part: what is dearest to his thinking is this paradoxical non-conscious 'continuity' that is unattributable to 'direct communication and tradition', but since that idea might seem to invalidate the very premises of psychoanalysis to the extent that those premises concern the way in which mechanisms of development go wrong in individuals, it is necessary to make this apparently straightforward qualification.

The two elements of retheorization come together shortly after *Totem and Taboo* with the concept of 'primal phantasies' that is elaborated in the *Introductory Lectures* (although it depends on the Wolf Man case history, which was underway but not yet published). In formulating the concept, Freud confirms that the sexual abuse of children by male relatives is a fact that psychoanalysts are able, on occasions, to establish 'unimpeachably'. But abuse is not a necessary event for the onset of illness whose manifestations suggest such incidents:

> If they have occurred in reality, so much to the good; but if they have been withheld by reality, they are put together from hints and supplemented by phantasy. The outcome is the same, and up to the present we have not succeeded in pointing to any difference in the consequences, whether phantasy or reality has the greater share in these events of childhood. Here we simply have once again one of the complemental relations that I have so often mentioned; moreover it is the strangest of all we have met with. Whence comes the need for these phantasies and the material for them? There can be no doubt that their sources lie in the instincts; but it still has to be explained why the same phantasies with the same content are created on every occasion. I am prepared with an answer that which I know will seem daring to you. I believe these are *primal phantasies*, as

> I should like to call them, and no doubt a few others as well, are a phylogenetic endowment. In them the individual reaches beyond his own experience into primaeval experience at points where his own experience has been too rudimentary. It seems to me ... possible that all the things that are told to us today in analysis as phantasy – the seduction of children, the inflaming of sexual excitement by observing parental intercourse, the threat of castration (or rather castration itself) – were once real occurrences in the primaeval family times of the human family, and that children in their phantasies are simply filling in the gaps in individual truth with prehistoric truth. I have repeatedly been led to suspect that the psychology of the neuroses has stored up in it more of the antiquities of human development than any other source. (**16: 370–1**, 1: 417–8)

These are the steps that lead to the consolidation of Freud's theory of inherited memory, which will remain a fixed part of his work thereafter. Of the two theoretical developments, by far the more destabilizing is the second – the contention that memories may be endowments from the prehistoric past. The idea that fantasy may replace an act in eventually triggering neurosis involves a displacement of significance from, one might say, act to idea, event to imagining, but either way experience is the large and circumscribing category in which everything takes place. That is no longer the case when it comes to the concept of primal fantasy. With that concept, experience is no longer all-embracing. Experience can indeed be just 'rudimentary', 'withheld' by the world, in need of supplementation.

Two documents

The initially extended psychoanalytic understanding of experience as being constituted by thought processes – imaginings, dreams, desires – involves an enlargement of experience to include more than events and their perception; but the further extension requires that experience be understood as potentially insufficient to account for the mind's contents. And so remembering – if, by that word, one understands in this context something personal, self-referential, the thought process in which experience (in the enlarged sense) is called back to mind in whatever way (which is to say, in whatever relation or non-relation to conscious awareness) – requires to be distinguished from memory, the latter being now something overarching and excessive of personal experience even if, by Freud's account, this memory still involves a kind of knowing, the 'special' kind he refers to in *Moses and Monotheism*. To put the problem in a concise way: what is at stake is a transition from a theory concerned with memory deficit to one concerned with memory surplus.

In the famous early declaration by Freud and Breuer, which Freud is still using in *Five Lectures on Psycho-Analysis* (1910 [1909]), *'hysterical patients suffer from reminiscences'* (**11: 16**), it is a matter of unremembered experience pressing, in the form of manifestations of illness, to be avowed: in the remembering of the experience, whether it be real or imagined, is the healing. But remembering is not an option for the non-experienced realm of memory Freud claims to discover: that realm is, precisely, beyond experience, unrememberable. Or, otherwise said, it is not one's own; it is outside of identity and we cannot conceive of any idea of identity in the light of Freud's inherited-memory theory now unless it is to be at the cost of the idea of experience constituting memory.

It is worth considering this problem in respect of the account of thought in the 'Project'; there, Freud explains thought as transitional – its aim is to retrieve pre-established coordinates, to cross-refer. It is instrumental, purposive, directional: it is expeditionary but only in the selfsame, known country of experience. With the hypothesis of the transgenerational inheritance of others' experience, which is not remembered, what emerges is ... another country. That country, which has never been mapped by personal perception or cognition, even if it is somehow known, is both historically far distant – an ancient country without roads, tyrannized by a violent patriarch – and, in a different but equally wide sense, not within familiar borders; it is outside personal identity. And yet it is known in Freud's 'special way'. How is thinking to travel this country? On the basis of the goal-directed and expeditionary account of thinking in the 'Project' and *The Interpretation of Dreams*, it would seem that thinking becomes impossible to conceive of. Or perhaps one had better say that because thinking would now, in the light of inheritance of others' experiences, not have familiar roads to travel to familiar destinations, it is impossible to conceive that it is able to finish its journeying.

It may be helpful at this point to juxtapose early and late remarks by Freud that emphasize both the radical upsetting of the ground of personal experience and also suggest the problems of thinking and erroneous self-knowing that ensue, including the disturbances of psychoanalytic theorizing. First there is this statement in the *Studies on Hysteria*:

> It was as though we were examining a dossier [*Archiv*] that had been kept in good order. The analysis of my patient Emmy von N. contained

> similar files of memories [*Erinnerungsfaszikel*] though they were not so fully enumerated and described. These files form a quite general feature of every analysis and their contents always emerge in a chronological order which is as infallibly trustworthy as the succession of days of the week or names of the month in a mentally normal person. They make the work of analysis more difficult by the peculiarity that, in reproducing the memories, they reverse the order in which these originated. The freshest and newest experience in the file appears first, as an outer cover, and last of all comes the experience with which the series in fact began.
>
> I have described such groupings of similar memories into collections arranged in linear sequences (like a file of documents [*Aktenbündel*], a packet, etc.) as constituting 'themes'. These themes exhibit a second kind of arrangement. Each of them is – I cannot express it in any other way – stratified concentrically round the pathogenic nucleus. (**2: 288**, 3: 374, *1: 292*)

Here the relationship between memory and experience is reducible to a bounded idea of personal identity. That identity may be multiform but its organization is 'infallibly trustworthy' so that it is explicitly a matter of cross-reference and the internal interrelationship of discretely framed parts. We may see here a recurring aspect of Freud's theorizing (discussed in Chapter 4) which is concerned with topography: the nuclear centre, the peripheral covering, the concentric stratification. The orderedness is likewise historically intelligible, even though it is unexpectedly arranged in reverse order; and yet all the same it is as familiar and cogent as 'the succession of days of the week or names of the month'. And Freud's analogy here with documentation and archiving – as if he were a librarian or a bureaucrat – is a somewhat charming instance of explanatory self-confidence: it is just a question of the proper retrieval of well-arranged textual information.

By the time of *Moses and Monotheism*, the texts being spoken of are entirely different and so is their world. The texts are not the jacketed and labelled files in a consulting room or an office, they are the antiquarian's scraps and fragments, barely decipherable, like hieroglyphics which (as Freud mentions in an aside in the *Introductory Lectures*) 'betray vagueness in a variety of ways which we would not tolerate in our writing today' (**15: 230**, 1: 268). In reconstructing, as he asserts, the murder of the Egyptian Moses and a subsequent Jewish abandonment of monotheism, Freud refers to the Biblical Hexateuch (Genesis, Exodus, Leviticus, Numbers, Deuteronomy, Joshua) in terms of its 'distortion', its occlusions and omissions – these books 'have mutilated and amplified' historical events in the service of 'their secret aims', leaving however evidence of this secret work in the form of 'noticeable gaps, disturbing repetitions and obvious contradictions'. Overall, Freud writes, the distorting effect 'resembles a murder: the difficulty is not in perpetrating the deed, but in getting rid of its traces' (**23: 43**, 13: 283).

Striking changes have taken place in Freud's work in an interval of more than 40 years and they are highly conspicuous in this juxtaposition. There is the shift in the idea of explanation, which is focused in the differing accounts of textual evidence: from the well-kept files with their internal logic and topology to the ravaged sacred writings. Intelligibility is no longer what is highlighted, but complex kinds of undecipherability. There is a shift therefore also in historical perspective and in milieu: the quasi-bureaucratic and modern keeper of orderly records is transformed into the scholar of antiquity, poring over enigmatic documents – but we can see how there is continuity here with the way Freud describes modern technology (as discussed in Chapter 1). And there is, most apparently of all, a whole other thematic in the late work: the murder and mutilation. It is helpful to register just that topical development and the way its concern is not just to the notional event of the primal killing but also, as if to assert itself still further by the postulated resemblance, to its inaccurate memorialization. The Hexateuch, in Freud's interpretation of it, murders the murder by its work of distortion. Or, more precisely, it murders the murder that it nonetheless memorializes and, as Freud would have it (referring now to the Yahwist and Elohist narratives), interns. The biblical texts 'were like mausoleums beneath which ... the true account of those early things ... was, as it were, to find its eternal rest' (**62**, 303–4).

By Freud's own account, form repeats and actually re-enacts content here. The memorializing texts do not name the murder the knowledge of which nonetheless, secretly, they conserve. This intricate idea combined with its part in a wide-ranging, long-reaching, ancient-minded death awareness in Freud's later writings underlines the psycho-Lamarckian theorizing. It is the dead's knowledge that shatters the identity of personal experience. However incongruous or uncanny that may sound, however out of place it may seem in a discussion of theories of mental states, it is nevertheless what Freud means by the inherited-memory theory, especially in *Moses and Monotheism*:

> I must admit that I have behaved for a long time as though the inheritance of memory-traces of the experience of our ancestors,

> independently of direct communication and of the influence of education by the setting of an example, were beyond question. When I spoke of the survival of a tradition among a people or of the formation of a people's character, I had mostly in mind an inherited tradition of this kind and not one transmitted by communication. Or at least I made no distinction between the two and was not clearly aware of my audacity in neglecting to do so. My position, no doubt, is made more difficult by the present attitude of biological science, which refuses to hear of the inheritance of acquired characters by succeeding generations. I must, however, in all modesty confess that nevertheless I cannot do without this factor in biological evolution.
>
> If we assume the survival of these memory-traces in the archaic heritage, we have bridged the gulf between individual and group psychology; we can deal with peoples as we do with an individual neurotic. Granted that at the time we have no stronger evidence for the presence of memory-traces in the archaic heritage than the residual phenomena of the work of analysis which call for a phylogenetic derivation, yet this evidence seems to us strong enough to postulate that such is the fact. (**23: 99–100**. 13: 345–6)

There are some disingenuous flourishes here: the 'present attitude of biological science' sounds as if psycho-Lamarckism were not so controversial as it clearly was (as Freud well knew); and there is something very unconvincing about the claim to have 'bridged the gulf between individual and group psychology', the metaphor suggesting unification and cohesion and happy conjunction when what is at stake is the dismembering of personal experience. It is also worth noting the phrase 'not... transmitted by communication'. It is used elsewhere, as we shall see in Chapter 4.

To be sure, Freud concedes a certain audaciousness in his theorizing, but not so as to give the impression that what is proposed is in fact very disconcerting. And yet he is cutting the last of the rational ground away and making sure that we know it. Freud might have allowed for some attenuated form of cultural awareness of the prehistoric happenings, some cabalistic whisperings, say, some possibility that what is universally known in the special way of inherited memory might not in fact have been so completely forgotten. Or he might have, more credibly and predictably, placed much less emphasis on the historical reality of the event whose record is inherited, relying on some communal tendencies of individual imaginative capacity. But Freud makes no such qualifications. These dreadful forgotten memories that are not one's own, not to be remembered, must, in his account, be assumed to persist despite not being communicated in any intelligible way.

The foregoing quotations make clear how great a change has occurred between the beginning and the end of Freud's work. The crucially displaced idea is that of personal experience: it has deteriorated, been weathered down to very little in terms of its grounding function for personality. The really weighty memories, the ones that source the crucial individual desires and imaginings, now are rooted in prehistoric experience. Freud never gives up on experience to this extent. The primal murder was committed; it was a real event; actions were taken, witnessed, other events followed... until the original violence was *forgotten*. Once the inherited-memory theory is in place, then, there is an astonishing dual revision of the relationship between personal experience and memory. In respect of the contemporary individual self, the experience that matters is someone else's (or, rather, a number of others') that, in fact, *no one remembers*. Selfhood becomes constituted, according to Freud's later theory, by what is not, by what *can never be* – if thought and remembering are to be taken to have a retrieving, functional relationship to personal experience – one's own. Someone else's forgotten experience always penetrates one's own.

An indispensable idea

Freud's psycho-Lamarckism is scientifically discredited. Although it has been argued that Freud's adherence to the theory of inherited memory can be shown to be consistent with Darwinian evolution or the science of DNA,[11] it is mostly accepted that, in historian of science Frank Sulloway's words, it is a matter of 'outmoded' and 'erroneous biological assumptions'.[12] Or, as Stephen Jay Gould puts it: 'Freud's theory was a wild speculation, based upon false biology and rooted in no direct data at all about phylogenetic history.'[13] It has therefore become customary to reject this aspect of Freud's work[14] – to minimize its significance and, more questionably, to play down its very presence.[15] In going on to look at some responses to the inherited-memory theory, I want to hold a simple question in mind: what if we take Freud at his word in *Moses and Monotheism* – that he 'cannot do without' his psycho-Lamarckism?

There is a temptation to edit psycho-Lamarckism out of psychoanalysis, to wish it away. One might think of it in this way: psycho-Lamarckism is like a river in the country of psychoanalysis. Perhaps it is not so navigable a river, perhaps it is torrential and perilous, but if one is to map that country the river cannot, just because it is more dangerous than useful, be omitted from the cartography. And yet this is just what often happens in accounts of Freud's work: the inherited-memory theory is dismissed, ignored or wilfully misinterpreted. In my view, Freud's Lamarckism involves, as in one respect the 'cannot do without' makes clear, a multifold question of compulsion, necessity, obligation. Freud's psycho-Lamarckism is a theory of obligation – to the past, to ancestral experience – that he came to feel under some kind of obligation to restate and honour in spite of its discredit and (as we shall see) its dysfunction as far as yielding conclusive explanations goes, and despite how little is left in its wake of the self of identity and experience. Freud's persistence in holding to the theory of the inheritance of memory-traces wreaks havoc with his explanatory project, even as it does so in the name of explanation and neat, well-organized knowledge. The question of the absolute validity of Lamarck's scientific hypotheses is different from the question of what the actual effects of these hypotheses are in the spaces of Freud's writing, and to foreground the first will mean we risk not being able to answer the second.

Psycho-Lamarckism was, in fact, discredited (as Freud's remarks in *Moses and Monotheism* make clear enough) already by the 1930s (though it would continue to have currency in the Soviet Union under the guise of 'Lysenkism'). This just did not matter to Freud. It is not that he was unaware of the problem. Ernest Jones makes it all very clear in his biography:

> Freud never gave up a jot of his belief in the inheritance of acquired characters. How immovable he was in the matter I discovered during a talk I had with him in the last year of his life over a sentence I wished him to alter (in the Moses book) in which he expressed the Lamarckian view in universal terms. I told him he had of course the right to hold any opinion he liked in his own field of psychology, even if it ran counter to all biological principles, but begged him to omit the passage where he applied it to the whole field of biological evolution, since no responsible biologist regarded it as any longer tenable. All he would say was that they were all wrong and the passage must stay.[16]

Jones was embarrassed by Freud's stubborn persistence and he feared for the reputation of psychoanalysis, as he had also done a few years before when Freud decided that there was merit in the idea of telepathy (which I shall discuss in Chapter 5). He did his best therefore to persuade Freud to recant or at least to tone down the theory. Jones indeed begged, yet

Freud remained unmoved. There would continue to be embarrassment but, in succeeding years, it would become acceptable in fact to begin to ignore Freud's theorizing in this respect, as Richard Wollheim mostly does in his synoptic monograph.[17]

Even when the theory is mentioned and explored, it is often downplayed or treated as aberrant, absurd. This is the case with perhaps the most sustained scholarly commentary on the subject to have been published in recent years, Yerushalmi's. Yerushalmi, a historian of Judaism, in fact explicitly calls Freud's theory absurd but his engagement is all the same concerted and intense in its attempt to rebut and seek to refute the substance of what Freud argues, especially the idea of cultural history 'not... transmitted by communication' – cultural history, that is, which is not in the hands of, for example, a hierarchically organized religion. Yerushalmi objects entirely to the proposition that cultural history may work through undisclosed, indeed forgotten secrets. He writes:

> Peoples, groups, at any given time or in any generation, can only 'remember' a past that has been actively transmitted to them, and which they have accepted as meaningful. Conversely, a people 'forgets' when the generation that currently possesses the past does not convey it to the next or when the latter rejects what it has received and does not pass it onward. The break in transmission can occur abruptly or by a gradual process of erosion. In either case the process is rarely, if ever, simultaneous for the entire group, for the group has neither the biological nor psychological homogeneity of the individual. Many and mighty things have been truly and totally forgotten in the course of human history, and these are irretrievable. Other things *seem* to have been forgotten over long periods... only to resurface. When such a reemergence takes place other factors must account for it. For even when most 'forget,' there remain those, be they only individuals, who 'remember'; or... even after most have repressed, some have not, and at certain historical junctures those few to whom they have actively transmitted what they know may play a key role in the anamnesis... among the group as a whole.[18]

It is worth noting here that, in a scintillating intervention in the debate, the Egyptologist Jan Assmann has argued, contrary to Yerushalmi (whom he discusses), that in fact it can be shown that certain historical events can be utterly forgotten but all the same be retrieved, many centuries later, as was the case with the Egyptian monotheistic religion of Akhenhaten (which, of course, is a key element in Freud's argument in *Moses and Monotheism*), and moreover that 'the experience was traumatic enough to produce legendary traditions which – because of their unlocatability in the official cultural memory – became free-floating and thus susceptible to being associated with a variety of semantically related experiences. They formed a "crypt" in the cultural memory of Egypt.'[19] I am not in a position to evaluate these contesting arguments; all I can say here is that Assmann's book is a wonderful challenge to the imagination and it prompted in me the question, what else might have been forgotten? What great and convulsive cultural moments have perished without record, without even fragments and debris? *Moses and Monotheism* encourages that kind of question too and it is worth just registering how Freud's sense of the ancient past is full of mystery and hidden secrets.

Such mystery and secrecy are anathema to Yerushalmi because they are at odds with the authoritative knowledge of cultural and religious groups – knowledge which, in his account, is maintained and transmitted consciously, rationally, didactically, ritualistically, above all purposefully. These are the practices and attitudes that Yerushalmi reasserts in the face of Freud's psycho-Lamarckianism and so one may see, if only on the basis of the reassertion, the extent to which it is difficult to entertain Freud's ideas unless one is prepared to jettison or at least bracket off fundamental ideas of rationality and identity. But it is not as if Freud had been imprecise or tentative. He insists that this is a theory which he cannot do without – this theory of endless remorse and forgetting and unsupposed knowledge finding hiding places in the mind. For the truly radical and hard-to-assimilate element of Freud's theory is not really its hypotheses about incidents in antiquity or their cultural representation (as interesting or baffling as one may find these), but rather its implications for how we conceive of the psychoanalytic theory of an individual mind. Yerushalmi's objection to Freud is, it seems to me, not really to do with the nature of traditional and religious knowledge at the group level, but with the very premises of Freud's individual psychology. Yerushalmi's response to a theory of the unsuspectingly self-divided mind – I mean by this Freud's early account of psychology, as it emerges in *The Interpretation of Dreams*, say, in advance of *Totem and Taboo* – is actually a theory of the purposeful transmission of doctrine, a theory of education as opposed to a theory of uncommunicated memory which is irreducible to rational understanding. There is very little common ground, Yerushalmi's solicitous monologue notwithstanding, between the two sets of ideas and his book is not finally of much help for this reason – except that it emphasizes the extent to which Freud's theory is commonly held to be objectionable.

A specific disagreement among commentators may usefully be brought forward here. Frank Sulloway, in his exhaustive account of Freud's place in the history of science, interprets Freud's psycho-Lamarckism as follows:

> Freud's later works on primitive man and on the origins of religion, law, and civilization are simply a continuation of the basic shift in reductionistic explanation that occurred in his psychoanalytic thinking between 1895 and 1905. That was a shift from *proximate*-causal theory to *ultimate*-causal theory within Freud's abiding ambition of attaining a synthetic, psychobiological solution to the problems of the mind.[20] And Sulloway therefore concludes that, even if he was mistaken in certain of his phylogenetic and anthropological theories, his appeal to those ultimate-causal solutions marks him as a shrewd thinker who fully understood the task of constructing a universal theory of human behavior.[21]

Sulloway's tribute to Freud as an ambitious 'shrewd thinker' is an oddly insubstantial kind of praise, as if ingenuity combined with grand explanatory ambition were in themselves virtuous.[22] That suggestion rings hollow, given Sulloway's emphasis on the theoretical discredit of Lamarckism, but it has the great merit of accepting the presence of Freud's unpopular theories.

Paul Robinson has objected to Sulloway: 'Phylogeny, in effect, is the argument of last resort – not, as Sulloway would have it, of first preference.' This is indeed so (see below): in the Wolf Man case history, Freud clearly states that the history of the species should not be appealed to until an exploration of personal experience has been fully concluded. But the conclusions Robinson draws on the basis of his precise observation are not necessarily justified:

> No doubt Freud believed in his speculations. But they remain, nonetheless, residues of his nineteenth-century scientific education, relegated to the digressive margins in his new psychological science. Even if we were to accept Sulloway's argument that phylogenetic ideas such as the suppressed sense of smell were dearer to Freud than his textual subordination of them implies, we must ask whether Freud's claims to greatness could possibly rest on such speculations.[23]

It is just not the case that Freud marginalizes his psycho-Lamarckism. Despite the protests of those close to him, Freud makes a point of reiterating and underlining the inherited-memory theory as when he says, plainly: 'I cannot do without this factor.' The question of Freud's 'claim to greatness' therefore surfaces as something that may override the problem of psycho-Lamarckism; perhaps in anticipation of the objection that not only did Freud not marginalize his theory, but he also made a point of insisting on their significance in his work (such that they become a kind of compulsively returned-to theme), Robinson invokes the factor of reputability in order to treat Freud's psycho-Lamarckism as an aberrant anomaly that one can reasonably discard.

Yerushalmi's and Robinson's arguments have the merit of clear disbelief and objection; they are on this account to be preferred, in my view, to a particular defence of Freud's position that they have prompted, to be found in a book by Richard J. Bernstein, a philosopher, which has its own contrivance of intimacy (a 'Dialogue with Yerushalmi'). Bernstein asserts that:

> "Applied psychoanalysis" may mislead us into thinking that first we develop the concepts required for the psychoanalysis of neurotic individuals and then we apply them in a straightforward manner to group and cultural phenomena. But Freud is much more dialectical and subtle in what he actually does. His cultural analyses in *Totem and Taboo, Civilization and its Discontents,* and *The Man Moses and the Monotheistic Religion* supplement, modify, and *deepen* our understanding of the dynamic conflicts of the ego, the id, and the super-ego in *individuals.* Our understanding of these dynamic conflicts in individuals is enhanced by the study of culture.[24]

This is a fine rational defence of Freud's theory of irrationality and it seems to me to be unconvincing. Instead of dismissing Freud's psycho-Lamarckism as an anomalous or absurd obsession that is incompatible with the observant and rational explanation to be found elsewhere in psychoanalysis, Bernstein claims that it is in fact after all a kind of helpful observant, reasonable theorizing. Robinson and Yerushalmi say in effect: Freud's ideas on the subject of species inheritance are strangers that have no true place in psychoanalytic theory. Bernstein's response is to suggest that the apparent strangers are in fact familiar old friends. And indeed familiarity in the sense of 'dialectical and subtle' theorizing – theorizing that recognizes phenomena to be intelligible rather than alien, say – is Bernstein's basic concern. He does not sanction 'straightforward' application of concepts but only because that may not be the most effective way to 'supplement, modify, and *deepen* our understanding' so that it can be 'enhanced'. It is all very progressive and genial, appealing to figures that emphasize fit and orderly change and depth and improvement. But such ideas may not work in this context, failing to account not only for the somewhat dismaying quality of compulsion Freud describes as corollary to the inherited-memory theory, but also for the disorderliness that ensues from the theory (notably as regards the status of personal experience). Or, to put this another way, Bernstein makes an appeal to identity or integrity ('enhanced' understanding) at the level of the figure of theory to account for what is Freud's most radical challenge to a notion of personal identity.

We might recall here what Freud has to say about the paradoxical kind of enhancements provided by modern technology and that troubling image of trouble – the prosthesis around which there has not been fully successful healing. What is not considered in the responses to Freud's psycho-Lamarckism that I have discussed is an account of it that does not require an organizing concept of fit or identity, an account that would, for example, work with a concept of irreducible strangeness – as with an unrecognized stranger who is neither welcomed nor dismissed, or a hidden secret memory.

Contraband

Bernstein is in fact taking a cue from Freud, who does not present his psycho-Lamarckian theories as being startling – as when he confidently bridges that gulf, or so he tells us, in *Moses and Monotheism*. Quite the reverse. He says they derive from the observation of evidence obtained in psychoanalytic inquiry. And he says that there is no great difference between one's own experience and others' long-forgotten, long-ago experience. The two may be complementary, fitting together, mere interchangeable pretexts for the important business of the universal business of growing up. If personal experience is 'rudimentary', ancestral experience can make up the deficit. If childhood fantasizing does not take particular directions, ancestral forbidden desires can reawaken to provide the necessary rerouting. And always there will be filial remorse based on a forgotten and therefore all the more powerful, deep-lying, inescapable event: 'the dead father,' as Freud famously writes in *Totem and Taboo*, 'became stronger than the living one had been' (**13: 143**, 13: 204), and the forgotten father becomes more influential than the remembered one had been.

In the texts where Freud deals explicitly with the hypothesis of the prehistoric murder, he does so openly and proudly, in defiance of any objections. But elsewhere, I think, it as if he smuggles this utterly extraordinary contention – with all the implications it has for a new impossibility of experience-derived identity – into psychoanalysis under the guise of something, paradoxically, based on evidence and observation. It is no wonder that so many commentators have refused to accept the smuggled goods. And we can see precisely when, where and in what disguise the contraband arrives. Or, in other words, to rely a little less on the metaphor, Freud often refers to the inherited-memory theory (and therefore to the primal-murder hypothesis) as if it were rather unremarkable.

We have already seen one example of this smuggling, when Freud states in *Totem and Taboo* that 'we simply have once again one of the complemental relations that I have so often mentioned' (albeit that he adds that this one is 'the strangest of all we have met with'). Roughly contemporaneous with that remark, in the 1914 preface to the third edition of the *Three Essays on the Theory of Sexuality* (1905), he furthermore writes:

> Ontogenesis may be regarded as a recapitulation of phylogenesis, in so far as the latter has not been modified by more recent experience. The phylogenetic disposition can be seen at work behind the ontogenetic process. But the disposition is ultimately the precipitate of earlier experience of the species to which the more recent experience of the individual, as the sum of the accidental factors, is super-added. (**7: 131**, 7: 40)

And, in 'The Dissolution of the Oedipus Complex' (1924):

> [One] view is that the Oedipus complex must collapse because the time has come for its disintegration, just as the milk-teeth fall out when the permanent ones begin to grow. Although the majority of human beings go through the Oedipus complex as an individual experience, it is nevertheless a phenomenon which is determined and laid down by heredity and which is bound to pass away according to programme when the next pre-ordained phase of development sets in.... There is room for the ontogenetic view side by side with the more far-reaching phylogenetic one. It is also true that even at birth the whole individual is destined to die, and perhaps his organic disposition may already contain the indication of what he is to die from. Nevertheless, it remains of interest to follow out how

> this innate programme is carried out and in what way accidental noxae exploit his disposition. (**19: 173–4**, 7: 315)

Finally, most breezily speculative of all (to the point of Freud referring to his ideas here as being a 'fantasy'), in the discarded 'Overview of the Transference Neuroses', written in 1915 but not published (and to a small extent reconstructed) until 1987:

> When the constitutional factor of fixation comes into consideration, acquisition [is] not eliminated thereby; it only moves into still earlier prehistory, because one can justifiably claim that the inherited dispositions are residues of the acquisitions of our ancestors. With this one runs into problem of the phylogenetic disposition behind the individual or ontogenetic, and should find no contradiction if the individual adds new dispositions from his own experience to his inherited disposition <acquired> on the basis of earlier experience. Why should the process that creates disposition on the basis of experience cease precisely at the individuals whose neurosis one is investigating? Or <why should> this [individual] create [a] disposition for his progeny but not be able to acquire it for himself? Seems rather <to be> necessary complement.[25]

(It is worth emphasizing again how clear it is in the last passage that the concept of experience is not at all dispensed with: what is laid aside is rather the importance of experience of one's own. And, however much this is a theoretical 'fantasy', it is extremely rigorous. Freud is addressing here, as he does not tend to do elsewhere, the logical inference that the process of transmission of ancestral experience will continue from generation to generation: dispositions and memories go on being bequeathed. The process does not cease.)

What interests me here are the ideas and analogies of organization and intelligible correlation. 'Earlier experience' and 'recent experience' can be seen to make a 'sum', 'super-added'. Ontogenetic and phylogenetic exist 'side by side'. There is 'no contradiction' between inherited and personally experienced factors. It all seems very neat and well-fitting and it is this assertion that I think is in fact disingenuous. But it is important to watch what Freud is doing, or attempting to do. He is introducing a figure of theory to do with ordered, coherent identity to justify his theorizing: these ideas, Freud claims, interrelate. They commingle without obstructing one another. They may be reduced without contradiction. They may be added to one another almost arithmetically.

An aside on other figures of theory is useful here. We have seen already some examples of Freud's explanatory self-consciousness in his claims for successful understanding – the recognizing and riddle-solving and undoing. But there are also numerous examples of Freud declaring his understanding to be provisional (see Chapter 4), uncertain to the point of mystification, stalled or blocked. In the celebrated discussion in *The Interpretation of Dreams* of the 'navel' of a dream, for example, 'the spot where it [dream] reaches down into the unknown', Freud asserts that the 'dream-thoughts to which we are led by interpretation cannot ... have any definite endings; they are bound to branch out in every direction into the intricate network of our world of thought' (5: 525, 4: 671–2). Freud's remarks here about the 'tangle of dream-thoughts which cannot be unravelled' (Ibid.) foreshadow some comments in the 'Rat Man' case history, 'Notes upon a Case of Obsessional Neurosis' (1909): 'It was impossible to unravel this tissue of phantasy thread by thread' (10: 207n, 9: 88). At a level of greater generality in *Inhibitions, Symptoms and Anxiety* (1926 [1925]), Freud writes:

> Why are not all neuroses episodes in the development of the individual which come to a close when the next phase is reached? Whence comes the element of persistence in these reactions to danger? Why does the affect of anxiety alone seem to enjoy the advantage over all other affects of evoking reactions which are distinguished from the rest in being abnormal and which, through their inexpediency, run counter to the movement of life? In other words, we have once more come unawares upon the riddle of which has so often confronted us: whence does neurosis come – what is its ultimate, its own peculiar *raison d'être*? After tens of years of psychoanalytic labours, we are as much in the dark about this problem as we were at the start. (**20: 148–9**, 10: 307)

This disclaiming rhetoric also appears in less technical contexts, as when Freud speaks of gender in the *Outline*:

> We are faced here by the great enigma of the biological fact of the duality of the sexes: it is an ultimate fact for our knowledge. It defies every attempt to trace it back to something else. Psycho-analysis has contributed nothing to clearing up this problem, which clearly falls wholly within the province of biology.... The fact of psychological bisexuality, too embarrasses all our enquiries into the subject and makes them harder to describe. (**23: 188**, 15: 422–3)

Freud is here reprising remarks made in *The Ego and the Id* (1923) about the 'complicating element introduced by bisexuality that makes it so difficult to obtain a clear view of the facts in connection with the earliest object choices and identifications and still more difficult to describe them intelligibly' (**19: 33**, 11: 372). And, finally, there are remarks about art. In 'Dostoevsky and Parricide' (1928 [1927]), Freud writes: 'before the problem of the creative artist analysis must, alas, lay down its arms' (**21: 177**, 14: 441) – reminding one of his more embellished commentary in *Leonardo da Vinci and a Memory of his Childhood* (1910) on Leonardo's pictures of Bacchus, Leda and John the Baptist, which 'breathe a mystical air into whose secret one dares not penetrate' (**11: 117**, 14: 210).

Freud's figures of theory in these remarks are like a counterpoint to the figures of undoing, right-naming and elucidation discussed in Chapter 1. Those figures involve the reduction of complexity to simpler forms of meaning or they concern the act of understanding what is for the moment apparently without meaning. In either case it is a matter of order, rationalization, simplification – as with the supposed concentric arrangement of Freud's patient's 'files of memory'. The rhetoric of entanglement, blockage, secrecy (and the rest) is rather a matter of complexity that is irreducible – and it is thus more redolent of the intransigent scriptural textuality described in *Moses and Monotheism*.

It is against this background that one may question Freud's claim to neatness and fit in theorizing transgenerational memory and inherited experience, especially insofar as this is chiefly a theorizing of causes. Freud cannot, on the occasion when he most assiduously tries it, in the Wolf Man case history, decide between alternative explanations of the 'primal scene' of parental intercourse that, under the various disguises that Freud claims to penetrate, besets his patient. In discussing the scene in question, Freud decides that it is possible that his patient actually witnessed it or that he extrapolated it from the observation of animals or that he imagined it on the basis of an inherited 'primal phantasy'. As to which of these in fact happened, however, Freud is undecided. In an interpolated and bracketed postscript to the case history, he famously writes: 'I intend on this occasion to close the discussion of the reality of the primal scene with a *non liquet*' (**17: 60**, 9: 295) and then refers readers to the theory of 'primal phantasies' in the *Introductory Lectures*.

At the end of the case history, Freud comes back to the problem:

> I should myself be glad to know whether the primal scene in my present patient's case was a phantasy or a real experience; but, taking

> other similar cases into account, I must admit that the answer to this question is not a matter of very great importance. These scenes of observing parental intercourse, of being seduced in childhood, and of being threatened with castration are unquestionably an inherited endowment, a phylogenetic heritage, but they may just as easily be acquired by personal experience. [...]
>
> All that we find in the prehistory of neuroses is that a child catches hold of this phylogenetic experience where his own experience fails him. He fills in the gaps in individual truth with prehistoric truth; he replaces occurrences in his own life by occurrences in the life of his ancestors. I fully agree with Jung in recognizing the existence of this phylogenetic heritage; but I regard it as a methodological error to seize on a phylogenetic explanation before the ontogenetic possibilities have been exhausted. I cannot see any reason for obstinately disputing the importance of infantile prehistory while at the same time freely acknowledging the importance of ancestral prehistory. Nor can I overlook the fact that phylogenetic motives and productions themselves stand in need of elucidation, and that in quite a number of instances this is afforded by factors in the childhood of the individual. And, finally, I cannot feel surprised that what was originally produced by certain circumstances in prehistoric times and was then transmitted in the shape of a predisposition to its re-acquirement should, since the same circumstances persist, emerge once more as a concrete event in the experience of the individual. (**17: 97**, 9: 337–8, *12: 131*)

Freud's rhetoric here is plain but nonetheless artful. It passes off rather remarkable propositions without much demur – and especially, as with the idea quoted above of experience that is too 'rudimentary' (as if experience were a skill), the proposition that experience may have 'fail[ed]' Freud's patient in not providing him with sufficiently shocking 'concrete' events to witness. But the notion of failure is congruent with the overarching figure here, which is to do with 'fill[ing] in the gaps in ... truth' – truth, that is, not one's experience, whose failure it would be in this case (not truth's). Thus the somewhat beguiling statement that 'I should myself be glad to know ... but ... the answer to this question is not a matter of very great importance'. One does not need to look very far further to discover the extent to which personal experience has been undermined as a key concept for Freud. And we can see again the way in which Freud smuggles paradoxical and irreducible or undecidable arguments under the guise of coherent or selfsame knowledge or truth, that overarching concept being buttressed by an explanatory rhetoric of self-assurance that also includes such cues as 'I cannot see any reason for obstinately disputing... Nor can I overlook the fact... I cannot feel surprised'. The blandness of the language is its chief rhetorical feature.

Freud's *'non liquet'* is comparable to his references to tangles and riddles and secrets but it is, as with the figures of theory involving side-by-sideness or 'super-added' elements in relation to psychological and inherited-memory theories, all the same reconceptualized in Freud's conclusion to the Wolf Man case history as being part of some larger coherence (or identity). But the problem of the origin of his patient's illness is not the less undecided for that reconceptualization. Freud's overview of his method renders the difference of opinion between Sulloway and Robinson moot. It confirms Sulloway's point to the extent that it shows how inherited memory may be the ultimately instigating factor in the case where personal experience is 'rudimentary'; it also confirms Robinson's assertion that inherited memory in this context provides an explanation as a 'last resort' ('I regard it as a methodological error to seize on a phylogenetic explanation before the ontogenetic possibilities have been exhausted').

But, either way, the problem is that Freud is not in fact giving us a genetic explanation. What is in fact on offer here is an implicit theory of alternative beginnings – not genetic explanation, that is to say, but something more of the order of 'genetigenic' explanation: explanation (if the word may still be used in this context) that ends with more possible beginnings than it started with, explanation whose work is (despite its plain-spoken and level-headed rhetoric of coherence) generative of self-revision and complexity rather than reductive of it. Peter Brooks has commented on the indecision of the case history:

> We have here one of the most daring moments of Freud's thought, and one of his most heroic gestures as a writer. He could have achieved a more coherent, finished, enclosed, and authoritative narrative by sticking by his arguments of 1914–15, never adding the bracketed passages. Or, given his second thoughts of 1918, he could have struck out parts of the earlier argument and substituted for them his later reflections. What is remarkable is that, having discovered his point of origin, that which made sense of the dream, the neurosis, and his own account of them, Freud then felt obliged to retrace the story, offering another and much less evidential (and 'eventimential') kind of origin, to tell another version of the plot, and then finally leave one juxtaposed

> to the other, indeed one superimposed on the other as a kind of palimpsest, a layered text that offers differing versions of the same story. A narrative explanation that surely foresaw that much of its celebrity would come from its recovery of so spectacular a moment of origin doubles back on itself to question that origin and indeed to displace the whole question of origins, to suggest another kind of referentiality, in that all tales may lead back not so much to events as to other tales, to man as a structure of the fictions he tells about himself.
>
> A narrative account that allows the inception of its story to be either event or fiction – that in turn opens up the potential for another story, anonymous and prehistoric – perilously destabilizes belief in explanatory histories as exhaustive accounts whose authority derives from the force of closure, from the capacity to say: here is where it began, here is what it became.[26]

This is a much better description of the Wolf Man case history in particular and the problem of the inherited-memory theory in general. That theory is presented as cogent and gap-filling, but its implications are disruptive of the notional coherence of experience-based thinking and identity, and its repercussions, in spite of Freud's rhetoric of fit and explanation, are highly disruptive of the purposiveness and fulfilment of Freud's own theorizing.

Guilt and theory

It is all very well saying that Freud's anthropological ideas add to a multifaceted sense of psychology and history or that he reaches for an 'ultimate-causal' explanation when a 'proximate-causal' one eluded him, but to do so is to edit out the fact that, in practice, Freud tends to invoke phylogenetic explanation in order to propose alternative solutions to a problem such that it becomes impossible to decide from a causal point of view which solution is valid. Truth in the form of a definitive explanation is deferred in favour of this work of alternation. It is crucial, I think, to go in the opposite direction to Bernstein (taking his cue from Freud): not to insist that it all adds up neatly and illuminatingly, but to accept the explanatory dysfunction. One can, turning this way, usefully cite some different observations on Freud's psycho-Lamarckism. Michel de Certeau remarks that *Moses and Monotheism*

> provides for a plurality of possible interpretations. What it "means" can only be *silenced*, infinitely *repressed*, forever remaining *to be*

> *expressed*. In its form, the text upholds the terms of a contradiction that... aims at the blind spot of an *I don't know* reiterated in respect every one of its objects'.[27]

René Girard is rather more direct in *Violence and the Sacred* (1972): 'The overlapping of theories in Freud's work, their profusion and multiplicity, can only be interpreted as a sign of failure.'[28] And Philip Rieff, more sympathetically, concurs: 'scarcely anything Freud discovered in the constitution of individual minds requires the Lamarckian hypothesis'.[29] These comments are not quite the same. They imply different kinds of deliberateness in Freud's theorizing. For Certeau, there is a purposeful 'uphold[ing]' of contradictory meanings; Girard also emphasizes overflowing of meaning, but takes it to be a limitation – Freud did not manage to pare down multiple meanings in order to arrive at a definitive explanation; Rieff suggests that Freud may have been driven by some obscure motive in his 'novel and daring' essays in 'psychohistory', concluding that little was accomplished in the process apart from the bewildering, annoying or even offending of readers.[30]

As we have seen, it is common for commentators to sequester Freud's psycho-Lamarckism as a *sui generis* exception to the rest of psychoanalysis, a weird eccentricity: it simply does not belong, or so the suggestion goes, with other Freudian theories. An alternative tactic, more generous but in my view unsustainable, is to finesse the whole question in the name of industrious attempts at ever-more-comprehensive understanding. Psycho-Lamarckism may be discredited, it is asserted, but its presence in Freud's writing has nevertheless some benefit, prompting readers to further thought (so long, at any rate, as it does not prompt outrage). What both of these responses preclude is a reading that considers how the outdated, outmoded, non-functional, perverse, failed theory might make a kind of sense *in its very failure*. One may move towards such a reading by way of the commentaries that I quoted in the previous paragraph; each has the merit of recognizing the extent to which Freud's inherited-memory theory is transgressive. Freud's stubborn elaboration of the theory works against unitary explanation and especially against a coherent account of beginnings.

How then is one to treat Freud's psycho-Lamarckism if one is not to edit it out or simply regard it as failed or outdated? I propose that the idea of countersense is an especially useful one here because it allows for a countervailing sense that is at once transgressive of and intimately belonging to a more conventional idea. The countersense here is the dispossession of experience, the marring of personal identity. And yet, by means of neatly arithmetical figures of theory, Freud uses exactly the idea of identity to introduce into psychoanalysis a conceptualization of how personal identity is ruined. The ideas are not simply in conflict; they do not simply clash or contradict. The sense of identity is, as it were, tidal; the countersense of marring is its undertow. Such, I would argue, is the complex rhetorical machination; the rhetoric is, like the minds being imagined, appropriately not selfsame.

Cathy Caruth suggestively addresses the problem of Freud's psycho-Lamarckism like this:

> But what kind of crime [the primal murder] is this, that can never be discovered in a memory, but only in a kind of forgetting, in an *unconscious* feeling? And what kind of past moreover is constituted by a crime that, as Freud will insist, is never committed by the individual as such but only by what he calls the primal horde of prehistory – a past, therefore, which never, for the individual, *occurs* as such?
>
> These questions, in effect, are not simply about experience but about the way in which experience (in its error) comes to know itself, that is, about psychoanalytic inquiry and theory.[31]

In my account of Freud's psycho-Lamarckism, the problem is not so much a matter of experience's erroneous self-knowing, as the impossibility, in the wake of the idea of original others' memories, of any successful such knowledge. Experience and knowledge come to stand in a new relationship to one another, the latter increasingly dispossessing the former. One needs to begin to conceptualize the individual mind as being preoccupied by the memory of incidents that are beyond the frame of its own experience so that thinking can no longer travel back to the identity of a personal experience. And so it is a matter of the individual mind being no longer a selfsame unit, being instead encroached upon by others' memories and so by a burdening ancient past. Caruth's emphasis on guilt suggests a similar sense of obligation and a similarly weighed-down thinking which is no longer able to travel swiftly and surely.

In exploring Freud's psycho-Lamarckian theory of inherited memory, I have emphasized the way it subverts a concept of personal identity. And although Freud uses another, organizational concept of identity to describe the presence of inherited-memory theory in psychoanalysis, it seems more adequate to look for other descriptions. So, in particular, it is necessary to note that the psycho-Lamarckian ideas complicate Freud's explanatory schemes rather than simplifying them by, for example, referring different phenomena to the same ultimate cause. There is this referral, but its effect is to generate further alternative accounts of causality and so make the past in which Freud always seeks explanation more rather than less mysterious. And so his work, with what Jean Laplanche calls its 'passion for the phylogenetic',[32] becomes more and more preoccupied by the past, more and more retrospectively fascinated with historical meanings. But these meanings are intransigent so that the attempt to retrieve them becomes seemingly self-perpetuating, as if retrospection rather than explanation had become a purpose in itself. There is, as Laplanche and J.-B. Pontalis put it in a superb essay, 'a passion for investigation, pursued ever deeper', a 'search for chronology, going backwards', during which, instead of there being a culminating moment of revelatory discovery of event or occurrence, 'the "scene" ... disappears over the horizon'.[33]

Caruth makes a further observation from which one may take a lead: 'The problem *of* guilt is also the guilt of the theory: if the murder of the primal father is thus the locus of a convergence between the originating *act* and the *knowledge* of that origination, between guilt and theory.'[34] What might guilt mean in this context? It might be another way of describing the accumulation of alternative explanations that results from the cherished psycho-Lamarckism. It might be said that guilt involves, or at least is indicative of, a particular sort of retrospective theorizing. In Freud's myth of origins, guilt is the attitude to the primal murder that progressively builds that event into a monolith of memory. The past, by this account, becomes a force field that both repels and attracts a fascinated looking-back. Guilt successively repudiates and yearns for the past. It cannot exactly recall what it longs to recover. Guilt as a mode of theorizing would thus be self-complicating, self-replicating. In Freud's account of his work in this area, the guilt is finally dispelled; the primal murder is uncovered as a historical fact; the force field loses its energy. But it might be more accurate to say that the guilt regenerates in one particular sense – because its uneasy relationship to the past revives in the multiplications of explanations of the past that are bred by Freud's theorizing (insofar as this theorizing is not forcibly divested of its psycho-Lamarckian aspects). More: the import of the theory is that the individual mind must, in spite of its own integrity, at the cost of great damage, at pain of forceful intrusion, be formatively inhabited by the traces of the violent past. History breaks into the mind; others' memories are stockaded in the world of experience. And so ideas of species-history invade an experience-based psychology that would otherwise have a coherent identity.

Describing the composition of *Moses and Monotheism*, Freud writes that the work 'tormented me like an unlaid ghost [*ein unerlöster Geist*]' (**23: 103**, 13: 349, *16: 210*), echoing a passage written some thirty years previously in the 'little Hans' case history, 'Analysis of a Phobia in a Five-Year-Old Boy' (1909): 'In an analysis ... a thing which has not been understood inevitably reappears; like an unlaid ghost [*ein unerlöster Geist*], it cannot rest until the mystery has been solved and the spell broken' (**10: 122**, 8: 280, *7: 355*). In purporting to lay to rest the ghosts of human prehistory, Freud constructs an account of psychology that makes a strange space for others' memories. As his compulsively retrospective theorizing proceeds, minds are increasingly conceptualized as overburdened and deformed by the past, resembling thus the very theorizing in which they are imagined.

3
Mourning as Ethics and Argument

Freud himself draws attention to the compulsive and burdening quality of his inherited-memory theory. The arguments in *Moses and Monotheism* 'tormented' him 'like an unlaid ghost', obliging him to write them out; he could not do without them. Fully aware that psycho-Lamarckism was viewed by scientists with disdain, Freud held fast to the idea that one's own experience is not the measure of memory. How to account for this fastness and fixity of purpose? Anti-Freudian commentators claim that the psycho-Lamarckism, especially in the Wolf Man case history, is evidence of dogmatic obstinacy. Malcolm Macmillan states that 'a postulate for which there was no evidence other than the gaps in his speculative reconstructions is at once a measure of the weakness of the developmental schema and of the strength of the grip the conformity assumption had' on Freud.[1] Frank Cioffi bemoans 'an appearance of intricate coherence where the items are not genuinely related'.[2] John Farrell speaks for many when he interprets Freud's theorizing as gratuitously forceful, concerned above all to assert the truth of pre-existing psychoanalytic theory:

> Lamarckian evolution, Fechner's law, Fleiss's theories of sexual cycles, the 'bio-genetic' doctrine that 'ontogeny recapitulates phylogeny', these errant principles themselves now look, even to the Freudian, like narcissistic projections or 'secondary revisions' imposed upon the data in order to provide an intellectual context satisfying to the mind's sense of coherence.[3]

Farrell uses psychoanalytic concepts in order to attack psychoanalytic theory and this significantly diminishes his attack. But even if this were not the case, I wonder how seriously we can take the suggestion that

Freud's compulsive theorizing had 'coherence' as its object, let alone its effect. That assessment is at odds with the fact that the inherited-memory theory is a disruptive factor in the Wolf Man case history: it means that Freud cannot make up his mind about the exact cause of his patient's illness. The theory does not tend towards coherent explanation just as it does not promote consensus or scientific creditability.

I will come back to the problem of coherence – with reference to Freud's interest in topology – in the next chapter. At this point, what is more important is to emphasize that what is at stake, as the discussion of supposedly genetic explanations in the last chapter will have begun to indicate, is a problem of retrospective knowledge. The problem is the past and, more specifically, its obscurity, density and weight. In this respect, I find Freud's references to ghosts (quoted in the previous chapters) especially suggestive. The idea of the past that they evoke is particular. One does not infer from these references a sense that the past is easily intelligible or that it prompts a dispassionate surveying. Instead, the past seems unyielding, misty, a place of apparitions and perilous obscurities. It resists explanation and understanding, or it prompts repetitious incomplete reckonings.

Ordeals of retrospection

Elsewhere in the Wolf Man case history, Freud is at pains to distinguish his approach from those of Carl Jung and Alfred Adler, from whom he was by now estranged. In a footnote, Freud writes:

> I did not require the contributions of Adler or Jung ... to bear in mind the possibility that what analysis puts forward as being forgotten experiences of childhood (and of an improbably early childhood) may on the contrary be based upon phantasies created on occasions occurring late in life. According to this view, wherever we seemed in analyses to see traces of the after-effects of an infantile impression of the kind in question, we should rather have to assume that we were faced by the manifestation of some constitutional factor or of some disposition that had been phylogenetically maintained. On the contrary, no doubt has troubled me more; no other uncertainty has been more decisive in holding me back from publishing my conclusions. I was the first – a point to which none of my opponents have referred – to recognize both the part played by phantasies in symptom-formation and also the 'retrospective phantasying' of late impressions into childhood and their sexualization after the event.... If, in spite of

> this, I have held to the more difficult and more improbable view, it has been as a result of arguments such as are forced upon the investigator by the case described in these pages or by any other infantile neurosis – arguments which I once again lay before my readers for their decision. (**17: 103n**, 9: 344n)

All the emphasis in this passage is on the obstructions in the way of full explanation: 'doubt', 'uncertainty', 'the more difficult and improbable view'. It is the very ease of the explanations of his dissident former colleagues that Freud says bothers him. But one may infer further that Freud is ill at ease with the view of the past that Adler and Jung champion – the view (approximately summarized) in which the individual mind is, beneath consciousness, in some mystical communion with a vast treasury of ancient symbols and archetypes.[4] Freud's psycho-Lamarckism is on occasion read in these terms by admiring commentators as well as detractors:

> Although he ultimately rejected it, the hypothesis of Freud's Lamarckian phylogenesis was simple and powerful: All individuals carry with them the whole of human experience. With this, Freud envisioned a transparent universe, one available to total comprehension, in which the past and the future were linked in an endless circle governed by a collective, organic, immortal memory.[5]

The assertion here about Freud's rejection of the theory is inexplicable and inaccurate, and the emphasis on 'total comprehension' incompatible with the uncertainty summed up in Freud's '*non liquet*'.

Freud's view of the ancient past is rather, as he says in 'Thoughts for the Times on War and Death' (1915), 'filled with murder' (**14: 292**, 12: 81). And it is not a clear view that he claims; there is no communion or straightforward communication. On the one hand, what can be reconstructed of the past exists only as fragments and lies and buried secrets; and, on the other hand, according to his revision and displacement of experience, it is 'known' by one only in a memory that defies all remembering. Nothing adds up very well and the past is more an ordeal that needs to be endured than anything more consoling or illuminating. As Philip Rieff puts it:

> While Adler favored Lamarck over Darwin because the former's teleology supported his own evolutionist optimism, Freud's version had a consistently gloomy cast. What appealed to Freud was not its

> teleological verve but the near-fatalism of the theory which supposes, in William James's famous definition, 'the same emotions, the same habits, the same *instincts* [to be] perpetuated without variation from one generation to another.' Lamarck (and Darwin too) offered 'serviceability' as an explanation for the persistence of certain emotional forms and accidentally produced tendencies to action. For Freud, archaic and individual memories are neither efficient nor serviceable. Once acquired, they persist in the individual (and through the generations) as the final cause of neurotic misery.[6]

Melancholy, I think, or misery for that matter, much better describe the kind of retrospection which is at stake than 'the mind's sense of coherence'. Rieff's observations bring to mind Freud's description of Saint Paul in *Moses and Monotheism*: 'the dark traces of the past lurked in his mind' (**23**: 87, 13: 331). The great merit of Rieff's account of Freud's psycho-Lamarckism is that it looks to understand how the inherited-memory theory is consistent with trends elsewhere in Freud's work. What are the theory's reasons? What sense do they make in relation to other parts of Freud's work? Rieff detects in particular Freud's 'attitude' as it is revealed in the hypothesis of the murder of the tyrannizing father:

> If we look to the manner in which evolutionists disclose the origin of a thing in order to detect their attitude toward it, then Freud's elaborate description of society in a 'primal crime' discloses his basic attitude toward the history of society as a murder mystery, and toward the main problem of humanity as that of aggression.... Every part of Freud's theory, from his child psychology to his political psychology, is affected by the attitude veiled in this romance of origins. The doctor living quietly in Vienna proposed a myth of human existence as terrifying as any of those he loved to read in world literature.[7]

Even if anthropological theories are in fact the cause of uncertainty in Freud's work, they are nevertheless consistent with Freud's own tendency to reveal uncertainty as much as clearly evidenced truth or meaning. One way of accounting for Freud's theorizing is to regard, for example, the proliferation of alternate explanations of the Wolf Man's illness in Freud's presentation of it not as an explanatory failure but as an indication of Freud's recurrent interest in the breakdown or irreducible entanglement of meaning.

Rieff emphasizes the frightfulness of Freud's anthropology, its 'terrifying' features as a 'myth' of human existence, a Victorian 'murder mystery'. The downplaying, in the face of Freud's own claims, of scientific or historiographical rigour to a large extent marginalizes this element of Freud's writing; but it does so only having noted unequivocally the consistency of Freud's psycho-Lamarckism with '[e]very part of Freud's theory'. Rieff means by this chiefly that it shares with the theory of child development, for example, martial rather than pastoral themes. That is surely right; but what interests me even more is Rieff's observation that 'archaic and individual theories are neither efficient nor serviceable' in relation to the further idea of Freud's consistent 'attitude'. For it is not just that Freud consistently rediscovers, in his terms, homicidal intentions or taboo sexuality; it is the habit of a mode of theorizing that is in the business of remaking its own status as provisional or undecided or given to self-refraction. The dismal attitude, in short, may often be said to apply to the form as well as the content of Freud's writing; the pessimism reveals itself in themes of violence, incest and all the rest of it – but also in inconclusiveness or in a certain secretive complexity (as with figures of theory that, as I argued in the last chapter, provide the alibi of identity to ideas that are wildly at odds with identity).

It is useful to explore this point in relation to the primal murder. Freud insists on the reality of the murder as an historical event that is both repeated and secretly acknowledged and 'known'. A recent philosophical reading of Freud by Jonathan Lear emphasizes how problematic Freud's insistence is mostly taken to be:

> Freud is making a bold assertion, but there is really no basis for it. And if we consider the place of this speculation in the larger framework of his thought, Freud is in effect attacking his own life's work. He has spent his career showing the power of unconscious fantasy to shape a life, but when it comes to our religious lives, he claims this cannot be explained by the power of human imagination, culture and rituals alone. He is talking particularly about Judaism and Christianity: religions in which God intervenes in history and interacts with specific human individuals. Freud agrees with the religions to this extent: for these religions to be possible there must have been a significant *actual* historical event. These religions cannot, he thinks, be understood simply as a product of the human imagination. But he takes that actual event to be utterly secular: the murder of the primal father, followed by subsequent re-enactments with Moses and then with Jesus.

> If Freud's argument had been sound, he would have given a thoroughly naturalist account of religious experience. Obviously, it is in principle possible to give a naturalist account only invoking human imagination and culture. But by invoking an actual event Freud thought he had really nailed these fantasies down: this is what they are really about. This enabled him to think that he had given a secular and naturalist counterpart to original sin (the primal crime) and to the transmission of hereditary sin (phylogenetic inheritance). Without the actual crime, there would always be a question of why human imagination and culture took this form rather than some other – and there would be no place to look other than further delving into imagination and culture. Freud wants the primal crime to serve as an Archimedean point: religious experience is supposedly about that. But this isn't an Archimedean point; it's a fantasy of having achieved one. In effect, Freud is constructing his own myth of origins. But he hides this fact from himself by cloaking his myth in the garb of a naturalistic account of human development.[8]

This reading seems to me to be unconvincing. It alternates between amateur psychoanalysis and an apparently more robust philosophizing that is really no more effective as commentary. 'Freud,' we are told, 'is attacking his own life's work,' as if he suffered from some mental disorder, or at any rate a 'fantasy' (and after all, as I pointed out in the last chapter, Freud used the word himself to describe his psycho-Lamarckism – but his adherence to the theory is no less dogged for that). And if it were not a matter of some stubborn, childlike wilfulness, then there is for Lear the failure of sturdy, 'sound' reasoning: the 'Archimedean point' that is like a mirage. Freud cannot even 'nail… down' the matter at hand. If he is not in a delirium, then Freud in this realm is a shoddy workman.

My approach to the problem is different. It seems to me that what is important is not Freud's 'Archimedean' idea or 'fantasy' of a specifiable real event to which all religion and culture refers, but rather that the hypothesis of the real event allows Freud to argue that both culture and individual minds are always in a pained retrospective attitude – guilty, remorseful, confused. However absurd or groundless the hypothesis may seem (and thus how embarrassing and unacceptable to, for example, Lear) it is the conceptual anchor of a retrospective theory of subjectivity that, at whatever cost to identity, is constituted in a crisis of retrospection (with regard to others' memories). The hypothesis of the primal murder – and the insistence that it is a real event and not just a hypothesis – makes better sense if one thinks about Freud's work in terms of pained retrospection rather than Lear's nailing-down or sound explanation. This is at the heart of my project here: to draw attention to what I call the countersense of Freud's work, and above all its complex defiance of good sense and fixed, unitary explanation.

Lear's account of Freud's work will not allow persistent contradictions and alternations to go unresolved; so he simply conceptualizes these features in terms of self-delusion. There is, in my account, an element of trickery or sleight-of-hand (in Freud's use of figures of theory that invoke identity) but this element of his work seems to me to be especially interesting, no matter how much of an affront it is to the protocols of professional philosophy. Freud is self-deluded, Lear claims; but one might just as well say his work discloses a theory according to which something rather like delusion, a hauntedness – which is to say, in the terms of my argument, both the notionally incommensurate relation between experience and memory, and also the gyrant theorizing in which the incommensurability rises in and out of view – is fundamental. Like Rieff, Lear writes about a 'myth of origins', but using 'myth' to denote an unsupportable hypothesis that needs to be categorized as aberrant and illegitimate, to be discarded from Freudian theory. It is worth noting that post-structuralist commentators also invoke the idea of myth in this area, but without the straightforward repudiation that then follows in Lear's work. As Derrida puts it:

> [T]his pure and purely presumed event nevertheless marks an invisible rent in history. It resembles a fiction, a myth, or a fable, and its relation is so structured that all questions as to Freud's intentions are at once inevitable and pointless ('Did he believe in it or not? did he maintain that it came down to a real and historical murder?' and so on). The structure of this event is such that one is compelled neither to believe nor disbelieve it. Like the question of belief, that of the reality of its historical referent is, if not annulled, at least irremediably fissured.[9]

Original anguish

As his work develops, Freud gets more and more pessimistic until, by the time of *Civilization and Its Discontents*, he has become committed to an idea, for example, of the inherent and indestructible animosity underlying social organization. Violence is deferred (if it is), according to this view, only because the individual mind is shackled and disciplined internally according to the 'second topography', which imagines the tyranny of the superego (see Chapter 5). The technological advances of modern life seem to promise easier living, greater comfort, but they bring their own pain. Such is the trend of Freud's cultural theory; it is gloomy and grim indeed, but it is progressive in its way, a view of culture and society that develops over time in an orderly way as Freud appears to consolidate insights and arrange them theoretically. But in other respects, there is no such progression – only, rather, dispersion, disruption, fragmentation. This other trend, which is especially evident in Freud's stubborn psycho-Lamarckism, is clearly exemplified by the different texts Freud imagines, as we saw, in *Studies on Hysteria* and *Moses and Monotheism*, the first set organized, contemporary and legible, the second set mutilated, ancient and not only ambiguous but positively dissimulating. Freud moves from a sense of self-evidence to one of secrecy – or, actually, secret secrecy.

What kind of theorizing is this that seems to move away from cogent explanations towards undecidable alternatives and which is preoccupied by the terror and violence and barely intelligible documents of antiquity? Derrida has proposed the term 'archive fever' in his reading of Freud and Yerushalmi:

> [T]o be *en mal d'archive* can mean something else than to suffer from a sickness, from a trouble or from what the noun *mal* might name. It is to burn with a passion. It is never to rest, interminably, from searching for the archive right where it slips away. It is to run after the archive, even if there's too much of it, right where something in it anarchives itself. It is to have a compulsive, repetitive, and nostalgic desire for the archive, an irrepressible desire to return to the origin, a homesickness, a nostalgia for the return to the most archaic place of absolute commencement.[10]

Derrida's formulation tumbles forward in imitation of the frantic, distressed pursuit it describes: in its own movement, it asserts a solidarity or even a complicity with what it finds to be Freud's relentless yearning for an irretrievable archive. But 'nostalgia' and 'homesickness' are not, it seems to me, sufficiently strong words to describe the ordeal that is being noticed and reimagined – this impossible passion for knowledge of origination and evidence which, in grasping for what it cherishes, can only find that it has vanished. Vanished or was never there, like a memory of something not experienced, like an hallucination. I find Derrida's idea helpful in suggesting how the theory of transgenerational memory may not be just an isolatable hypothesis, but also, in its 'nostalgia' and also in its self-perpetuating search, a defining mode of Freud's theorizing.

The assertion by Freud in the mid-1890s that imagining may be as illness-inducing as actual experience (whether of abuse or, say, of witnessing something unbearable or incomprehensible) leads directly to the further contention in the Wolf Man case history that the imagining may not have any basis in experience. There may be a surplus of memory and a deficit of experience – and not the other way round. By relinquishing a primary idea of event-based experience that belatedly shocks someone into illness, Freud is able to conceive that the shock – whether the shock of observed sex or of witnessed murder – does not need to be experienced to be felt and 'known' by... everyone, even if it is not the cause of illness. One does not need to have experienced it oneself to feel the guilt, the grief, the dismay. And not only that, therefore, but also there is the constitutive 'hurt' which I have referred to in terms of a notionally unfinishable thinking that cannot find its way to experience, involving the idea of a self which is not its own. And so a practical, scientifically rooted therapeutic procedure begins its self-elaborating journey towards becoming a theory of the unavoidably agonized mind. A psychological theory whose stated purpose is the quasi-anatomization of the mind, the 'dissection' of personality, begins to become a theory of selves with no ultimate identity of their own, paralysed by 'nostalgia' – by a retrospective imperative that, formatively, must seek to remember what it has not experienced.

I have discussed alternation and proliferation, blocked or tangled understanding, explanation that, like the initially imagined expeditionary, cognitive thought processes, cannot be done with its work. But this does not really do justice to the sense that one can catch in Freud's work of desolation and inconsolability, of a grim substratum of negativity and distress. Is this too much, too freely interpreted? Consider, then, what seems like the ubiquity of anguish as a state of origination. Freud is constantly reaching back to a different past, often the oldest pasts he can imagine, in his retrospective search for origins and meanings. But what he finds there is anguish: terror, grief, remorse, helplessness.

One may look at a number of fundamental beginnings: of spoken language, writing, critical thinking and religion. (I will refer to another beginning, of consciousness itself, in the next chapter.) I have already quoted Freud's opinion in *Civilization and its Discontents* that '[w]riting was in its origin the voice of an absent person'. In the 'Project', Freud locates speech as having its origin in an infant's powerlessness:

> At first, the human organism is incapable of bringing about the specific action [e.g. feeding itself]. It takes place by *extraneous help*, when the attention of an experienced person is drawn to the child's state by discharge along the path of internal change [Strachey adds a footnote, 'e.g. by the child's screaming']. In this way the path of discharge acquires a secondary function of the highest importance, that of *communication*, and the initial helplessness of human beings is the *primal source* of all *moral motives* (**1: 318**, first interpolation is editorial).

I emphasize this passage not so much for its contribution to language theory or child development, but as a very early instance of Freud's emphasis on intense distress as a formative state out of which intellectual and expressive attributes develop.

Context and timeframe are very different in the next theory of origin, but the emphasis is very similar. Religion, as Freud describes it in *Totem and Taboo*, starts with remorse:

> Totemic religion arose from the filial sense of guilt, in an attempt to allay that feeling and to appease the father by deferred obedience to him. All later religions are seen to be attempts at solving the same problem. They vary according to the stage of civilization at which they arise and according to the methods which they adopt; but all have the same end in view and are reactions to the same great event with which civilization began and which, since it occurred, has not allowed mankind a moment's rest. (**13: 145**, 13: 206)

Again distress is the defining condition: a fearful, restless guilt belonging to both child and culture. Suffering and pathos define these origins; at the beginning is an experience of brutalization, a hurt inflicted or perceived or intimated in the condition of the world. In another passage, in 'Thoughts for the Times', it is critical thought in general that Freud understands as a modality of existential pain and more specifically that agony that is in the 'persisting memory of the dead':

> What released the spirit of inquiry in man was... the conflict of feeling at the death of loved yet alien and hated persons. Of this conflict of feeling psychology was the first offspring. Man could no longer keep death at a distance, for he had tasted it in his pain about the dead. (**14: 293–4**, 12: 82)

These are very different descriptions of thinking than the identity-based processes found in the 'Project' and *The Interpretation of Dreams*, but are they not in keeping both with 'archive fever' and with the ghosts and death awareness referred to in Chapter 1? And do they not concur with the subversion of Freud's initial account of experience-based identity by the theory of inherited memory? We may see here therefore some corroboration for the argument I outlined in Chapter 1. The freezing grave and the bloodthirsty ghosts in *The Interpretation of Dreams* begin to seem like approximate prefigurings both of Freud's idea of inherited memory and of his contention that communication and thinking are, in their origins at least, ineluctably species of grief, guilt, remorse, desolation. Freud's figures may be seen to be more than mere rhetorical ornament; they are forerunners of arguments he will later make explicit.

It is useful to make reference here to a 1975 essay, 'Notes on the Phantom: A Complement to Freud's Metapsychology', by the psychoanalyst Nicolas Abraham, whose work – including a remarkable reinterpretation of the Wolf Man case, co-written with Maria Torok – is concerned with what he calls 'transgenerational haunting', a process he outlines in terms of a 'metapsychology of secrets':

> The belief that the spirits of the dead can return to haunt the living exists either as an accepted tenet or as a marginal conviction in all civilizations, ancient or modern.... From the brucolacs, the errant spirits of outcasts in ancient Greece, to the ghost of Hamlet's vengeful father, and so on to the rapping spirits of modern times, the theme of the dead – who, having suffered repression by their family or society, cannot enjoy, even in death, a state of authenticity – appears to be omnipresent (whether overtly expressed or disguised) on the fringes of religions and, failing that, in rational systems. It is a fact that the 'phantom,' whatever its form, is nothing but an invention of the living. Yes, an invention in the sense that the phantom is meant to objectify, even if under the guise of individual or collective hallucinations, the gap produced in us by the concealment of some part of a love object's life. The phantom is therefore also a metapsychological fact: what haunts are not the dead, but the gaps left within us by the secrets of others.[11]

Abraham's rich and suggestive ideas are indeed revisions of Freud, in which he introduces new concepts (notably the metapsychological idea of the 'crypt'). But they may be adduced here to give ballast to a reading of Freud. I am arguing that Freud's references to ghosts, for example, are not at odds with his psychological theories. They are, rather, like premonitions of the theory. It is not that Freud is secretly superstitious. In emphasizing inherited-memory theory, Freud does not abandon psychoanalysis. It is still a matter of psychological theory, of mapping the spaces and processes of the mind. Only they are increasingly complex and irreducible spaces and processes. And is not Freud's psycho-Lamarckism rather precisely, especially in respect of personal experience, to do with 'the gaps left within us by the secrets of others'?

But they also indicate, recalling Rieff's term, the 'cast' of Freud's mind – not only the way his theorizing is ncreasingly retrospective to the extent that it becomes so concerned with anthropology and the history of religion, but also its kind of retrospection. For all Freud's assertions of explanatory comprehensiveness and for all the detail and specificity of his hypotheses with respect to specific prehistoric events, his work is inconclusive, self-revising, formally complex (as with the way he adds problematizing interpolations and footnotes to the Wolf Man case history or with the complex structure of *Moses and Monotheism*, with its prefaces not at the beginning but in the middle). Would one not say that there is something rather 'haunted' about such writing and theorizing, by dint of their compulsive retrospection, which manifests itself in books which are like palimpsests or even mausoleums? The retrospective theorizing is moreover a theory *of* retrospection. What is so fascinating, therefore, is that we may discern an uncanny self-reflexiveness in Freud's writing. The way his theorizing is elaborated seems somehow to replicate hypotheses in his psychological theory. Just as Freud is drawn to the ancient past, so his inherited-memory theory is a theory of individual obligation to primaeval experiences.

In his account of the beginnings of thought and communication, Freud emphasizes loss and bereavement; it is therefore a type of grief, albeit grief that is self-divided by mixed feelings. Grief is complicated by remorse and unavowed satisfaction. This complex distress leads, in Freud's account, to more or less extensive and intricate acts of communication, narrative or theorizing – as intricate, for example, as religion, with its great stories and doctrines that are appeasements of guilt that ceaselessly re-enact their own guilt by finding again the murdered father. What is at stake here may be said therefore to be a problem of mourning, a problem which Freud treated in distinctively psychoanalytic terms as both a paradoxically interpersonal process and also as a specific form of thinking – of, indeed, theorizing – rather than an emotional outpouring or state of unthinking shock.

Safekeeping

In Derrida's later work, mourning became a crucial topic, although its roots lie in work from the 1970s, especially his commentary on Abraham and Torok from 1976:

> Introjection/incorporation: Everything is played out on the borderline that divides and opposes the two terms. From one safe, the other; from one inside, the other; one within the other; and the same outside the other.... According to Freud's *Mourning and Melancholy*...the process of incorporation into the Self provides an economic answer to the loss of the object. The Self tries to identify with the object it has 'incorporated.' Thanks to what Maria Torok calls 'temporization,' the self recuperates its previous cathectic investments from the lost object, while waiting for a libidinal reorganization. Sealing the loss of the object, but also marking the refusal to mourn, such a maneuver is foreign to and actually opposed to the process of introjection. I pretend to keep the dead alive, intact, *safe (save) inside me*, but it is only in order to refuse, in a necessarily equivocal way, to love the dead as a living part of me, dead *save in me*, through the process of introjection, as happens in so-called normal mourning. The question could of course be raised as to whether or not 'normal' mourning preserves the object *as other* (a living person dead) inside me. The question – of the general appropriation and safekeeping of the other *as other* – can always be raised as the deciding factor, but does it not at the same time blur the very line it draws between introjection and incorporation, through an essential and irreducible ambiguity?[12]

I will shortly come to 'Mourning and Melancholia', but first I want to point out that Derrida does not give a proper account of that essay. In setting his ethical theory of mourning – or, rather, of what he calls *demi-deuil*, 'half-mourning' – against Freud's discussion, Derrida, it seems to me, may be said to understate the extent to which Freud is himself equivocal about what happens in mourning. Moreover, Derrida does not really (except for some passing comments later in *Archive Fever*) correlate the theory of inherited memory with the question of mourning. And yet, as I suggested in relation to Abraham's metapsychology, is not that theory in its own way to do with 'safekeeping' the dead?

In the discussion in Chapter 1 of Freud's references to telephones, I looked at how those references always involve the troubled interrelationships between individuals: the individual who, in a panic, is isolated from help, the person who is too closely and therefore deterimentally involved with another, the lonely individual far away from loved ones, and finally the scenario in psychoanalytic practice where there is a kind of blending of persons. Derrida's idea of safekeeping does not share Freud's premise in speaking about interrelationship. Though Freud is especially sensitive to the problem of loneliness, he is always concerned (as the example of the patient who is forbidden to telephone his lover illustrates) with what may be thought of as the proper separation and boundedness of persons. The concern is with identity, just as it is when Freud initially theorizes thought processes as functionally referring to the known orbit of experience. This is what makes the inherited-memory theory so difficult in the context of his work because the theory, if it is to be taken seriously, demands a rethinking of identity. It is not the case, as his remarks about Jung and Adler make clear, that Freud proposes to relinquish the idea of identity. There is a recurrent tension between versions of personal identity and selfsame experience, on the one hand, and others' memories and tormented retrospection, on the other; likewise, there is the replayed tension between fluent, successful explanation and explanation that gets blocked or can only come upon a tangle of alternatives.

Therefore Freud's psycho-Lamarckism involves surely some version of the idea of 'safekeeping of the other *as other*', but it is not a version that will ever definitively replace the theory of identity. However, to make sense of the hypothesis of inherited memory, it is necessary to imagine not only the idea of others' experiences interfering with one's own, but also, as Freud insists, their 'otherness' – which is to say, in Freud's terms in *Moses and Monotheism*, that what is part of one is 'subject matter' that is forgotten, inaccessible to remembering, hidden and secret and knowable only in the 'special way' of noncommunication. Derrida celebrates the painful and forever inconclusive process of incorporation, in which he says the dead person is kept safe and distinct inside one. Freud imagines something similar in respect of others' memories but cannot welcome the idea or be reconciled to something so disruptive of identity. It may have to do with love in Freud's account – but the complex love that he refers to in 'Thoughts for the Times': love indistinguishable from guilt and hate, each perpetuating the other, dragging painful mourning out.

Although I believe a reading of 'Mourning and Melancholia' brings Freud nearer to Derrida than Derrida himself will allow, there is no question of trying to suggest that Freud was some kind of proto-deconstructionist. Freud remained committed to explanation and experience and identity; those ideas start to become undone in spite of that commitment. And Freud repeatedly draws attention to this, emphasizing uncertainty or failed understanding – not, however, in order to valorize them (as Derrida does), but rather perhaps because to do so is not to evade the compulsive retrospection of his theorizing. That compulsiveness, however, is unthinkable against any backdrop other than the desire for proper and conclusive explanations that will unify psychoanalytic understanding. It is just that each new retrospective theory seems to defer and complicate that understanding, no matter that Freud asserts that all the pieces fit together.

Mikkel Borch-Jacobsen has called attention to this aspect of Freud's theorizing:

> The various topographies erected since the 'Project for a Scientific Psychology' are testimony to this constant substratification of the psychoanalytic subject, ever more fragmented and shattered, yet ever more deeply driven back to its own primordiality. In this sense, the multiplication of topographic agencies and 'characters' does much more to presume than to contradict the unity and identity of the subject: the subject can be divided only because it is first of all *one* subject. Finally, neither the theme of a 'primal repression' nor even that of an *après-coup* (*Nachträglichkeit*) would have been enough to make Freud question the stubbornly maintained notion of an already given subject, already present to (already subjacent to, underlying) its representations. In this respect, we can guess that the idea so dear to Emmanuel Lévinas – that of a 'trauma' predating and seizing subjectivity before any representation or any memory, and therefore also before any repression – would have seemed completely nonsensical to Freud. The unconscious, for Freud, *is* memory, a storehouse of traces, inscriptions, remembrances, fantasies. And this memory, traumatic and fractural though it may be, must be underlaid, re-membered, by a subject to whom and in whom it represents itself.[13]

Borch-Jacobsen's powerful work is directed at questioning what he argues to be the one indivisible unit in Freudian theory: the subject. Freud may separate a self out into multiple parts, may describe it as an entity of contending pressures and pulsations, may imagine it transected or striated, but it is still, in this account, an intact entity, integral, selfsame at least in its role as a remembering or reconstituting agency. I am not aware that Borch-Jacobsen has written about Freud's psycho-Lamarckism as a factor that complicates the assertion that there is always a core concept of subjectivity in psychoanalysis – but in any case, I do not dispute the suggestion, well made, that there is any fit between the ideas proposed by Levinas and those explored by Freud. I would assert that what I argue to be the Freudian countersense of thinking that cannot achieve its purpose of finding a way back to experience is a much more radical development than is generally allowed – not least because it comes out of psycho-Lamarckism, which is characterized as the most retrograde and absurd of Freud's ideas. But this, for me, is the fascination: the drama of the theorizing, as with all the refurbishing of the Wolf Man case history, occurs in the tension that is generated by Freud's revisions and compulsive (haunted) elaborations. The palimpsest metaphor is apt: layers of modification accrete. But there is also the dynamism of, in particular, the interplay between the self of experience and the inherited-memory theory. Both stay on the stage even as one confounds the other.

Freud's premises are, at first (in the 'Project'), to do with a limited questioning of mental identity. He begins with a purposive or expeditionary idea of thinking: thought travels between perception and personal experience in order to unite them and in so doing be finished with its work. That idea, especially its concern for personal experience, is progressively eroded – first by the notional substitution of experience by imagining, then, more radically, by the hypothesis of 'primal phantasies'. Others' experiences and indeed others' imaginings become, hypothetically, instigating agents in the individual mind. It is, as Borch-Jacobsen points out, always a question of the individual mind, the subject. But we have to conceive of this subjectivity, reading both with the grain of Freud's writing (by, for example, noting his concern for suffering as the origin of consciousness and communication) and against it (by exploring, in my account, figurative countersense), as being increasingly not united. Its identity is compromised; it is not selfsame, especially because one's own experience has had to give way to others' in Freud's theorizing. Freud does not let go of an idea of the subject or of identity. And I am arguing that in particular he does not let go of identity as a figure of theory – as with the way he presents the relationship between psychological theory and inherited-memory theory, psychoanalysis and psycho-Lamarckism. But this overarching figure of theory – like its counterpart ideas of recognition, elucidation, right-naming and so forth – can hardly do the work of unifying: there is too much elsewhere that counteracts it. Purposive thinking, for example, becomes almost unimaginable given the dispossession of personal experience; one begins to conceive of thinking – to the extent that it is purposive – as ever unable to extinguish itself, however temporarily, through uniting stimulus and remembered experience. And that unself-extinguishing retrospective thought is conspicuous both in Freud's self-revising theorizing that often cannot decide between alternative explanations, and in figures of anguish, loneliness, beleaguering. I therefore propose an account of Freud's writing that emphasizes not, for example, a wholesale deconstruction of the idea of subjectivity, but rather an account of agonized identities – and one whose guiding references are what I am calling figurative countersense's own erosion or countermanding of organizing ideas of explanatory identity.

Freud increasingly has unconsoling things to say: the pain grows more intense and far-reaching, anguish becomes the originating mode of thought. His explanatory pragmatism and ambitions for scientific understanding therefore contend with both the deepening pessimism and what I have called an ordeal of retrospection. Though I think there are parallels, it is not possible to imagine Freud sharing the almost rapturous sense Derrida has of safekeeping the other as other.

Loyal grief

Derrida finds in the idea of incorporation – presented as being, in psychoanalytic terms, a pathological process – a fundamental basis for a radically altruist ethics, which indefinitely prolongs the state of bereavement, shattering personal identity in so doing, as the price of staying loyal to someone who has died. This loving loyalty, for Derrida, is a kind of tender memorialization that gives a berth to the dead loved one. What is crucial in his theory of mourning, however, is the idea that the memory of the other does not fade or diminish. This is the cruel work of '"normal" mourning', which is therefore analogous to an annihilating devouring rather than an ongoing, cherishing hospitality. In *Mémoires for Paul de Man*, Derrida writes:

> Upon the death of the other we are given to memory, and thus to interiorization, since the other, outside us, is now nothing. And with the dark light of this nothing, we learn that the other resists the closure of our interiorizing memory. With the nothing of this irrevocable absence, the other appears *as* other, and as other for us,

> upon his death or at least in the anticipated possibility of a death, since death constitutes and makes manifest the limits of a *me* or an *us* who are obliged to harbor something that is greater and other than them; something *outside of them within them*. Memory and interiorization: since Freud, this is how the 'normal' 'work of mourning' is often described. It entails a movement in which an interiorizing idealization takes in itself or upon itself the body and voice of the other, the other's visage and person, ideally *and* quasi-literally devouring them.[14]

In contrast to this enclosing, absorptive, nullifying kind of mourning, Derrida posits an 'impossible' mourning:

> What is an impossible mourning? What does it tell us, this impossible mourning, about an essence of memory? And as concerns the other in us…where is the most unjust betrayal? Is the most distressing, or even the most deadly infidelity that of a *possible mourning* which would interiorize within us the image, idol, or ideal of the other who is dead and lives only in us? Or is it that of the *impossible mourning,* which, leaving the other his alterity, respecting thus his infinite remove, either refuses to take or is incapable of taking the other within oneself, as in the tomb or vault of some narcissism?[15]

In this ethics of impossible or unfinishable mourning, the dead one is neither wholly outside of oneself nor inside, since were it inside, as a result of the 'interiorization' by which the other one becomes just an ideal or a memory and so begins to dwindle to nothing, it would no longer be removed and so…other. The ethical injunction is therefore not to mourn 'normally' and so not betray (or kill) the other one; instead, at the cost of personal identity, 'the limits of a *me* or an *us*', the self makes room for 'something that is greater and other'.

Derrida affirms the paradoxes that emerge in his theory of faithful unfinished mourning and then goes further still by celebrating paradox as the basis for an ethical theory in which there is almost nothing left of identity. As is always the case in his work, Derrida's paradoxes are intertwined like some kind of a multiple helix. It is nevertheless worth trying to separate them out in order to see the extent to which identity is repeatedly refused as a concept and, in the very intertwining paradox play and also the highly unstructured syntax of his writing, as an organizing idea. There is 'the closure of our interiorizing memory' and 'interiorizing idealization' that Derrida psychologizes in terms of 'narcissism' and spatializes in terms of a 'tomb or vault'. Identity is here a matter of an imagined three-dimensional space or structure like a box or a room or, perhaps most appropriately, an oubliette. That structure may be accessed or it may be sealed (and there might be more complicated arrangements too – as with a hidden entrance or a secret door). Derrida formulates ideas of non-enclosure, of something other than 'interiorizing' whereby a structure maintains its solid boundaries so that it has a space inside. That space would permit of being occupied by an object, for example an 'image, idol, or ideal' which is either more or less material – such as a figurine or a framed picture, on the one hand, or a disembodied shape or intangible apparition (a ghost, a shadow), on the other. Derrida also formulates ideas of disintegration or indistinctness, of something other than a self-contained thing that could, even if it were non-material, be enclosed. Relating object and space is an idea therefore of enclosure – of process, action, movement. Once more, however, the idea entertains both physical and imaginary alternatives. It is a question of 'taking' – 'takes in itself or upon itself the body and voice of the other', 'ideally *and* quasi-literally devouring' – and therefore, notionally, of consumption and of 'introjection' (as opposed to non-devouring 'incorporation'), both of which are, in Derrida's account of them, kinds of inclusion that further imply appropriation and assimilation, as with eating or 'libidinal reorganization'. Derrida propounds an idea of non-assimilative admission or taking-in such as, in his use of the term, incorporation, safekeeping or 'respecting ... infinite remove'. And there is a final refusal of identity in Derrida's paradoxical figures of theory, as with 'quasi-literally' and (a typical formulation) 'the deciding factor ... [which] at the same time blur[s] the very line it draws', and above all with the recalcitrant syntax (with its repeated questions and accumulated qualified propositions) and elaborately restated paradoxes and puns: 'From one safe, the other; from one inside, the other; one within the other; and the same outside the other' and so on.

Derrida's writing is ingenious, inventive and for all its repetitiveness and syntactic disorderliness remarkably precise and consistent in what one might call its hunt for any last vestige of identity. As an exegetical method that is also an innovative and experimental mode of writing, Derrida's work is both valuable and rewarding, but as a general theory of ethics it is open to rebuttal. An instance of that rebuttal, by the political scientist Gillian Rose, is helpful in getting at the problem of Freud's much more equivocal and non-affirmative erosion of identity. Rose writes of Derrida's theory of mourning:

> *This is no work of mourning*: it remains baroque melancholia immersed in the world of soulless and unredeemed bodies, which affords a vision that is far more disturbing than the salvific distillation of disembodied 'spirit' or 'spectre'. For if all human law is sheer violence, if the law is no positive or symbolic law to be acknowledged – the law that decrees the absence of the other, the necessity of relinquishing the dead one, returning from devastating inner grief to the law of the everyday and of relationships, old and new, with those who live – then there can be *no work*, no exploring of the legacy of ambivalence, working through the contradictory emotions aroused by bereavement. Instead, the remains of the dead one will be incorporated into the soul of the one who cannot mourn and will manifest themselves in some all too physical symptom, the allegory of incomplete mourning in its desolate hyper-reality.[16]

(Rose's use of the phrase 'work of mourning' here and elsewhere in her book is not referenced to Freud. Rose's work is philosophical rather than psychoanalytic and, given my own avoidance of psychoanalytic terminology, I make no objection to the usage. But 'work of mourning' – *Trauerarbeit* – is, according to Laplanche and J.-B. Pontalis,[17] Freud's own coinage, so the omission is noteworthy.) Rose's key ethical idea is expressed in 'salvific' and 'unredeemed' (as opposed to 'damnific'), as with Christian doctrines of redemption from sin. It is to be contrasted (though both ideas seem to me to be quasi-Christian) with Derrida's emphasis on faithfulness and altruism, the difference being to do with individualism (which is to say, identity and subjectivity) and Rose's concern for the process of 'working through ... contradictory emotions' (another arguably psychoanalytic concept which is not attributed as such) – with something like what Derrida might call 'interiorizing idealization'. Rose valorizes 'the law that decrees the absence of the other' in contrast to Derrida's condemnation of the 'unjust betrayal' of completed mourning. But what seems to me most important in Rose's rebuttal of Derrida – especially given that the philosophical, religious and psychological subjects being discussed are as large as justice and redemption and emotion – is the concern for 'devastating inner grief'.

In Derrida's theory of mourning what is overridingly important is interpersonal loyalty and its continuation in anticipation of and after the death of loved ones. What follows from or is implied by this loyalty is the deconstruction of identity and personal integrity: the consequence is subjectivity which is not selfsame. Derrida imagines this as a form of love. This has considerable relevance to Freud's theories which also (as we have seen) are preoccupied by problems of bereavement but which emphasize remorse rather than love – though they are no less concerned with faithfulness, however reluctant or ambivalent; and which involve imagining how one is beholden somehow to others' memories, interpersonally dependent in a kind of impossible retrospection that must forfeit the ground of personal experience. But Freud, like Rose in this sense, retains a concept of identity: it is incessantly either stated or implied even though it is repeatedly countermanded, especially in figures and ideas that are to do in rather precise ways with 'devastating inner grief'. Each of Rose's words has significance for my reading of Freud. Derrida is interested in refusing it, but Freud is clear in his sense of there being something as intelligible as interiority (though it may, as I shall discuss later and as Borch-Jacobsen suggests, be increasingly subdivided) – there is an 'inner' space, even if it needs to be understood as a space that is unstable or transgressed. And 'grief' is also key, emphasized as much by Freud as love and loyalty are by Derrida – grief in terms of loneliness, abandonment, regret and hurtful retrospection. And therefore what I am giving special emphasis to is the 'devastating' aspect of Freud's theories – the problem of pain, of agonized states of mind which Rose rues and laments but which Derrida valorizes.

'Mourning and melancholia'

I will come back to Derrida's discussions of mourning in the next chapter. For now, I want to question the way he characterizes Freud's theory of grieving. Elsewhere in *Mémoires*, Derrida alludes to 'the gesture of faithful friendship, its immeasurable grief, but also its life: the sublimity of mourning without sublimation and without the obsessive triumph of which Freud speaks'.[18] And, discussing the collapse of the Soviet Union, he refers again to 'the manic, jubilatory, and incantatory form that Freud assigned to the so-called triumphant phase of mourning'.[19] Such discussion of triumphalist mourning involves a partial misreading of Freud's work. Derrida neglects the basic distinction Freud makes between the mania that can overtake melancholy and the relatively unostentatious features of normal mourning. For Freud, in fact, writes in 'Mourning and Melancholia': 'normal mourning, too, overcomes the loss of the object, and it, too, while it lasts, absorbs all the energies of the ego. Why, then, after it has run its course, is there no hint in its case of the economic condition for a phase of triumph?' (**14: 255**, 11: 264).

The task of mourning is to come to terms with the death of a loved one. As Freud puts it in *Totem and Taboo*: 'Mourning has a quite specific psychical task to perform: its function is to detach the survivors' memories and hopes from the dead' (**13: 65**, 13: 122). It is necessary not to linger over the dead, not to become preoccupied by the memory of the one who has died because the dead do not return; love cannot resuscitate them or preserve them in the present. Prolonged mourning represents, as Freud says in the *Five Lectures*, 'an abnormal attachment to the past' (**11: 17**). The deceased do not live on – they have become lifeless, inorganic, insensible and silent. Nothing remains of them. However, it is the strange habit of incomplete mourning precisely to allow for the persistence of the dead. During mourning something like the memory of the deceased inhabits the minds of the bereaved so that – subjectively – it is almost as if the death has not occurred. Mourners are preoccupied with the dead. Preoccupation suggests introspection, a withdrawal into self, an intensive activity of thought, a time-consuming labour of reflection as Freud describes it in *Totem and Taboo*: 'Mourning... tends to be preoccupied with the dead man, to dwell upon his memory and to preserve it as long as possible' (**13: 57**, 13: 113). But preoccupation also suggests the manner in which, say, something takes up residence somewhere – in the manner, for instance, of a sentry-post in an occupied territory or of an intrusive element lodged within the space of the mind, 'preserved' no matter what the cost to identity, holding its ground as it were by force, unsynthesized or unassimilated.

For Freud mourning has a great deal to accomplish: successful mourning restores the efficiency of understanding in spite of desire, successful mourning seals the past away from the present. But failed mourning – interminable or unfinished mourning – results in excessive introspection, in the partial unintelligibility of history and the entanglement of mind and world, mind and body, what remains alive and what has died. Unsuccessful mourning is an exemplary failure of interpretation and understanding. However, Freud remarks in 'On Transience' (1916 [1915]): 'Mourning... however painful it may be, comes to a spontaneous end' (**14: 307**, 14: 290).

Freud's stated concern for an ending to mourning is complicated, however, by the idiosyncracies of his most sustained exploration of the process, the 'Mourning and Melancholia' essay. For a start, the essay's chief concern is with 'melancholia': with, that is, an aberrant form of mourning. Freud is fascinated not by successful mourning but by its distorted, distended variants. Secondly, it is only at the beginning of the essay that Freud announces the proper course of normal mourning. Once he has established this course, he does everything that he can to emphasize that mourning is enigmatic, that it goes its own ways. He repeatedly mentions the need, for example, to correlate mourning with an 'economics of pain'; but he stresses that he has no idea what the economic considerations are as regards pain. Again: at the beginning of the essay, Freud insists that he will discuss melancholia only insofar as it is 'psychogenic' rather than 'somatic'. And yet, in order to describe the 'complex' of melancholia, he uses the images of a wound and of disease – as if it were 'somatic' after all. He goes on to repeat the image of the wound in the last paragraph – and this image (despite being, for the reasons I gave in Chapter 1, highly confusing in the context) is what lingers in the mind, and what is so often singled out from the essay. Having thus confused the postulated distinction between the 'psychogenic' and the 'somatic', Freud exacerbates this by declaring that mental pain is 'analogous' to physical pain. Finally, the essay palpably fails to end satisfactorily. The principal rhetorical device in the essay is not 'pious' moralizing, but a repetition of disclaimers at odds with any 'injunction' whatsoever. Reading the essay, it is amazing how fragile the announcement of the proper course of normal mourning finally seems.

In Freud's account mourning involves leaving a loved one to death in order to turn again towards the world. This involves an intensive activity of research. All the memories associated with the loved one who is dead must, in Freud's account of the process, be revisited, compared to the real and permanent absence of the loved one, and then consigned to the periphery of awareness:

> Each single one of the memories and situations of expectancy which demonstrate the libido's attachment to the lost object is met by the verdict of reality that the object no longer exists; and the ego, confronted as it were with the question whether it shall share this fate, is persuaded by the sum of the narcissistic satisfactions it derives from being alive to sever its attachment to the object that has been abolished. We may perhaps suppose that this work of severance is so

> slow and gradual that by the time it has been finished the expenditure of energy necessary for it is also dissipated. (**14: 255**, 11: 265)

The mourner must learn again the work of understanding. With the death of a loved one thought turns inward and the mind rages against itself, overcome by an inner fury (**257**, 267). Thinking ricochets in the chambers of the mind, harmfully, such that, Freud writes: 'we rely on… [mourning] being overcome, and we look upon any interference with it as useless or even harmful' (**244**, 252); mourning becomes pathological if there is not an end to the 'inhibition and circumscription of the ego' – if there is 'an exclusive devotion to mourning' (Ibid.). If the mind is so absorbed with itself, it no longer has the capacity for 'understanding', for intervening effectively between body and world, reconciling perception against the archive of memory. In the place of this understanding there is 'internal work… consuming… [the melancholic] ego' (**246**, 255). Freud's essay dwells not on the efficiency of self-reflection and the fluent intervention of thought in preparation for action but on almost every imaginable form of intellectual prevarication and self-inspection: 'self-regarding feelings', 'self-reproaches and self-revilings', 'self-regard', 'self-criticism', 'self-abasement', 'self-reproach', 'self-exposure', 'self-denigration', 'self-respect', 'self-evaluation', 'self-accusations' (**243–8**, 252–6).

Troubled mourning exhibits, in other words, a mental crisis which estranges the mind from itself such that the mind is capable of taking itself as an object. This self-critical propensity in mental life is described by Freud famously in terms of the 'shadow of the object' falling. Instead of a self-reflexive luminescence prevailing within the mind, there are areas of darkness. Self-evidence or identity is marred. However, this marring allows for death to be denied, even invalidated: 'the existence of the lost object is psychically prolonged' (**245**, 253). Within the bereaved mind, death is an effect of successful mourning rather than its cause. 'The object… has been abolished' but it continues to inhabit the minds of those who mourn such that it is necessary, Freud suggests, to *kill* the dead individual:

> Just as mourning impels the ego to give up the object by declaring the object to be dead and offering the ego the inducement of continuing to live, so does each single struggle of ambivalence loosen the fixation of the libido to the object by disparaging it, denigrating it and even as it were killing it. It is possible for the process in the *Ucs.* to come to an end, either after the fury has spent itself or after the object has been abandoned as valueless. (**257**, 267)

As I suggested above, in mentioning Abraham's work, Freud can conceive of a catastrophe within the mind allowing for the continued interaction with individuals who have died (in a manner perhaps not entirely unlike that in which Derrida conceives of such an interaction).

Freud, then, announces the teleology of normal mourning but dwells upon its troubled variants. The litany of possible self-inspecting scenarios, the textual preoccupation with the failures of instrumental thought and cognition corresponds with something like the introspective thinking which Freud identifies as symptomatic of incomplete mourning or its melancholic variants. The presentation of Freud's essay has an affinity with the thought processes of unfinished mourning. Not the least of the affinity is the inconclusive manner of the essay's ending: mourning remains to some degree unintelligible because the 'economics of pain' (**244**, 252) are so hard to understand.[20] And so, when he ends 'Mourning and Melancholia', it is with a gesture of explanatory failure, an announcement of thinking to come, as unfinished as melancholy:

> The conflict within the ego, which melancholia substitutes for the struggle over the object, must act like a painful wound which calls for an extraordinarily high anticathexis. – But here once again, it will be well to call a halt and to postpone any further explanation of mania until we have gained some insight into the economic nature, first, of physical pain, and then of the mental pain which is analogous to it. As we already know, the interdependence of the complicated problems of the mind forces us to break off every enquiry before it is completed – till the outcome of some other enquiry can come to its assistance. (**258**, 267)

At the beginning of the essay Freud had distinguished between 'somatic rather than psychogenic affections' (**243**, 251). But at the point at which the essay abruptly terminates, the somatic and the psychogenic have become indistinguishable, reinforcing the sense – the mournful sense – of inconclusiveness.

I would argue in the first instance that, broadly, it is viable to describe Freud's work as having a melancholic cast or attitude. That is to say: Freud is greatly concerned to describe the power that the dead exert, an instigating power, even, that sets the spark to fire reasoning. This is a key theme. But there is, in addition to that, a pronounced retrospective orientation in his writing. Compulsively, ever-restlessly, Freud ploughs into the past. It is as if there can be no end to the work of going back.

Theorizing, mythmaking, hypothesizing, imagining: however one might categorize Freud's speculativeness, it is always falling down towards the vortex of a far-distant past – or, rather, a multifilament past, for it is the nature of the past in Freud's work that it is composite, an amalgamation of timeframes and perceptions of time, of experience in recurrent iterations. Melancholy, then, as if in mourning in its retrospective preoccupations.

I am, however, concerned with the character of Freud's rhetoric and argument in its specific manifestations; to attribute a certain mournfulness to Freud, as if he were a literary writer, is not entirely the point. It is not just that Freud is retrospective. He is, more distinctly, prone to arriving at the sort of inconclusive endings and unresolved explanations that are said to characterize mourning that has not managed to terminate. Therefore, contrary to Derrida's ascription of a generalizing normativity, Freud's theory here is significantly more open-ended (and so more conducive in fact to Derrida's idea of non-triumphant, non-devouring 'half-mourning') than it is allowed in that ascription. Of what exactly does this open-endedness consist? It signally does not involve the joyous affirmation of aporia, undecidability. The crisis of explanation in Freud's work is elided wherever possible. The way closure and the restoration of cognition are emphasized in 'Mourning and Melancholia' is rather like the way what I called figures of theory involving identity escort the ruinous inherited-memory theory in other texts.

4
Across Limits

On 12 August 1904, Rilke wrote to Franz Kappus:

> If there is anything morbid in your processes, just remember that sickness is the means by which an organism frees itself of foreign matter [*ein Organismus sich von Fremdem befreit*]; so one must help it to be sick, to have its whole sickness and break out with it, for that is its progress.[1]

This analogy with convalescence – the young Kappus is struggling with religion, love and poetry – seems like the basis for kind sound advice. It promises an end to distress through the evacuation of alien things; like a physiologist or a doctor, Rilke reassures by urging patience as the body does its work of expulsive healing. The same logic applies in the analogy Freud makes in the *Studies on Hysteria*: 'treatment ... works like the removal of a foreign body [*die Entfernung eines Fremdkörpers*] from the living tissue' (**2: 290**, 3: 376, *1: 294*).

But elsewhere in the letter, Rilke has a much stranger observation to make:

> I believe that almost all our sadnesses are moments of tension that we find paralyzing because we no longer hear our surprised feelings living. Because we are alone with the alien thing [*dem Fremden*] that has entered into our self; because everything intimate and accustomed is for an instant taken away; because we stand in the middle of a transition where we cannot remain standing. For this reason the sadness too passes: the new thing in us, the added thing, has entered into our heart, has gone into its inmost chamber and is not even there any more, – is already in our blood. [*Darum geht die Traurigkeit*

> *auch vorüber: das Neue in uns, das Hinzugekommene, ist in unser Herz eingetreten, ist in seine innerste Kammer geganen und ist auch dort nicht mehr, – ist schon im Blut.*] We could easily be made to believe that nothing has happened, and yet we have changed, as a house changes into which a guest has entered. We cannot say who has come, perhaps we shall never know, but many signs indicate that the future enters into us in this way in order to transform itself in us long before it happens.[2]

In the sickness to which Rilke refers, the foreign matter that has entered the body is a hostile stranger doing harm, an affliction, and the patient must rest and wait while his immune system does its work to be rid of the harmful intrusion. In this way the body may restore both its equilibrium and its identity or homogeneity; it can be free of strangers. But in Rilke's picture of tense sadness something else occurs: the stranger comes in like a guest and not just in, but into the inmost chamber of the heart. From there it passes, dispersing, into the blood, which going-in is rendered in Rilke's antiquated punctuation – ',–' – the comma yielding to the more decisive forward movement of the rule, after which the penetration is complete. In the space of that rule it has happened, a crossing, and then the new thing is already in the blood. The strange thing, perhaps not even recognized as such, a mere shadow passing over the threshold, is absorbed into the body, instead of being expelled, and the body is not the same afterwards.

Letters to a Young Poet is a beautiful book of exhortation: to live, to wait, to be still as change happens, to believe, to love, to watch the world and welcome its strangeness. It is a book full of consolation and compassion. And yet in this passage Rilke has stringent and unconsoling things to say, which are hard to understand, the kinds of things to be found everywhere in the *Duino Elegies* (1923) and the *Sonnets to Orpheus* (1922), for example in the ninth elegy:

> *Zeig ihm, wie glücklich ein Ding sein kann, wie schuldlos und unser,*
> *wie selbst das klagende Leid rein zur Gestalt sich entschließt,*
> *dient als ein Ding, oder stirbt in ein Ding –, und jenseits*
> *selig der Geige entgeht. – Und diese, von Hingang*
> *lebenden Dinge verstehn, daß du sie rühmst; vergänlich,*
> *traun sie ein Rettendes uns, den Vergänglichsten, zu.*
> *Wollen, wir sollen sie ganz im unsichtbarn Herzen verwandeln*
> *in – o unendlich – in uns! Wer wir am Ende auch seien.*

> Show him how happy a thing can be, how innocent and ours;
> how even grief's lament purely determines its own shape,
> serves as a thing, or dies in a thing – and escapes
> in ecstasy beyond the violin. And these things, whose lives
> are lived in leaving – they understand when you praise them.
> Perishing, they turn to us, the most perishable, for help.
> They want us to change them completely in our hearts,
> oh – forever – into us! Whoever we may finally be.[3]

Rilke's language is much more ornate and unyielding than in the letters but the figure of absorption by the heart is the same, and there is a comparably uncanny undertow to the pathos of departure and diminishing and succour. The 'things' in the poem are hardly things: 'even grief's lament ... serves as a thing.' The anthropomorphism that gives them grateful knowledge and desire, which is in the nature of rueful pleading for transformation, is counterpointed by a materialization of 'us', whose substance is subject to deterioration – it being less a matter of persons than some organic transforming-chamber or a -machine of the heart. The departing of things is also an entering or a yearning to enter and be changed, as if by passing over a threshold and passing swiftly into the bloodstream. Rilke's dense poetic language in the *Duino Elegies* is less directly pertinent to Freud than the more ordinary epistolary style, but the figural complexity that is implied in Rilke's comment about an 'alien thing' is worth adducing in its more elaborate manifestation.

Freud, too, had a sense of strangers coming into one without invitation. He writes in 'A Difficulty in the Path':

> In certain diseases – including the very neuroses of which we have made a special study – things are different. The ego feels uneasy; it comes up against limits to its power in its own house, the mind. Thoughts emerge suddenly without one's knowing where they came from, nor can one do anything to drive them away. These alien guests even seem to be more powerful than those which are at the ego's command. They resist all the well-proved measures of enforcement used by the will, remain unmoved by logical refutation, and are unaffected by the contradictory assertions of reality. Or else impulses appear which seem like those of a stranger, so that the ego disowns them; yet it has to fear them and take precautions against them. The ego says to itself: 'This is an illness, a foreign invasion.' **(17: 141–2)**

Freud's metaphor of the house recalls what Rilke has to say about illness and expulsion: the mind's 'alien guests' are hostile and unruly; and they are insubordinate, oblivious to 'enforcement' or 'refutation', they resist the householder's 'command'. The metaphor is both domestic or familial and political and the strong sense (as with Rilke's description of the 'progress' of illness) is that the 'invasion' needs to be defended against. But what Freud imagines is not expulsion but rather that the stranger be 'disown[ed]' – as if ejection were not possible, only an uncomfortable disregard. There is then implicitly something of Rilke's more disturbing formulation: the strange thing that has gone so far in that it is 'not even there any more'.

Freud makes other such remarks. In 'A Disturbance of Memory on the Acropolis' (1936), in a discussion of the 'feeling of derealization [*Entfremdungsgefühl*]' (**22: 244**, 11: 453, editor's interpolation), Freud refers to the phenomenon whereby 'the subject feels either that a piece of reality or that a piece of his own self is strange to him [*entweder erscheint uns ein Stück der Realität als fremd oder ein Stück des eigenen Ichs*]' (**245**, 453, *16: 254*). And, in 'Thoughts for the Times on War and Death', where Freud considers the age-old problem of bereavement. As it was for 'primaeval man,' Freud says, so it still is in the deepest part of the individual mind: there is a multilayered fear of loved ones dying:

> a parent or a partner in marriage, a brother or sister, a child, or a dear friend. These loved ones are on the one hand an inner possession [*ein innerer Besitz*], components of our own ego; but on the other hand they are partly strangers, even enemies [*Fremde, ja Feinde*]. (**14: 298**, 12: 87, *14: 353*)

Jacqueline Rose has glossed these remarks in the following way: 'what belongs to us most intimately is also a stranger or enemy, a type of foreign body in the mind'.[4] Very well, but what type of 'foreign body'? And how would it have found its way, not into the bodily organ of the brain, but into the *mind*?

The problem of strangeness is also a problem of writing and theorizing. If *Moses and Monotheism* was like 'an unlaid ghost' besetting Freud (in his account of the compulsive way in which he wrote the book), it was also a kind of stranger: 'the author's creative power does not always obey his will: the work proceeds as it can, and often presents itself to the author as something independent or even alien [*fremd*]' (**23: 104**, 13: 350, *16: 211*). And, in a letter to Sándor Ferenczi dated 31 July 1915, Freud writes: 'I maintain that one should not make theories – they must fall into one's house as uninvited guests while one is occupied with the investigation of details'.[5]

Topologies

Freud's account of mourning as a self-completing thought process is clear enough in principle. Grief and introspection are transitional states, like the expeditionary thinking he refers to elsewhere. They preoccupy the mind as it adjusts to death; and for the time of that adjustment, they impair and do damage to the mind. It is necessary therefore for the mind to be reconciled to the fact of death in order not to remain turned in upon itself, its identity compromised, wounded.

The ethical imperative set out in Freud's essay is one of self-reassertion. It is not compatible as such with Derrida's ethics of mourning. But the essay's own presentation seems to countermand the imperative of restoring identity. It therefore can be said to epitomize a wider issue: the way Freud endlessly complicates his own psychological schema with hypotheses that compromise them, and the way his project of explanatory undoing is also a project of entanglement and proliferation. But the complex idea of mourning set out in Freud's essay is more than just an example of self-revising theory. Its concern with the way the mind can hold on to the memory of a dead person to the detriment of identity is clearly consistent with the theory of inherited memory, in which it is also a matter of imagining the mind's preoccupation with the dead. As Jacqueline Rose puts it, though not in relation to Freud's psycho-Lamarckism:

> Mourning appears … almost as a metaphor for psychoanalysis itself, or at least for the mental processes it describes: estrangement of conscious from unconscious thinking, the symptom as 'alien', the 'foreign body' of the repressed. More important, the thought provoked by mourning takes the form of a dissociation. The thought provoked by mourning … is not thought as assured knowledge, but a form of thinking unable, in any single or singular way, to own or possess itself.[6]

I would want to add to this account the matter of retrospection. Mourning, in Freud's terms, is a painful combination of introspection and retrospection and, as such, it seems to describe well Freud's own troubled theorizing, with its recurring emphasis on failed knowledge and its persistent sense of the heavy weight of the past.

In one of Derrida's most sustained discussions of mourning, he emphasizes the topological dimension of his theory. Mourning, in its 'safekeeping', is a paradoxically intersubjective state, but its work is a matter of spatial knowledge. The work of 'normal' mourning:

> consists always in attempting to ontologize remains, to make them present, in the first place by *identifying* the bodily remains and by *localizing* the dead (all ontologization, all semanticization – philosophical, hermeneutical, or psychoanalytical – finds itself caught up in this work of mourning but, as such, it does not yet think it...). One has to know. *One has to know it. One has to have knowledge.* Now, to know is to know *who* and *where*, to know whose body it really is and what place it occupies – for it must stay in its place. In a safe place.... Nothing could be worse, for the work of mourning, than confusion or doubt: one *has to know* who is buried where – and *it is necessary* (to know – to make certain) that, in what remains of him, *he remain there*. Let him stay there and move no more![7]

As always, Derrida's formulation involves the affirmation of contradictions. His interest is to theorize in terms of heterogeneity what is often considered in terms of homogeneity or identity, and then to celebrate the paradoxes that ensue – as with the irreconcilable play of inside and outside, self and other in the passages quoted in the previous chapter. Freud is never so at ease with contradiction. The fascination of his contradictoriness is to do with its declared concern for selfsameness and its assumption that identities may eventually be found to obtain even where this does not at first seem to be the case.

Derrida's remarks, however, usefully lead to an extensive rhetorical vein in Freud's work, comparable to the rhetoric of recognition, undoing or right-naming I referred to in Chapter 1. One of Freud's most characteristic ways of theorizing is topological. He thinks of spaces and how they interrelate, of borders and boundaries and frontiers, breaches and incursions, defence and obstruction, and so forth. We saw instances of this in Chapter 2 – the files that are arranged counter-chronologically but in sequence, one following logically after another and also the more complex and architectural idea of the textual containment of secret sense in a 'mausoleum'. These, though, are elaborate figures involving the imagination of objects and Freud's topological theorizing is often more abstract, mathematical rather than architectural.

In one of Breuer's contributions to the *Studies*, he writes:

> Out of [a] persisting hypnoid state unmotivated ideas, alien to normal association, force their way into consciousness, hallucinations are introduced into the perceptual system and motor acts are innervated independently of the conscious will. This hypnoid mind is in the highest degree susceptible to conversion of affects and to suggestion, and thus fresh hysterical phenomena appear easily, which without the split in the mind would only have come about with great difficulty and under the pressure of repeated affects. The split-off mind is the devil with which the unsophisticated of early superstitious times believed that these patients were possessed. It is true that a spirit alien to the patient's waking consciousness holds sway in him; but the spirit is not in fact an alien one, but a part of his own. (**2: 250**, 3: 332)

Breuer's invocation of the 'devil' has a certain derisoriness; there is no trace here of the fascination that, despite his contempt for superstition and animism, Freud seems to have had with, for example, the ghosts in the *Odyssey* (see Chapter 1). His scientific rationalism is more certain, or so we might think. And that shows in the topology outlined – the distinction between what is alien or 'split-off' and what is one's own. Breuer's figure is fundamental; it is as basic as known and unknown, familiar and unfamiliar, same and not-same – preliminary concepts of cognition. And Breuer holds to a project of familiarization. The insight that he brings is a matter of showing that what seems to be diabolically alien is in fact one's own, selfsame. The insight is an assertion of identity where there seemed to be none. It is barely topological, having only two elements and no concept of boundary beyond what is same and what is not (but in fact is).

Freud's topologies are always more complicated than this, as the earlier quotes, with their internal subdivisions in addition to their concept of strangeness, already make clear. Freud's imagination required a more complex, topographical figurative language. I want to look at some examples of this topographical thinking in terms of three categories: concepts of subdivided identity, concepts of boundary and concepts of breach.

Subdivided identities

Although Freud is more complex in his topologizing than Breuer, the difference can in fact be moot. Freud may subdivide more multiply and precisely, but it is often only to arrive at a more internally differentiated idea of identity (Derrida would call this 'ontologization'). One of the crucial starting points for psychoanalysis is its hypothesis that the mind is 'dynamic' – it has several parts which interact rather than being a single, static entity. Freud attributes the latter description to philosophy, as in *An Autobiographical Study* (1925 [1924]):

> Psycho-analysis regarded everything mental as being in the first instance unconscious; the further quality of 'consciousness' might also be present, or again it might be absent. This of course provoked a denial from the philosophers, for whom 'conscious' and 'mental' were identical, and who protested that they could not conceive of such an absurdity as the 'unconscious mental'. There was no help for it, however, and this idiosyncrasy of the philosophers could only be disregarded with a shrug. (**20: 31**, 15: 214–5)

The starting point is that there is strangeness in the mind. As Freud puts it in 'Dostoevsky and Parricide': 'So alien [*fremd*] to our unconsciousness are the things by which our unconscious mental life is governed!' (**21: 184**, 14: 449, *14: 408*).

In the last phase of his work, Freud's subdivisions become more intricate, as in a discussion of symptoms – 'what is, of all the contents of the mind, most foreign to the ego [*Ichfremdesten*]' (**22: 57**, 2: 88, *15: 62*), or some general remarks in the *New Introductory Lectures on Psycho-Analysis* (1933 [1932]): 'the repressed is foreign territory to the ego – internal foreign territory – just as reality (if you will forgive the unusual expression) is external foreign territory [*äußeres Ausland ist*]' (**22: 57**, 2: 88, *15: 62*).

In Breuer's account of the matter, the point is to recognize what seems to be strange as actually familiar. For Freud it is rather a matter of containment and demarcation. His figures (though they are sometimes only barely metaphorical) retain the element of strangeness and differentiate types of it: strangeness inside, strangeness outside, the foreign within and without. In the passage quoted, Breuer finally dispenses with the concept of strangeness – 'the spirit is not in fact an alien one, but a part of his own' – and so arrives at a redoubled idea of selfsame ownership. Identity is reappropriated, having seemed at first to be at risk. Freud does not perform such a reappropriation in the remarks I have quoted. Strangenesses remain (and this is especially and transgressively the case in the second topography, with its introduction of the concept of the superego, which I will discuss in the next chapter).

But – be it inside or out, component or extraneous – it is mostly a known, circumscribed strangeness, as can be seen in remarks in 'The Unconscious' (1915):

> [A]nalysis shows that the different latent mental processes inferred by us enjoy a high degree of mutual independence, as though they had no connection with one another, and knew nothing of one another... [W]e have to take into account the fact that analytic investigation reveals some of these latent processes as having characteristics and peculiarities which seem alien [*fremd*] to us, or even incredible, and which run directly counter to the attributes of consciousness with which we are familiar.
>
> Like the physical, the psychical is not necessarily in reality what it appears to us to be. We shall be glad to learn, however, that the correction of internal perception will turn out not to offer such great difficulties as the correction of external perception – that internal objects are less unknowable than the external world. (**14: 170–1**, 11: 172–3, *10: 269*)

Freud starts with a mind's own sense of itself – of what it knows of its inner make-up. The idea of 'mutual independence' is already a departure from Breuer's idea of a coherent entity from which some part has been detached (though it will later be shown not to have been): there is indeed detachment and dislocation of a radical kind. The mind's components are distinct from one another, adjacent territories rather than simply on one side or the other of a division between the strange and the familiar (or inside and outside, or one's own and not one's own). The significantly more minute demarcating involved is exemplified in the fact that strangeness in 'The Unconscious' is no longer attributed to the mind's component parts, but rather to aspects of functioning within or between these parts. And so there is a reconceptualizing of 'alien' here: it is in a sense a smaller idea, more localizable and 'ontologizable' – a property of certain effects or agitations that occur in relation to a complex system of interrelated sectors. And the components of the internally subdivided whole, for all that they may be independent, permit of being self-perceived or at least mutually perceived. This is therefore the sense in which Freud's more intricate topologies are not so different from Breuer's selfsame-versus-nonselfsame scheme. There can, in Freud's account of it, finally be said to be coherence and a kind of identity – the coherence, above all, which can arise from psychoanalytic investigation, facilitating internal self-perception even as it theorizes in general terms the nature of that perception. The mind is ultimately knowable, more so than the world, in psychoanalytic terms.

It is worth looking at one of Freud's most interesting and topologically complex late accounts of mental functioning in relationship to psychoanalytic knowledge, which is to be found in the *New Introductory Lectures*:

> In thinking of this division of the personality into an ego, a superego and an id, you will not, of course, have pictured sharp frontiers like the artificial ones drawn in political geography. We cannot do justice to the characteristics of the mind by linear outlines like those in a drawing or in primitive painting, but rather by areas of colour melting into one another as they are presented by modern artists. After making the separation we must allow what we have separated to merge together once more. (**22: 79**, 2: 112)

These are especially inventive figures of theory. Alternative figurative accounts of psychoanalytic explanation are juxtaposed and their merits compared. There is one simile then another and they are organized by a metaphor (the re-merging) that is in one sense rather simple (though abstract) but is also complicated by deriving its terms from one of the similes. Freud says that psychoanalysis can subdivide the mind, as if by dissection, and so separate its constituent parts one from another. That quasi-dissection can be the basis for a kind of mapping of the mind, as in 'political geography'. That quasi-geography, though, is overschematic and must be reconceptualized in nonlinear ways – without the 'artificial' concepts of 'frontier' and 'outline' – in terms, that is, of overlap, merging or indeed of 'bleeding' (as would be said of colour fields).

This is not in one respect an especially characteristic passage: Freud is not often to be found discussing modern art, let alone imagining psychoanalysis in terms of abstract painting. What is much more characteristic is the seriality and complexity of Freud's figures for his own interpretative work: medicine, cartography, drawing and painting. Through these figures Freud's theorizing may be said to explore itself and also elaborate itself, even in the uncanny fashion that I am describing in terms of figural countersense. The value of scrutinizing the figures lies, it seems to me, in deducing from them terms that give nuance to conceptual problems elsewhere in Freud's writing – especially problems that may, for example, not be presented as problems – as with the way Freud discusses the inherited-memory theory in terms of being only and simply a 'super-added' factor. Against that idea of complementarity one can set, for example, the figure of the murderous text (having shown how complex that figure is when compared with the figure of the well-ordered files) and argue that it is the second idea, with its violence and its inscrutability, that better accounts for some crucial features of Freud's theorizing. I am not sure that the analogy with modern painting is quite so useful. It does, however, show how intricately Freud sets out to give topological accounts of the mind – and then to reflect on those accounts, seeking figurative terms for his own interpretative figures. Freud has multiple and complex topological concepts; he is a much more enthusiastic subdivider than Breuer and he has further concepts of interrelationship and transgression (as with the blending of colours). But even the idea of blending or merging is one that is demarcated or notionally confined. No matter the bleeding on the canvas, that is to say, the picture imagined here is nevertheless enclosed within a frame. That frame would be an analogy for the overriding concept of coherence or identity – multiply internally subdivided though it may be – which is so often in place in Freud's theorizing.

Boundaries

Freud subdivides identity, but he does so in the name of knowledge and increasingly precise and accurate demarcations. The spatial rhetoric is a delimiting one. In addition, however, Freud also has somewhat more provisional concepts of boundary, what Harold Bloom calls 'frontier concepts'[8] – and, most notably, the concept of the drive as it is elaborated in *Three Essays* as 'one of those lying on the frontier between the mental and the physical' (**7: 168**, 7: 83). Another example of such a concept is to be found in *Beyond the Pleasure Principle,* in which Freud gives a spatial account of 'the system *Pcpt.-Cs.*' (perception and consciousness, in other words, as opposed to memory and the unconscious, which is Freud's preliminary pair of concepts): 'It must lie on the borderline between outside and inside; it must be turned towards the external world and must envelop other psychical systems' (**18: 24**, 11: 295).

However, as well as there being technical concepts like these, there is a sense in which 'psychoanalysis' is also a concept of boundary in a way that allows again for a questioning of Freud's commentary on his own theorizing. To get the problem, it is useful to quote a passage from the *Outline*:

> We know two kinds of things about what we call our psyche (or mental life): firstly, its bodily organ and scene of action, the brain (or

> nervous system) and, on the other hand, our acts of consciousness, which are immediate data and cannot be further explained by any sort of description. Everything that lies between is unknown to us, and the data do not include any direct relation between these two terminal points of our knowledge. If it existed, it would at the most afford an exact localization of the processes of consciousness and would give us no help towards understanding them.
>
> Our two hypotheses start out from these ends and beginnings. The first is concerned with localization. We assume that mental life is the function of an apparatus to which we ascribe the characteristics of being extended in space and of being made up of several portions – which we imagine, that is, as resembling a telescope or microscope or something of that kind. Notwithstanding some earlier attempts in the same direction, the consistent working-out of a conception such as this is a scientific novelty. (**23: 144–5**, 15: 375–6)

Freud's analogy with scientific instruments emphasizes the extent to which the allusion to abstract painting is to a degree anomalous. 'Apparatus' in the sense of a piece of machinery or equipment is, after all, Freud's chosen metaphor for the mind, and it is a metaphor that is consistent in a general way with his allusions to telephones and, to take another example, to printing machinery. The analogy with 'a telescope or microscope' is pertinent to Freud's psychology because it is a matter of an object made up of multiple component parts – in these cases ones that are engineered precisely, carefully built out of smaller pieces that must be assembled together expertly in order for the instrument to function. This is therefore another topological figure, indicative in the first instance of the way the mind is said to be internally subdivided. But both telescope and microscope are instruments of scientific knowledge and observation (and, indeed, their different purposes, or rather their different scope, are suggestive of the relationship between anthropology and psychology in Freud's writing) and they therefore suggest questions of epistemology as well as psychological theory.

Those questions are posed throughout this passage, and posed topologically. Freud is interested in 'exact localization', imagining that it may be possible not only to give consciousness a position in space – by which Freud means a notional representative position, as on a map – but also to localize its position in the physical matter of the brain, bringing together anatomy and the metaphorical 'anatomy' or 'dissection' of the mind. This emphasizes the figurative nature of Freud's theoretical descriptions but it also foregrounds the question of liminal positionality: not subdivision in its arrangement of sectors but subdivision as a conceptualization of intersection – not territories but borderlines or frontiers (as with the 'sharp frontiers' and 'linear outlines' in the *New Introductory Lectures*). Moreover, those concepts need themselves to be conceptualized topologically. Thus Freud is concerned with the position of consciousness as a delimitable entity, whether the delimiting be notional or actually anatomical (and this involves the further question of analogy itself as a form of transposition), but he is also concerned with the position of psychoanalytic knowledge.

Freud writes about 'ends and beginnings' and these concepts here are spatial ones as is made clear in reference to 'any direct relation between these two terminal points of our knowledge'. There are mirrored topologies here: the notional topology of the mind, the topology of the mind's relationship to the brain and the topology of the relationship between psychoanalysis and anatomy (or other scientific disciplines). What Freud does in respect of the last of these is to emphasize that there is a distinct space for psychoanalysis. Between this point or that, in relationship to terminal limits of knowledge, psychoanalysis can make room for itself. This is its 'novelty'; it has a place of its own.

As mentioned in Chapter 1, the idea of psychoanalytic distinctiveness occurs throughout Freud's work. So it is interesting to note that it is at issue regarding the theory of inherited memory. In the unfinished draft of 'Overview of the Transference Neuroses', Freud writes:

> The possibility exists as well that such fixation is brought along in pure form and that it [is] also produced by early impressions and, in the end, that both factors work together. All the more since one can claim that both kinds of elements are actually ubiquitous, inasmuch as, [one the one hand,] all dispositions are constitutionally present in the child and, on the other hand, the operative impressions are allotted to large number of children in like manner. Is thus a case of more or less, and an effective coincidence. Because no one is inclined to dispute constitutional factors, it devolves upon ψA to represent forcefully the interests of early infantile acquisitions.[9]

It may be noted in passing that Freud once more theorizes his theories according to a calculus of intelligible 'superaddition' ('more or less') and according to a concept of coincidence: 'both factors work together'. But what is more important for my purposes is rather the comment that there is a need for psychoanalysis 'to represent forcefully the interests' of its own theories about 'infantile acquisitions' – about, that is, a child's personal experience. The figure here is forensic but it implies the topology of psychoanalysis taking its place between terminal points of other areas of knowledge, demarcating the boundary between its own insight and that of other disciplines: psychoanalysis begins at one point and ends at another and so it is distinctive, novel, proper. It is in this sense, in its separating off of one discipline from another (even as its theoretical business is in further separating, subdividing and delimiting) that psychoanalysis is a concept of boundary.

But the boundary being imagined is an unstable one, or rather it is provisional. Beginning and end are also of course temporal concepts and time, in Freud's account of the matter, is likely to nullify boundaries. This can be demonstrated once more in respect of the inherited-memory theory and one of Freud's only remarks about it explicitly to name its intellectual provenance. In a letter to Ferenczi dated 28 January 1917, Freud remarks: 'My impression is that we are coming completely into line with the psycho-Lamarckists... and will have little to say that is completely new. Still ψA will then have left its calling card with biology.'[10] This problem of not having anything distinctive to add to psycho-Lamarckism seems to have been behind Freud's abandonment of his draft paper: psychoanalysis did not have something of its own to add. But, of course, the question of inherited memory would, in spite of Freud's properly psychoanalytic concern for personal experience, return and would do so with force, especially in *Moses and Monotheism*.

Freud's sense of disciplinary limits is, in other words, provisional. The borders may not prove to hold. Freud demarcates his theoretical territory only to imagine the ruin of his delineations. That imagining is recurrent in his writing. Consider a remark in *The Interpretation of Dreams*: 'Even when investigation shows that the primary exciting cause of a phenomenon is psychical, deeper research will one day trace the path further and discover an organic basis for the mental event' (**4: 41–2**, 4: 105); or in 'On Narcissism: an Introduction' (1914): 'all our provisional ideas in psychology will presumably some day be based on an organic substructure. This makes it probable that it is special substances and chemical processes which perform the operations of sexuality' (**14: 78**, 11: 71, *10: 144*). In *Beyond the Pleasure Principle*: 'The deficiencies in our description would probably vanish if we were already in a position to replace the psychological terms by physiological or chemical ones' (**18: 60**, 11: 334); and again in the *Outline*: 'we are concerned with therapy only in so far as it works by psychological means... The future may teach us to exercise a direct influence, by means of particular chemical substances, on the amounts of energy and their distribution in the mental apparatus' (**23: 182**, 15: 416). As Paul-Laurent Assoun puts it: 'la psychanalyse comme forme de savoir, œuvrant dans l'espace de l'inachèvement, se réalisera dans sa mort, une fois atteinte la limite de sa perfection épistémique, absorbée par les autres savoirs'.[11]

Breaching

In the case of the delimitation of the territory and boundaries of psychoanalytic knowledge, then, Freud's writing puts in places concepts of threshold or boundary but also imagines the overriding of these limits; they are due to be breached.

We have already encountered problems of incursion and transgression, especially the hypothetical transgression of personal experience by others' memories. More specifically, it is worth recalling from Chapter 1 the way Freud writes about the telephone as an analogy for his psychotherapeutic technique. The psychoanalyst 'must adjust himself to the patient as a telephone receiver is adjusted to the transmitting microphone'. What is envisaged is the destruction of barriers between minds and an overpowering of consciousness. Psychoanalysis may make of its participants a kind of transmitting-machine.

Freud's references to the telephone are predated by Breuer, who uses the analogy (along with another one) in his theoretical contribution to the *Studies on Hysteria*:

> We ought not to think of a cerebral path of conduction as resembling a telephone wire which is only excited electrically at the moment at which it has to function (that is, in the present context, when it has to transmit a signal). We ought to liken it to a telephone line through which there is a constant flow of galvanic current and which can no longer be excited if that current ceases. Or better, let us imagine a widely ramified system for lighting and the transmission of motor power; what is expected of this system is that simple establishment of a contact shall be able to set any lamp or machine in operation. To make this possible, so that everything shall be ready to work, there must be a certain tension present throughout the entire network of lines of conduction, and the dynamo engine must expend a given quantity of energy for this purpose. In just the same way there is a certain amount of excitation present in the conductive paths of the brain when it is at rest but awake and prepared to work. (**2: 193–4**, 3: 268–9)

Breuer's analogy here is different to Freud's in 'Recommendations to Physicians' to the extent that he is describing a wholly internal system of functioning rather than the quasi-automatic telecommunication between two persons which is Freud's concern. But there are ideas here about the relationship between energy and machines that are useful to pick up: energy that is in 'constant flow', 'lines of conduction' and the idea also simply of 'work' as the expenditure of energy.

The figurative language Breuer uses derives from physics and specifically from mechanics and thermodynamics and it is not therefore necessarily of relevance to the question of topology (although one may note that the complex circuitry Breuer describes involves topographical considerations). However, it is a reminder of how Freud imagines a certain dissolution of boundaries between minds – this dissolution being what I am claiming is radically at stake in the inherited-memory theory – in terms of an analogy with the telephone. But the passage also helps to contextualize an often-quoted letter Freud wrote to Wilhelm Fliess on 20 October 1895:

> During an industrious night last week, when I was suffering from that degree of pain which brings about the optimal condition for my mental activities, the barriers suddenly lifted, the veils dropped, and everything became transparent – from the details of the neuroses to the determinants of consciousness. Everything seemed to fall into place, the cogs meshed, I had the impression that the thing now really was a machine that shortly would function on its own.[12]

This letter has a certain casual euphoric enthusiasm that is not necessarily of interest in itself. But it is also another instance of Freud's theoretical self-awareness, albeit of a fairly straightforward kind, lacking the figures of theory that are so much in evidence elsewhere. But there are all the same a number of typical figurative concerns. The ultimate pronouncement is to do with the idea of theorizing as an autofunctional machine which, though it would do work 'on its own', would depersonalize psychoanalytic explanation (as Freud imagines the natural sciences will one day dispossess psychoanalysis). That pronouncement, however, is reached by way of a description of the elimination or overriding of boundaries: 'the barriers suddenly lifted, the veils dropped'. The letter's figurative language indicates how theorizing can be figured in Freud's writing in terms of topology and, specifically, in terms of a kind of breach.

In proselytizing moments, Freud could call himself not just an explorer, but a conquistador, establishing dominion over new territory. The images, though, are not always so grandly heroic. So, at the end of the Wolf Man case history, for example, when Jung and Adler and inherited memory are once more on his mind, Freud writes:

> I am aware that expression has been given in many quarters to thoughts like these, which emphasize the hereditary, phylogenetically acquired factor in mental life. In fact, I am of [the] opinion that people have been far too ready to find room for them and ascribe importance to them in psychoanalysis. I consider that they are only admissible when psychoanalysis strictly observes the correct order of precedence, and, after forcing its way through the strata of what has been acquired by the individual, comes at last upon the traces of what has been inherited. (**17: 121**, 9: 364–5)

These remarks are redolent of Freud's idea, in the *Studies on Hysteria* (see Chapter 2), of packets of files which are arranged in an orderly fashion. The statement about 'the correct order of precedence' recalls the 'chronological order which is as infallibly trustworthy as the succession of days of the week or names of the month' and this succession is likewise imagined topologically. Freud's metaphor seems to be to do with mining, with breaking through layers or 'strata' of earth and rock in order to get at the ultimate causal ground, at bedrock. The breaching here is imagined to be the work of rigorous psychoanalytic understanding and we may associate the figure therefore with the explanatory work of recognition or unravelling (see Chapter 1), as well as with the autofunctional machinic theorizing that Freud writes about to Fliess, but the additional idea is that of 'forcing…through'. The barrier in question must be torn into, violently breached.

In Chapter 1, I noted the way in which there is a verbal kinship between two senses of 'involution' in Freud's writing. There is the figure of explanatory undoing of a joke and also the sense, or countersense, of a more primal destructiveness that Freud discusses as a kind of deathliness. Something similar may perhaps be at issue with Freud's concepts of breaching. If Freud imagines rigorous psychoanalytic explanation in terms of forcible breakthrough in the Wolf Man case history, elsewhere he envisages such breakthrough as something much more pernicious and damaging, as in the *New Introductory Lectures*:

> [W]e are familiar with the notion that pathology, by making things larger and coarser, can draw our attention to normal conditions which would otherwise have escaped us. Where it points to a breach or a rent, there may normally be an articulation. If we throw a crystal

> to the floor, it breaks; but not into haphazard pieces. It comes apart along its lines of cleavage into into fragments whose boundaries, although they were invisible, were predetermined by the crystal's structure. Mental patients are split and broken structures of this same kind. (**22: 58–9**, 2: 90)

The topological figure here is vividly to do with distress and a dangerous shattering, even though there is also a sense of how breaking apart is not altogether a matter of chaotic destruction so much as structured disarticulation. The context is again, furthermore, theoretically self-aware: the imagined hurling to the ground of a crystal is referred to as illustration of the heuristic device – a sort of magnification or thickening, as Freud describes it – of inferring 'normal conditions' on the basis of a pathological state. So, as we have already seen on various occasions, a figure of transgression is framed, so to speak, by a figure of theory involving explanation or identity (as with the idea of 'super-added' causes). But the figurative language here – 'breach or rent', 'cleavage', 'split and broken structures' – is not the less preoccupied by transgression and, for that matter, pain.

A brief digression is in order at this point because Freud's image of a split crystal has a precursor which is of interest in itself, and also because it is another figure of theory to do with a notional understanding of the interrelationship of what is individual and what belongs to the species. In *Totem and Taboo* – written while he had still to theorize inherited memory by way of the concept of 'primal phantasies' – Freud pauses to consider the relationship between individual mental disturbance and what may be its cultural equivalent:

> He [the psychoanalyst] has come across people who have created for themselves individual taboo prohibitions... and who obey them just as strictly as savages obey the communal taboos of their tribe or society. If he were not already accustomed to describing such people as 'obsessional' patients, he would find 'taboo sickness' a most appropriate name for their condition. Having learnt so much, however, about this obsessional sickness from psychoanalytic examination – its clinical aetiology and the essence of its psychical mechanism – he can scarcely refrain from applying the knowledge he has thus acquired to the parallel sociological phenomenon.
>
> A warning must be uttered at this point. The similarity between taboo and obsessional sickness may be no more than a matter of

> externals; it may apply only to the *forms* in which they are manifested and not extend to their essential character. Nature delights in making use of the same forms in the most various biological connections: as it does, for instance, in the appearance of branch-like structures both in coral and in plants, and indeed in some forms of crystal and in certain chemical precipitates. It would obviously be hasty and unprofitable to infer the existence of any internal relationship from such points of agreement as these, which merely derive from the operation of the same mechanical causes. (**13: 26**, 13: 79–80)

In the same way as the Wolf Man remarks have a kinship with the comments about explanatory undoing, this passage recalls the tangles and knots that psychoanalytic theorizing cannot seem to get past or unravel. It is an unusual and appealing passage, its self-declared formalism having something in common with the later reference to modern painting, the concern being momentarily for something other than component delimitation – for, instead, abstract and uncanny and nonlinear shapes and patterns. And the patterns here are evoked to describe Freud's theorizing. At this point in his work, Freud is still wondering about phylogenetics and in this passage he sets out the problem; his mode is questioning. What connection, if any, is there between these different phenomena, one personal, the other cultural? Soon Freud will arrive at his paradoxical answer: in spite of all the theoretical trouble introduced as a result (as with the alternative possible explanations of the Wolf Man's illness), it is a matter of inheritance and experience having to be thought of configurally rather than in the terms suggested in *Totem and Taboo* of mere apparent resemblance. I have questioned the viability of this configuration: it is not as easy Freud sometimes proposed to make it seem. And, in a comparable way, the explanatory forcing-through in the Wolf Man case history suggests to me other, injurious breaches.

In his letter to Fliess, Freud writes of 'that degree of pain which brings about the optimal condition for my mental activities' and it is the question of pain that I think is correlative to, or implicit in, the topological and figural writing under discussion. Breaching, in fact, would be a definition of pain, as Freud tries to understand it in the 'Project': 'cases where excessively large Qs break through the screening contrivances in O – that is, in cases of *pain*' (**1: 320**). Freud does not return to the subject very much more. When he does, as we have already seen in 'Mourning and Melancholia', it is only to say how mysterious the phenomenon remains. But there are some sustained remarks on pain in an addendum to *Inhibitions, Symptoms and Anxiety*:

> We know very little about pain either. The only fact we are certain of is that pain occurs in the first instance and as a regular thing whenever a stimulus which impinges on the periphery breaks though the devices of the protective shield against stimuli and proceeds to act like a continuous instinctual stimulus, against which muscular action, which is as a rule effective because it withdraws the place that is being stimulated from the stimulus, is powerless. If the pain proceeds not from a part of the skin but from an internal organ, the situation is still the same. All that has happened is that a portion of the inner periphery has taken the place of the outer periphery. (**20: 170–1**, 10: 331)

What is immediately striking again once more is the precision of the topological theorizing. By way of boundaries, there is skin and there are organ surfaces as well as both an inner and an outer periphery and a protective shield. All of these boundaries, though they are permeable, are effectively like carapaces: they are defensive shells whose function is to fend off stimulation.

But because they are permeable they may be breached and breaching is agonizing. It is to be contrasted with something else, another process: healing. The healing that is so hard to achieve around, for example, prosthetic technological appendages – and which is also the business of mourning, if it is ever to be complete.

Against the tide

In the fourth chapter of *Beyond the Pleasure Principle,* Freud tries to come at a view of the origins of consciousness by imagining 'a living organism in its most simplified possible form as an undifferentiated vesicle of a substance that is susceptible to stimulation' (**18: 26**, 11: 297).

> This little fragment of living substance is suspended in the middle of an external world charged with the most powerful energies; and it would be killed by the stimulation emanating from these if it were not provided with a protective shield against stimuli. It acquires the shield in this way: its outermost surface ceases to have the structure proper to living matter, becomes to some degree inorganic and thenceforward functions as a special envelope or membrane resistant

> to stimuli. In consequence, the energies of the external world are able to pass into the next underlying layers, which have remained living, with only a fragment of their original intensity; and these layers can devote themselves, behind the protective shield, to the reception of the amounts of stimulus which have been allowed through. By its death, the outer layer has saved all the deeper ones from a similar fate – unless, that is to say, stimuli reach it which are so strong that they break through the protective shield. *Protection against* stimuli is an almost more important function for the living organism than *reception of* stimuli.... In highly developed organisms the receptive cortical layer of the former vesicle has long been withdrawn into the depths of the interior of the body, though portions of it have been left behind on the surface immediately beneath the general shield against stimuli. These are the sense organs, which consist essentially of apparatus for the reception of stimuli, but which also include special arrangements for further protection against excessive amounts of stimulation and for excluding unsuitable kinds of stimuli. (**18: 27–8**, 11: 298–9)

This passage has received a great deal of attention over the years, not least because of Derrida's lengthy reading of it in *The Post Card: from Socrates to Freud and Beyond* (1980): on which he associates Freud's account of the vesicle being embattled by an overbearing external environment both with 'strategico-military' figurative language – and I will refer to Freud's blatant use of such figures in the next chapter – and with the question of the politics of psychoanalytic institutions. The primitive vesicle is like the beleaguered discipline of psychoanalysis whose survival requires defensive strategies. And so the metaphor of the unicellular organism, in Derrida's analysis, may:

> be transferred onto every corpus, every organization, for example... the Freudian corpus, or the organization of the psychoanalytic 'movement' protecting, in its tradition, the transmission of its protective vesicle, the pocket of a system sorting out the information from the outside, protecting against internal dangers, and that the same transference would pass along from one legatee to another, like the simulacrum of a secret.[13]

Derrida once more affirms contradictions and paradoxes, recalling his observations about Abraham and Torok's work and also his ethics of mourning in the play on inside and outside. The idea of a 'pocket', a further interior place of repository, and also of 'the simulacrum of a secret' are recognizably counterintuitive figures of problematized or inaccessible meaning and it is difficult to gloss them without being obliged to reconfigure them in equally paradoxical terms. Again, one may note that Freud never celebrates paradox even if he finally arrives at it. What will be clear from the review of his topological thinking is that, however complex and subdivided it becomes, it is always attempting precision and identity, under however great a threat of subversion.

The microscopic vesicle is unmistakeably threatened. One may note, for a start, that the vesicle is formed by violence – its capacity for differentiated existence comes about through a self-protecting defence against overwhelming force. It is all that can be done just to make a shield against 'the most powerful energies'. Such a shield is the only alternative to being killed, but it involves some dying: the 'outermost surface' must 'to some extent' die in order that there may be created a sufficiently robust exterior protecting cortex – which is hardly, in fact, a shield, more a mere 'membrane', as thin as an 'envelope' – for the organism to survive. It must be scorched (Freud refers a few sentences earlier to the cortex as a 'crust' that has been 'baked through'), cauterized, scarred in order to be able to resist being destroyed. It is decidedly a matter of pain or brutalization and I see a connection between this imagined origin and the others I quoted in Chapter 3. The context is an entity that can barely protect itself; it must suffer in order to survive. It is lost, abandoned, alone. In the beginning is an anguish of isolation that is like the bereft or remorseful loneliness that Freud claims to be at the origin of the appeasing cries of language and religion and critical inquiry. These are the states of mind and feeling that Freud so often invokes; the vesicle metaphor seems to me to be figuring them again. The organism is unprotected, direly threatened and it must harm itself in response to that state. It is another kind of violence altogether from what is imagined in terms of the primal murder, but it is violence nonetheless. It is also therefore a question of physical injury. There is an analogous relationship between this passage and the reference to wounding in 'Mourning and Melancholia' or to necrotic bone in 'Analysis Terminable and Interminable' (see Chapter 5).

And in this passage, Freud's topological imagination is in full flood, with all the main emphasis on the fundamental creation of a boundary that, despite the allowance for deintensifying permeability of the membrane, is principally a protective barrier, like a battlement – a fortification. Without such a 'screening contrivance', the vesicle will be killed. Freud's microbiological account foreshadows the extraordinarily acute sense of danger and peril in his books about civilization, especially *The Future of an Illusion*, with its notion of 'over-mighty and pitiless forces of nature' (**21**: **19**, 12: 198):

> [N]o one is under the illusion that nature has already been vanquished; and few dare hope that she will ever be subjected to man. There are the elements, which seem to mock at all human control: the earth, which quakes and is torn apart and buries all human life and its works; water, which deluges and drowns everything in a turmoil; storms, which blow everything before them; there are diseases, which we have only recently recognized as attacks by other organisms; and finally there is the painful riddle of death, against which no medicine has yet been found, nor probably will be. With these forces nature rises up against us, majestic, cruel and inexorable; she brings to our mind once more our weakness and helplessness, which we thought to escape through the work of civilization. (**15–16**, 195)

These remarks have none of the figurative complexity of *Beyond the Pleasure Principle*, but their intimations of catastrophe, which are hyperbolic to the point almost of being comical, can contextualize the microbiological topology. As with the topology of pain, one may see how defence or protection, on the one hand, and suffering or death, on the other, are the coordinates, often explicitly so, of Freud's topographies. The subdivisions, as in the vesicle passage (with its description of 'withdrawn' additional layers beneath or within the cortex), tend to be the interior, reinforcing component lines of a system of barely countervailing resistance. The topographies are topographies of emplacement. And I would once more suggest that they are therefore comparable to Freud's ideas about the self-protecting and tentatively consoling functions of language and thinking.

In imagining the microrganism's self-mutilating origin, Freud is precisely and explicitly imagining how a self comes to be. The vesicle is a metaphor for 'the system *Cs.*': this is a mind that is being formed. And one may note just how diminished a self this is – how tiny, reduced and restricted, how nearly exhausted its resources are, how eroded it is even if it were not so likely to be swept away altogether. It seems to me that in this respect, the vesicle metaphor has an affinity with a number of other aspects of Freud's work that I have already discussed. For in those contexts also it was often a matter of self-diminishment. The selfhood of personal experience is undermined and countermanded with the hypothesis of inherited memory. Experience therefore cannot delimit the compass of thinking and so we must imagine, as with Freud's failure to come up with a definitive explanation of the Wolf Man's statements and the extent to which they may actually be endowments of others' experience, an unfinished thinking unable to find its way to home and rest and identity. And such thinking resembles the painful introspection of mourning, which is also the kind of tormented retrospection Freud often discusses (in his own retrospective theorizing). In these contexts, the problem is inefficient thinking, thinking which may not be able to do its work – as Freud was unable to use the telephone – because it is too distressed, because it is instigated in grief and solitude. One might say that the vesicle in *Beyond the Pleasure Principle* is like a flimsy raft of a concept of personal identity, all its encrustations turned against a surging alien tide (which could be understood, as Bloom suggests, in terms of the weight of the past, in the sense that '[a]ll of us have too much behind us').[14] Freud is reduced to this mere fragment of a conceptualization of selfhood. But it is still, however diminished, such a concept. This must be underscored; and it should be a brake on the headlong paradox play that is to be found in Derrida's readings of psychoanalysis, which for all their value may be said to lose sight of the extent to which so much of the force of Freud's writing derives from the attempt to reaffirm identity and coherence in spite of the disfigurement, disruption or distress that is repeatedly found to throw these ideas into crisis.

Telepathy

It is time to begin to bring together the main elements of my reading: figurative language and its notional countersense, inherited memory and retrospection, pain and transgression, mourning, the self-revisions and complications of Freudian theorizing (including what I am calling figures of theory).

Freud's insistence that we inherit as memories the experiences of others is such an unsuspected, uncanny idea – no matter its origins in nineteenth-century science, its articulation in terms of anthropological speculation or the way Freud casually centres it in biological and topological terms – as, for example, he does in the 1919 paper '"A Child is Being Beaten": A Contribution to the Study of the Origin of Sexual Perversions', when he remarks that 'Man's archaic heritage forms the nucleus of the unconscious mind' (**17: 203–4**, 10: 192). But that offhand cellular metaphor is the heart of it: from the start, in its inmost nuclear centre, at its heart indeed, the self is not its own – or, one might say, it has no original privacy. A principle of heteronomy applies formatively: others, long-ago others, inhabit the vesicular self or instigate its very framing – like uninvited guests whom, as Rilke says, 'perhaps we shall never know'. What kind of selfhood is this that others' experiences may make a home there and not leave, may even become part of it, as if by passing into its body or its bloodstream?

It is, in my account, agonized, mournful. But one might also call it, in so doing now beginning to acknowledge, in respect of the radically non-private subjectivity being imagined, the force of figural countersense in Freud's writing – the idea that the self will have at some instigating moment access to, or at any rate possession of, the memory of others' experiences – *telepathic* selfhood.

Freud's interest in telepathy – or what he called 'thought-transference' – is elaborated in lecture 30, 'Dreams and Occultism', in the *New Introductory Lectures*. Freud explains what he has in mind: 'mental processes in one person – ideas, emotional states, conative impulses – can be transferred to another person through empty space without employing the familiar methods of communication by means of words or signs' (**22**: **39**, 2: 69). The discussion of telepathy is a version of Freud's psycho-Lamarckism. One need only recall the passage from *Moses and Monotheism* quoted in Chapter 2 – with its reference to how the memory of experience survives transgenerationally, 'independently of direct communication', 'not... transmitted by communication' – and then note its exact echo of the telepathy lecture's phrasing.

Although Freud presents his interest in occult phenomena here as being somewhat separate from psychoanalysis, his definition of telepathy is immediately reminiscent of remarks Freud makes elsewhere:

> The telepathic act is supposed to consist in a mental act in one person instigating the same mental act in another person. What lies between these two mental acts may easily be a physical process into which the mental one is transformed at one end and which is transformed back once more into the same mental one at the other end. The analogy with other transformations, such as occur in speaking and hearing by telephone, would then be unmistakable. (**55**, 85)

A number of Freud's preoccupations converge here. This passage highlights several questions that have emerged in previous chapters – or one might say it gives an account of these questions, as with a figure of theory. There is a distinction that needs to be made carefully here, a distinction which resembles the one I tried to make in Chapter 1 concerning Freud's autobiographical anecdotes of dismay. There I proposed to read certain personalized anecdotes as being indicative of widespread thematic and procedural elements of psychoanalysis: they are not just asides nor are they personal in a way that is separate from the supposedly disinterested theorizing. They give us terms – misrecognition, dismay, loneliness even – that figure abstract and impersonally expressed aspects of Freud's theorizing. I can see a connection, for example, having explored Freud's topological thinking, between Freud's railway carriage in 'The "Uncanny"', the beleaguered cellular unit of *Beyond the Pleasure Principle* and the figures of identity that Freud uses to account for the interrelationship between inherited-memory theory and psychoanalytic psychology.

In writing once more about the telephone, Freud seems to imagine how he can finally understand not just a series of notionally distinct problems but also their interrelationship – or even, in a sense, what interrelationship is: not just certain problems that converge but what convergence is. It is at this abstract level – one might use the term 'metaconceptual' as a correlative to 'figure of theory' – that Freud's telepathy lecture takes on very considerable significance. It might be put like this: Freud is startlingly and most unexpectedly confronting his most major themes and preoccupations – and the interconnection between them – in this apparently marginal text. Just as some of Freud's autobiographical anecdotes seem in their very nature to be incidental to his theorizing but may be said to be providing figural commentary on it, just as references to ghosts and spirits seem like inappropriate images in a psychoanalytic context but may be said to be suggestive of the large theoretical problem of psycho-Lamarckism, so arguably 'telepathy' in Freud's discussion may not be significant as an almost magical form of communication so much as an account of Freud's own theorizing. We may consider again the topics that emerge in the passage I have just quoted. There is the question of interpersonal interrelationship as a problem of communication but also 'instigation' (as with inherited memory); there is the ever-repeated problem of 'physical process' and so of the focus and expertise of psychoanalysis; and there is the analogical mode of presentation that presents itself in assured terms ('unmistakeable') that are in keeping with the dominating concept in this passage – 'transformation'. That concept is another concept of identity and I distrust it. For is it not in fact rather a concept of breaching, of pain? In any event, 'telepathy' begins to look like a name for the sense Freud's writing may have of itself.

As he nears the end of the lecture, Freud makes explicit the connection between transferral of thoughts in telepathy and the psycho-Lamarckian idea of inherited memory:

> If only one accustoms oneself to the idea of telepathy, one can accomplish a great deal with it – for the time being, it is true, only in imagination. It is a familiar fact that we do not know how the common purpose comes about in the great insect communities: possibly it is done by a direct psychical transference of this kind. One is led to a suspicion that this is the original method of communication between individuals and that in the course of phylogenetic evolution it has been replaced by the better method of giving information with the help of signals which are picked up by the sense organs. But the older method might have persisted in the background and still be able to put itself into effect under certain conditions – for instance, in passionately excited mobs. All this is still uncertain and full of unsolved riddles; but there is no reason to be frightened by it. (55, 86)

There is, it seems to me, a kind of deceptive confidence in this passage, at once thematic and in terms of Freud's ideas about his own ideas. There are, to be sure, some points of discord and irresolution – the 'passionately excited mobs', in particular, and also the recurrent 'unsolved riddles' (which, however, are at least a 'familiar fact' of psychoanalytic theorizing) – but otherwise Freud's writing is buoyant and confident as it presents a series of identities and ideas of identity. There is community and 'common purpose', there is the steady progress of unifying communication and information-giving in which perception and gesture, mind and body, increasingly coordinate. Individuals come together as if they might blend and correlate without difficulty and so do orders of time, the 'older method' sedimenting what has come after it. And so, overarchingly, there is the great hope for understanding in this imagined seamless plenitude of understanding: 'one can accomplish a great deal' with the idea.

The reference to 'great insect communities' reminds me of Rilke's 'tiny creatures / who stay in the womb that bore them forever' (see Chapter 1) and so it also suggests to me the dismayed and disconcerted loneliness that Freud describes in his consulting room and his train carriage. But that is not plainly expressed here. Indeed, something opposite seems to be under discussion: 'direct psychical transference', a form of interrelationship that would seem to preclude loneliness and misrecognition and fear – 'there is no reason to be frightened' – altogether. Are they nevertheless to be inferred?

Finally Freud arrives at an incident – not one from his own experience, it should be said, but one that was reported to him by Dorothy Burlingham – which he cannot explain away as superstitious wish-fulfilment. Burlingham, whom Freud calls 'a trustworthy witness', had been simultaneously treating a mother and her son:

> One day the mother spoke during her analytic session of a gold coin [*Goldstück*] that had played a particular part in one of the scenes of her childhood. Immediately afterwards, after she had returned home, her little boy, about ten years old, came to her room and brought her a gold coin which he asked her to keep for him. She had asked him in astonishment where he had got it from. He had been given it on his birthday; but his birthday had been several months earlier and there was no reason why the child should have remembered the gold coin precisely then. The mother reported the occurrence to the child's analyst and asked her to find out from the child the reason for his action. But the child's analysis threw no light on the matter; the action had forced its way that day into the child's life like a foreign body [*Fremdkörper*]. (**56**, 86–7, *60–1*)

Freud's evidence, if it can even be called that, is ultimately remarkably scanty: he has to rely on a second-hand report of an observed incident. Trustworthy his witness may have been, but one may imagine numerous other explanations for what supposedly happened – if indeed it did happen as Freud claims Burlingham claimed her patient claimed it did. It seems hardly credible that Freud could place so much emphasis on the report as confirmation of what is being argued to be a form of communication – or rather, given Freud's repudiation of explanations to do with 'direct communication', of something so strange as 'direct psychical transference'.

Something else is going on here and I think it is like the 'smuggling' I proposed in Chapter 2 to be occurring when Freud purports to sum up the relationship between personal experience and inherited memory, psycho-Lamarckism and psychoanalysis. Indeed perhaps it is the same smuggling. For the process of 'direct psychical transference' is the same process as Freud imagines in *Moses and Monotheism* to be the means of others' memories being secretly inherited.

5
The Foreign Bodies of Psychoanalysis

The British novelist Richard Hughes was influenced by Freud. Psychoanalytic ideas are woven into *The Fox in the Attic* (1961), which is preoccupied with the German experience of World War I. Hughes has passages that are extraordinarily interesting post-psychoanalytic accounts of psychological theory – and ones, incidentally, that resonate with Rilke's concerns (with birds and interiority, for example) in the *Duino Elegies*:

> Primitive man is conscious that the true boundary of his self is no tight little stockade round one lonely perceiving 'I', detached wholly from its setting: he knows there is always overspill of self into penumbral regions – the perceiver's *footing* in the perceived. He accepts as naturally as the birds and beasts do his union with a part of his environment, and scarcely distinguishes that from his central 'I' at all. But he knows also that his self is not infinitely extensible either: on the contrary, his very identity with one part of his environment opposed him to the rest of it, the very friendliness of 'this' implies a balancing measure of hostility in – and towards – 'all that'. Yet the whole tale of *civilized* man's long and toilsome progress from the taboos of Eden to the psychiatrist's clinic could be read as a tale of his efforts, in the name of emergent Reason, to confine his concept of self wholly within Descartes' incontestable cogitating 'I'; or, alternatively, recoiling rebuffed off that adamantine pinpoint, to extend 'self' outwards infinitely – to pretend to awareness of everyone as universal 'we', leaving no 'they' anywhere at all.
>
> Selfhood is *not* wholly curtailed within the 'I': every modern language still witnesses the perpetuity of that primitive truth. For

> what else but affirmations of two forms of that limited overspill of '*I*'-ness are the two words 'we' and 'my' (the most potent words we have: the most ancient meanings)? These are in the full sense 'personal' pronouns for they bring others right inside our own 'person'.[1]

These are exactly some of the issues that Freud sometimes struggles to address; is not the micro-organism in *Beyond the Pleasure Principle* a 'tight little stockade round one lonely perceiving "I"'? And as I have expounded it, the idea of others' memories being inherited is a matter of theorizing the presence of 'others right inside our own "person"' – this is what Freud insists on imagining without dispensing with identity both as a psychological concept and as a figure of theory. Hughes is interested in the topology of all this, though he precisely has concepts of topological complexity – which Freud cannot always find for all the elaborateness of his topological theorizing – such as, most notably, 'overspill of self into penumbral regions'. Hughes is perhaps freer and more deft in his language and indeed in his conceptualization than Freud; but the fascination of Freud's writing is that it requires and implies the strange and troubling ideas that it cannot always formulate so directly. One such idea is that of a 'foreign body', as I want to go on to show.

As with the inherited-memory theory, Freud's views on telepathy met with fierce objection from Ernest Jones. Again Jones argued in favour of majority rational opinion. And, as with the psycho-Lamarckian problem, Jones correctly predicted that Freud's published opinions on the subject would bring psychoanalysis into disrepute. Freud's response is fascinating and ironic: 'If anyone should bring up my Fall with you, just answer calmly that my acceptance of telepathy is my own affair, like my Judaism and my passion for smoking, etc., and that the subject of telepathy is not related to psychoanalysis.'[2]

In my account of 'Mourning and Melancholia', a paradox emerged: Freud describes mourning as a form of self-reasserting understanding that can put an end to painfully retrospective and introspective thinking. Such thinking is a form of lamentation and despair; its secret purpose is to try to keep a dead person alive. Freud's psychoanalytic theory of mourning cannot condone this tormented despair and yet the essay has its own introspectiveness and its own preoccupation with contradictions and unresolved ideas – especially the problem of hurt. Something similar happens with the inherited-memory theory. It is presented as fitting neatly together with Freud's theories of individual psychology, supplementing them, merely providing a fall-back explanation. And yet the theory leads to an unresolved account of alternative possible causes in the Wolf Man case history and, more widely, it dispossesses personal experience as the basis for identity. Another version of the paradox is evident in Freud's apparently casual dismissal of Jones's objections to the writings on telepathy. The 'private affair' remark looks like a way of stopping the conversation quickly. Jones might well have persisted with his objections: it is not a private affair because, on the one hand, the lecture on telepathy is, with its concern for uncommunicated thoughts passing transgenerationally between persons, another version of the inherited-memory theory – whose presence in psychoanalytic theory is very public indeed and very contentiously so. And, on the other hand, it is not private because what is at stake is a radical refusal on Freud's part of the idea of privacy at its most essential (personal experience constituting memory).

Again and again there is a crisis in Freud's argument; an element emerges that transgresses the orderly, selfsame identity of concepts and explanations. I have tried to show how this is so in a number of ways. There is the problem of metaphors of injury. There is the problem of speech, writing, religion, philosophy and subjectivity itself all being presented as modes of suffering, guilt, remorse, grief. And there is, at the level of Freud's conceptualization, a problem of painful breaching – a topological idea I have taken from Freud to describe the way ideas of coherence or identity are disrupted. Pain is, in this abstract way, a concept that can apply to the way Freud imagines the ruin of selfsameness, especially as a consequence of the inherited-memory theory. Freud may call inherited memory a 'nucleus' or a neatly 'super-added' supplementary component to experience (like, for example, 'prosthetic' technology) but it is actually more like an unassimilated foreign body. And that is the image which, in the lecture on occult phenomena, can be connected with Freud's psycho-Lamarckism by virtue of the recurrence of the idea of noncommunicated memory.

In Chapter 1, I spoke about a countersense in Freud's references to injury and ghosts – a countersense that can be claimed to overrun psychoanalytic theory. I want now to substantiate that claim, to show precisely how Freud centralizes the problem of transgenerational memory in the theory of the superego. In Freud's final theoretical revision of psychoanalysis, there is an unmistakeable emphasis on agonized and 'haunted' subjectivity, on selves in which a foreign body is lodged.

In the telepathy lecture the word *Fremdkörper* is used to describe one person's thought that secretly steals over a border into another mind. I have emphasized the way in which Freud may be said to be imagining again the falling-away of barriers between persons in a process whereby there would be no lonely, embattled, isolated self. But, as we have seen, for example in respect of the injurious 'auxiliary organs' of *Civilization and Its Discontents*, elsewhere such a process is lamented and regretted. Freud's 'dream' of knowledge or unity or indivisibility or integration or transformation becomes a 'nightmare', of a kind perhaps that Hughes describes later in his novel:

> A private nightmare too can begin nobly, pleasurably. Silver ponies skimming summer meadows…a soaring on wings among restless star-fronted towers, over alabaster domes mirrored in shining lakes…but then suddenly the dream changes phase, the wings shrink to a tight winding-sheet and the dreamer plummets, the topless towers turn to dizzy unbanistered stairways climbing to nowhere up nothing.
>
> Then the translucent lakes become the rocking oceans paved with accusing faces: then come the staring idiot monkeys and the hollow derisive parakeets, the stone coffin at the heart of the pyramid, the 'cancerous kisses of crocodiles' the slimy things and the Nilotic mud.…
>
> The *Flanders* mud, the slime of putrefying bodies. The accusing sunken eyesockets trodden in the trench floor. The gargled pink froth, and an all-pervading smell.[3]

Flanders and the Nile: these locales are Freudian ones too. I am reminded of the exploding ordnance and crushing earth in Freud's paper on war neurosis as well as his fascination with Egypt – a fascination that is never expressed in such fluidly horrifying terms as Hughes manages, but which is nevertheless perhaps consonant with Hughes's images of putrefaction; one can think of that ruined sacred text which is called a 'mausoleum' or indeed the ancient tombs and coffins with which I began in Chapter 1. And, as I have discussed, Freud is preoccupied, even inappropriately so given his psychological concerns, by images of the wounded body. It is the most important such image, expressed by *Fremdkörper*, that I want to go on to explore. I am interested in how Freud's writing 'changes phase', as with the last quotation from the telepathy lecture, at the end of which pain, almost unannounced, finds its way into Freud's account of undivided selves. We may note that the coin, the gold piece, described by Freud is a detail that connects this passage to one that I quoted at the beginning of Chapter 4, concerning the strange 'piece…of self' that is felt as unreal.

Someone else's memory is figured as an alien thing in the child's mind, which enters transgressively, by force.

With Freud's use of *Fremdkörper*, the lecture on telepathy may be said to change phase without fanfare and to change phase in something like the way Hughes imagines, just as the delightful coin becomes a foreign body, moving from unobstructed mind-to-mind communication to bodily injury and a highly physical and painful kind of obstruction.

Superego countersense

'Foreign body' has a history in Freud's writing, beginning with the *Studies on Hysteria*, but taking in also Freud's record of the aftermath of a botched operation that Fliess undertook (without, it seems, much cause) on a patient named Emma Eckstein.[4] Fliess surgically removed a bone from Eckstein's nose but failed to remove bandaging from the incision. The bandaging was only removed after the intervention of another physician. Freud was present and he recounted his reaction in a letter to Fliess on 8 March 1895:

> There still was moderate bleeding from the nose and mouth; the fetid odor was very bad. Rosanes cleaned the area surrounding the opening, removed some sticky blood clots, and suddenly pulled at something like a thread, kept on pulling. Before either of us had time to think, at least half a meter of gauze had been removed from the cavity. The next moment came a flood of blood. The patient turned white, her eyes bulged, and she had no pulse. Immediately thereafter, however, he again packed the cavity with fresh iodoform gauze and the hemorrhage stopped. It lasted about half a minute, but this was enough to make the poor creature, whom by then we had lying flat, unrecognizable. In the meantime – that is, afterward – something else happened. At the moment the foreign body [*der Fremdkörper*] came out and everything became clear to me – and I immediately afterward was confronted by the sight of the patient – I felt sick. [...]
>
> I do not believe it was the blood that overwhelmed me – at that moment strong emotions were welling up in me. So we had done her an injustice; she was not at all abnormal, rather, a piece of iodoform gauze had gotten torn off as you were removing it and stayed in for fourteen days, preventing healing [*hatte die Heilung verhindert*]; at the end it tore off and provoked the bleeding.[5]

It is important here to state the obvious: 'foreign body' in this letter is not metaphorical. The term refers to a gauze bandage left in a patient's body after an ineptly performed surgical procedure. The bandage could not be evacuated and so, as Freud describes, it led to infection and swelling. It had to be removed. Its removal was accompanied by major blood loss, a 'flood of blood'. But once it was removed, it was possible for Eckstein to recover. She duly did, without (so Freud, with relief, writes to Fliess in a letter of 13 March) holding Fliess's incompetence against him.

In Chapter 3, I briefly discussed Derrida's ethical theory of mourning as 'safekeeping of the other *as other*' and its additional variations on the paradox of, as one may say, the outsider inside. This paradox is elaborated in terms of fidelity, love, friendship and so on. I have tried to show how Freud's work discloses some comparable paradoxes – especially in terms of others' memories taking the place of one's own. But Freud does not or cannot go further and celebrate these paradoxes. For all the radical ideas that make it so hard to read Freud's work without being struck by its subversion of identity and unambiguous explanation (both of these being to do with the assumed instrumentality of thinking), there is nothing to indicate that Freud could conceive of the kind of metatheoretical play of paradoxes that is Derrida's habitual mode. Freud instead comes back again and again to fundamental ideas of coherence and self-identical explanation – even if, again and again, these tend to meet with their own disruption or undoing. I think it is impossible to conceive of Freud settling, as Derrida does (and Rilke also), with pleasure and even ethical valorization, on what is called 'aporia' in deconstruction – a.figure of ultimate undecidability. And, reading Freud's letter, it is especially unsurprising that Freud might ever imagine with enthusiasm a proposition involving what Derrida would call, with altruistic devotion, 'safekeeping' of a foreign body. What is unthinkable is not the foreign body as such but the idea that it could be cherished or lovingly harboured. It is clear in Freud's first use of the term: 'treatment... works like the removal of a foreign body from the living tissue' – as with the urgently necessary removal of the gauze bandage from inside Eckstein's face, because such a foreign body is agonizingly painful and the cause of life-threateningly dangerous infection and inflammation.

And yet Freud, all the same, comes to the point of imagining subjectivity in relationship to an unremoved foreign body.

Freud's descriptions of the superego are notable for their emphasis on ferocity and unstinting punitive aggression. And the superego is implacable. The more it is appeased, the more zealously and unforgivingly does it go about its castigation. There is no more chilling confirmation of the theme of suffering in Freud's work than his descriptions of the superego: a tyrannical internal patriarch, a violent bully, an unrelentingly sadistic parent in the imagination. It (or, rather, he) is also a kind of ghost – which is to say, the superego is the instrument of transgenerational inherited memory. Freud writes in *The Ego and the Id* that the superego is 'a reincarnation of former ego-structures [*Reinkarnation früherer Ichbildungen*] which have left their precipitates behind in the id' (**19: 48**, 11: 390, *13: 278*).

Whatever marginal status may be attributed to *Moses and Monotheism*, *The Ego and the Id* is in the mainstream of Freud's work, as is the final topographical theory of the self. But, no less than the theories in *Moses and Monotheism*, that topography is fundamentally psycho-Lamarckian. And the agent of inheritance is the superego, as Freud makes unmistakeably clear in *The Ego and the Id*:

> The super-ego, according to our hypothesis, actually originated from the experiences that led to totemism. The question whether it was the ego or the id that experienced and acquired these things soon comes to nothing. Reflection at once shows that no external vicissitudes can be experienced or undergone by the id, except by way of the ego, which is the representative of the external world to the id. Nevertheless it is not possible to speak of direct inheritance in the ego. It is here that the gulf between an actual individual and the concept of a species becomes evident.... The experiences of the ego seem at first to be lost for inheritance; but, when they have been repeated often enough and with sufficient strength in many individuals in successive generations, they transform themselves, so to say, into experiences of the id, the impressions of which are preserved by heredity. Thus in the id, which is capable of being inherited, are harboured residues of the existences of countless egos; and, when the ego forms its super-ego out of the id, it may perhaps only be reviving shapes of former egos and be bringing them to resurrection [*schafft ihnen eine Auferstehung*]. (**38**, 378, *266–7*)[6]

In my initial survey of figurative language in Freud's writing (see Chapter 1), I noted asides in which, paradoxically given his vehement polemic against superstition and religion, he refers to ghosts and evil spirits. These might be dismissed as rhetorical flourishes were it not for his theory of inherited memory, which argues in psychoanalytic terms for a kind of haunting. It does not involve apparitions and visitations;

instead it is, so Freud claims, a matter of supplemental or prosthetic memory. It is a psychological rather than a supernatural theory, but it is still a matter of dead persons' experiences finding a way to inhabit or displace or pre-empt one's own. Reading across from the texts on the history of religion and species memory to 'Mourning and Melancholia', one may draw a further connection. The agony of incomplete mourning – a form of thinking which is introspective and retrospective in a heightened way, self-consumingly preoccupied with a dead loved one – seems to describe the waylaid, grief-stricken or remorseful subjectivity that Freud describes elsewhere and can be inferred on the basis of the idea of a 'wounded' self no longer grounded in experience. Therefore, reading the figurative language speculatively for what I have called countersense, it is as if the allusions to ghosts and premonitions were kinds of intimations of the inherited-memory theory – and ones that illuminate that theory to the extent, at least, of furnishing the idea of haunting. But the inherited-memory theory may also be dismissed as marginal or aberrant. What really cannot be dismissed, I think, is the fact that one of Freud's definitive statements of his general psychological theory is explicitly psycho-Lamarckian. With the idea that the superego 'resurrects' the dead, the figurative countersense becomes the theory's explicit sense.

This is the case in a further way also. The other figures I referred to in Chapter 1 were metaphors of injury. They also are inappropriate to the extent that they might seem not to take into account the distinction between psychological and physiological explanation, the former being the terrain of Freud's work. However, it has been possible to see – especially in respect of the embattled and brutalized micro-organism of *Beyond the Pleasure Principle* – that those metaphors too make a kind of countersense, and one that resonates (as with the 'wounded' grieving mind) with the problem of others' memories.

As well as being an agent of 'reincarnation', then, the superego is also figured, in keeping with the descriptions of brutalization in *Beyond the Pleasure Principle*, 'Mourning and Melancholia' and elsewhere, as a foreign body. Freud does not, so far as I can see, use the metaphor directly, but he is only one step away from it. In *Civilization and its Discontents*, he writes:

> What means does civilization employ in order to inhibit the aggressiveness which opposes it, to make it harmless, to get rid of it, perhaps? We have already become acquainted with a few of these methods, but not yet with the one that appears to be the most

> important. This we can study in the history of the development of the individual. What happens in him to render his desire for aggression innocuous? Something very remarkable, which we should never have guessed and which is nevertheless quite obvious. His aggressiveness is introjected, internalized; it is, in point fact, sent back to where it came from – that is, it is directed towards his own ego. There it is taken over by a portion of the ego, which sets itself over against the rest of the ego as super-ego, and which now, in the form of 'conscience', is ready to put into action against the ego the same harsh aggressiveness that the ego would have liked to satisfy upon other, extraneous [fremden] individuals. The tension between the harsh super-ego and the ego that is subjected to it, is called by us the sense of guilt; it expresses itself as a need for punishment. Civilization, therefore, obtains mastery over the individual's dangerous desire for aggression by weakening and disarming it and by setting up an agency within him to watch over it, like a garrison [Besatzung] in a conquered city. (**21: 123–4**, 12: 315–6, 14: 482–3)

And again in the *New Introductory Lectures*:

> Restriction of the individual's aggressiveness is the first and perhaps the severest sacrifice of [the individual]. We have learnt the ingenious way in which the taming of this unruly thing has been achieved. The institution of the super-ego which takes over the dangerous aggressive impulses, introduces a garrison [*Besatzung*], as it were, into regions that are inclined to rebellion. (**22: 110**, 2: 144, *15: 118*)

The metaphor of garrison is suggestive in a number of ways. As with the microbiological metaphor in *Beyond the Pleasure Principle*, there is the idea of battle and danger. The mind is beset, only here the rebellious hostility comes from within the country (of the self). The superego is a colonizing entity and another analysis of Freud's rhetoric might draw attention to this as a paradoxically political account of psychology. I will confine myself simply to noting that this is a political metaphor and therefore it treats the individual mind in plural terms, implying in another sense the problem of others-in-the-self.

More important for the purposes of my argument is that the remarks in the *New Introductory Lectures* are a direct echo of a passage concerned with the formation of symptoms in *Inhibitions, Symptoms and Anxiety*, in which Freud plays on the word *Besetzung*, which means both 'occupation' in the militaristic sense of an occupying force and, specifically in a psychoanalytic context, 'investment' or channelling of psychical energy (which Strachey translates neologistically as 'cathexis'):

> It is ... only natural that the ego should try to prevent symptoms from remaining isolated and alien [*die Fremdheit und Isolierung des Symptoms aufzuheben*] by using every possible method to bind them to itself in one way or another, and to incorporate them into its organization by means of those bonds. A classical instance of this are those hysterical symptoms which have been shown to be a compromise between the need for satisfaction and the need for punishment. Such symptoms participate in the ego from the very beginning, since they fulfil a requirement of the super-ego, while on the other hand they represent positions occupied by the repressed and points at which an irruption has been made by it into the ego-organization. They are a kind of frontier-station with a mixed garrison [*Besetzung*].

And then Freud continues:

> An analogy with which we have long been familiar compared a symptom to a foreign body [*Fremdkörper*] which was keeping up a constant succession of stimuli and reactions in the tissue in which it was embedded.... The ego now proceeds to behave as though it recognized that the symptom had come to stay and that the only thing to do was to accept the situation in good faith and draw as much advantage from it as possible. It makes an adaptation to the symptom – to this piece of the internal world which is alien to it – just as it normally does to the real external world. It can always find plenty of opportunities for doing so....In this way the symptom gradually comes to be the representative of important interests; it is found to be useful in asserting the position of the self and becomes more and more indispensable to it. It is only very rarely that the physical process of 'healing' round a foreign body follows such a course as this. (**20: 98–9**, 10: 250–1, *14: 125–6*)

The figure of the garrison, then, fades into the figure of the foreign body. In this way the problems of ghosts and wounds come together, though it is coming-together that is also problematically at stake here. This foreign body, though indispensable and even 'the representative of important interests', cannot be absorbed into its host. There may be healing around the foreign body but that process – even if it is finished (and, as Freud says, this happens 'only very rarely', as with the failed healing around auxiliary organs and prostheses in *Civilization and Its Discontents*) – only seals off the foreign body, which remains intact.

What is the relationship between the use of the 'foreign body' non-metaphorically in the letter to Fliess and the later uses in respect of symptoms and telepathy? As I noted in Chapter 1, the term is first used as a simile by Freud and Breuer in the *Studies on Hysteria*. However, in the last, theoretical section – which was written without Breuer – of that book, Freud takes issue with the analogy:

> We have said that [the pathogenic] material behaves like a foreign body, and that the treatment, too, works like the removal of a foreign body from the living tissue. We are now in a position to see where this comparison fails. A foreign body does not enter into any relation with the layers of tissue that surround it, although it modifies them and necessitates a reactive inflammation in them. Our pathogenic psychical group, on the other hand, does not permit of being cleanly extirpated from the ego. (**2: 290**, 3: 376)

Freud here refuses the image in the interests of precision of the topological kind that he tries to establish wherever possible elsewhere. The peripheral boundary of tissue will not permit the foreign body's intrusion. It mounts whatever defence is necessary, swelling and inflaming, to keep the foreign body at bay. To this extent, therefore, Freud insists that the instigating component of illness is not a foreign body because it cannot be 'extirpated'. What Freud's commentary on the figure emphasizes is the extent to which he cannot at this point conceive of the paradox of an inextirpable foreign body that all the same has a 'relation' to what surrounds it; a foreign body around which there is 'healing' rather than 'reactive inflammation' (which would prevent any encirclement). To conceive of this paradox would be to dispense with... the idea of identity. In asserting that the 'material' of illness has a relation to the rest, he is relying on an extended concept of integral internal interrelationship. There can be a harmful component but it is nevertheless a component and therefore not a foreign body.

So Freud abandons the figure. On the one occasion between 1895 and 1929 that he uses it again, it is only to explain why it is not admissible. In the *Five Lectures*, he writes:

> Breuer adopted a hypothesis that hysterical symptoms arise in peculiar mental conditions to which he gave the name of 'hypnoid.' On this view, excitations occurring during these hypnoid states do not provide

> opportunities for the normal discharge of the process of excitation. There consequently arises from the process of excitation an unusual product – the symptom. This finds its way, like a foreign body, into the normal state, which in turn is in ignorance of the hypnoid pathogenic situation. Wherever there is a symptom there is also an amnesia, a gap in the memory, and filling up the gap implies the removal of the conditions which led to the production of the symptom.
>
> The last part of my account will not, I fear, strike you as particularly clear, But you should bear in mind that we are dealing with novel and difficult considerations, and it may well be that it is not possible to make them much clearer – which shows that we still have a long way to go in our knowledge of the subject. Moreover, Breuer's theory of 'hypnoid states' turned out to be impeding and unnecessary, and it has been dropped by psycho-analysis today. (**11: 20**)

As Freud will go on to explain, psychoanalytic theory holds that the patient is not 'in ignorance' of the problem, an intolerable memory. The problem is known, but elsewhere; it seems strange, a part of something else but it is in fact familiar, a lost or refused experience. It is not alien, but part of a selfsame field. Imagined or following on from an actual incident, the apparently alien element has a prior place in the selfsame field of experience. This is why the hypothesis of inherited memory is the truly radical development in Freud's thinking. It is that hypothesis, especially as it is centralized in the concept of the superego, which requires the readmission of the metaphor of the foreign body in *Inhibitions, Symptoms and Anxiety* in a fully paradoxical form – the foreign body that has 'healed over' – not been expelled or absorbed, but grown around, with all the associated trouble Freud alludes to in respect of prostheses.

The metaphor of foreign body returns, therefore, but it is reformulated in the process. For Breuer the figure makes sense only in terms of the necessity of its removal through treatment. For Freud the idea of removal is additionally problematic: it is in fact a matter of retrieving and reintegrating not removing and therefore there is no foreignness to speak of. The crucial figurative reimagining therefore is the return of the foreign body without the idea of removal. And this reimagining makes sense: it is required by the inherited-memory theory. And so the last occurrence of the term occurs in *Moses and Monotheism*:

> In my opinion there is an almost complete conformity… between the individual and the group: in the group too an impression of the past is retained in unconscious memory-traces.

> In the case of the individual we believe we can see clearly. The memory-trace of his early experience has been preserved in him, but in a special psychological condition. The individual may be said to have known it always, just as one knows about the repressed. Here we have formed ideas, which can be confirmed without difficulty through analysis, of how something can be forgotten and how it can then reappear only after a while. What is forgotten is not extinguished but only 'repressed'; its memory-traces are present in all their freshness, but isolated by 'anticathexes'. They cannot enter into communication with other intellectual processes; they are unconscious – inaccessible to consciousness. It may also be that certain portions of the repressed, having evaded the process of [of repression], remain accessible to memory and occasionally emerge into consciousness, but even so they are isolated, like foreign bodies out of connection with the rest. (**23: 94**, 13: 339)

This occurrence is perhaps less remarkable than the usage in *Inhibitions, Symptoms and Anxiety*. But the simple fact that the term appears here seems to me to be important. Of all Freud's books, it is *Moses and Monotheism* where one would expect to find 'foreign body'. And yet, as with the passages quoted in Chapter 2 to do with a notionally simple calculus by which the relationship of personal experience and others' memories may be 'super-added', the context for the foreign body is a figure of theory involving 'conformity'. Freud will not or cannot dispense with a topological metaphor of coherent organization – no matter that experience-based identity is no longer conceivable now and no matter that the paradox of the foreign body is, like 'wound' in 'Mourning and Melancholia', conspicuously naming the countersense of agonized non-identity and, in so doing, emblematizing itself as a principle of irreducible paradox in Freudian theorizing.[7]

Unending analysis?

The complexity of Freud's project, the recurrent strangeness, the hybrid character of his writing, the drifts and lapses of argument, the disturbances and uncanny effects are all to be discovered abundantly in 'Analysis Terminable and Interminable'. A long essay in eight sections, its instigating concerns are technical, concerned with the conduct of psychoanalytic treatment and the nature of the 'recovery' (**23: 218**) that such treatment can bring about in a patient, the 'analytic cure' (**223**) or 'deep-going alteration of…personality' (**224**). As in 'Mourning and

Melancholia', the question of conclusion, of a process that reaches a proper end in the form of attained understanding, is moot: the very formulation of the problem that Freud chooses – 'is there any possibility at all of bringing analysis to ... an end?' (219) – is indicative of a more pressing concern with what cannot be ended, with what is unintelligible or beyond explanation. The ending is provisional, emphasizing a 'great riddle' (252) that is invoked unexpectedly.

Like many of his major works, 'Analysis Terminable and Interminable' is digressive, speculative and punctuated by asides which delay or hold up the declared business of the argument. There are analogies and literary allusions; there are casual remarks that imply extraordinary propositions about psychoanalysis; there is a whole series of references to past and present collaborators. All of these to some degree impede the progress of the theorizing. The essay comes to seem like a scenario of the treatment that fails to end.

Like scarlet fever

Even at a first glance, it is clear how intricate and self-aware is the essay; in particular, it demonstrates different sorts of hypothesizing velocity. At times there is a concern for the minute interrelationships of particular assertions, a subclassificatory endeavour that seeks in detail to demarcate the stages and divisions of Freud's argument. At the beginning of the fifth section, for example, there is a summary. Freud indicates the progress of the discussion so far, which has moved from the question of whether it may be possible to abbreviate therapy, to that of the prevention of illness, to an attempt at inventorizing 'the factors which were decisive for the success of our therapeutic efforts' (234). In the name specifically of explanation, Freud invokes 'the paramount importance of the quantitative factor and ... the metapsychological line of approach' (Ibid.). The steadiness of this careful stacking-together of claims suggests the orderliness of accounting; the accent on quantity again sets theory out as if it were an arithmetical sum. This is indeed, plainly, a plain account of Freud's own argument, recognizable thus as a figure of theory and, moreover, one that may be less plain than it seems, especially in the reference to metapsychology as an overarching explanatory paradigm. With such thorough itemizing, such studious pegging of the forward movement of the argument, Freud gives the essay a solid-seeming grounding. Added to this is the incidental furniture of debate: for example, the throwaway disclaimer; 'everything I have said has long been familiar and self-evident' (226), which gives a character of rumination to the writing. More substantial are two large areas of deliberation, major components of much of Freud's work: literary allusion and reference to patients and colleagues.

If, then, one of the recurrent characteristics of 'Analysis Terminable and Interminable' is the language of systematic rigour, the back-and-forth of question-posing, recapitulation and summary, it is supplemented by an unhindered speculativeness that is all the more disconcerting on occasions because it is somewhat glib and unsurprised. Very startling propositions are made without much commentary on how startling they are. Two connected remarks in particular, having to do with notional outcomes of psychoanalytic therapy, stand out. There is, first, the way Freud entertains the idea of 'subjecting poor human creatures... to cruel experiments' under the authority of some 'plenary power' that a psychoanalyst might gain (**232**). Freud envisages the prospect, for example, of therapeutic treatment that would end up 'destroying a satisfactory marriage' (Ibid.) or ruining a patient's career because so to do might lessen the chance that a patient could fall ill again. Freud entertains the idea, but dismisses it: it would be, he writes, as if a doctor were deliberately to infect someone with scarlet fever in order to be able to ensure immunity to the disease. At issue here is the very nature of psychoanalysis as a therapy and this is broached in the second remark I want to underline. Very soon after Freud's dismissal of his own 'self-evident' remarks, he asks: 'Is it not precisely the claim of our theory that analysis produces a state which never does arise spontaneously in the ego,' a 'newly created state' (**227**), a 'deep-going alteration' (**224**). Freud wonders, in sum, whether the process of psychoanalytic therapy, far from returning a patient to some prior state of effectiveness and equilibrium, might not involve – at least potentially – a remaking of personality, a brainwashing, imagined quite frankly as an assault by the doctor. Though such ideas are now familiar in sceptical writing about psychoanalysis, they are not mostly to be found in Freud's work. Where they do surface, though in a more limited way, is in his numerous discussions of hypnosis – 'hackwork and not a scientific activity,' Freud declares in the *Introductory Lectures*, too much like 'magic, incantations and hocus-pocus' (**16: 449**), a clumsy if not abusive suppression – which aims at obscuring or burying something in the memory of a patient. 'Hypnotic treatment seeks to cover up and gloss over something in mental life; analytic treatment seeks to expose and get rid of something. The former acts like a cosmetic, the latter like surgery' (**451**). This 'newly created state' would in fact be more of a disfiguring veneer than a quasi-surgical extraction, psychoanalysis a remanufacturing, a coercive education, an indoctrination like a fever.

As diligent as he is elsewhere in tracking the movement of his argument, here Freud is blithe in formulating a truly overbearing idea. There is both a dynamism at stake therefore – the intercommunication of brief grand speculativeness and elaborate studiousness – and also a theme of harm that may be done to a patient, a theme in which may be heard the reverberation of earlier debates about the relationship between psychoanalysis and medicine. It is worth emphasizing, however, that Freud brings to the fore – as is also the case with the numerous earlier discussions of hypnosis – ethical questions. One of the recurrent topics in 'Analysis Terminable and Interminable' is a certain worldly civility of conduct that Freud makes a repeated point of upholding. Having made the dire analogy with scarlet-fever infection, he moves on to emphasize that the psychoanalyst should not behave 'in an unfriendly way to the patient' (**23: 233**); discussing his own treatment of Ferenczi (without naming him), he refers to the undesirability of 'some unfriendly piece of behaviour... on the analyst's part' as opposed to 'friendly relations' (**222**). Whatever view one may take on the ethics of psychoanalysis or on the therapeutic efficacy of its techniques, it should not be neglected that Freud gave significant emphasis to ethical questions; the concern for friendliness may be overlooked.

A sliding scale

Freud does not fail in the essay to put into play ideas of successful treatment or understanding. Indeed the two are sometimes equated, care being to a degree a function of explanation. Variously hermeneutic or therapeutic, there is a spectrum of scenarios of conclusion presented, different efforts towards an end. With the Wolf Man (though that patient is not specifically identified in the text), Freud records that 'I had to help him master a part of the transference which had not been resolved' (**218**). In more general terms, he then summarizes the process of treatment in this way: 'the analyst shall judge that that so much repressed material has been made conscious, so much that was unintelligible has been explained, and so much internal resistance conquered, that there is no reason to fear a repetition of the pathological processes concerned' (**219**). This is a definition of what Freud calls the 'natural end' (Ibid.) of psychoanalytic treatment. There may be a 'gratifying outcome' (**220**). When an illness is 'predominantly traumatic', the psychoanalyst may 'succeed in replacing by a correct solution the inadequate decision' (Ibid.) the patient had been forced to make in early life. So analysis offers 'critical illumination' and is sometimes able to achieve 'a completely successful result' (**221**), or at least 'radically to exhaust the possibilities of illness' (**223**). The work is retrospective and penetrative; it is concerned to 'go below the surface and uncover the influences of the past' (**232**), 'uncovering... what is hidden in the id' (**238**). The work is disciplinary or pacifying (if not militant), concerned to 'subdue portions of his [patient's] id which are uncontrolled' (**235**). Finally, a conventional explanatory rigour is underlined: 'the analytic relationship is based on a love of truth... a recognition of reality' (**248**).

As he is accustomed to do therefore, Freud lays out interrelated concepts of interpretative efficacy and professional competence, concepts that are in the manner mostly of plain statements, though they become more metaphorical: the uncovering, militarism and excavation. There are fundamental figures of theory. Yet in this essay they are notably unstable assertions because, as elsewhere but not for the most part with quite such accumulated force, there are concepts and formulations, hypotheses and rhetorical devices, which weather away the integrity of the assertions of competence.

There is a kind of sliding scale of countervailing tendencies in 'Analysis Terminable and Interminable'. At one end are outright statements of explanation or treatment in trouble. And at the other end is a cluster of elements in which a transgressive countersense makes a covert way into the essay, compounding its already pronounced emphasis on a crisis of knowledge, overrunning it – though I will shortly describe the movement as a retrograde one: the manoeuvre, so to speak, is a doubling-back. In the rhetoric of this text, the retrospective impasse that I have tried to identify as crucial to Freud's work is enacted in a kind of disguised ricochet movement that, at last, brings one back to a crisis at the beginning.

At that former end of the notional scale is the matter of expediency and specifically what Freud calls the 'limited horizon' (**222**) of psychoanalysis. For although 'analysis... is always right in theory' (**229**), there are always likely to be practical reasons why the theory cannot be explored in the human encounter of treatment. This theme is familiar from earlier in Freud's writing, notably in a footnote in which Freud is dealing with phylogenetic questions, which I quoted in part in Chapter 2, to the Rat Man case history: 'It was impossible to unravel this tissue of phantasy thread by thread; the therapeutic success of the treatment was precisely what stood in the way of this' (**10: 207n**, 9: 88). Treatment may be successful in such a way that the core of an illness is unapproached, its battlements unbreached. The theme is repeatedly amplified in 'Analysis Terminable and Interminable'; the essay is strewn with remarks that involve stalled understanding or obstructed treatment. So Freud warns that therapy may become too comfortable for a patient, who may thus lose an incentive to get well, creating a situation of 'the treatment inhibiting itself: it was in danger of failing as a result of its – partial – success' (**217**). The opposite situation may also arise: therapy may be sufficiently successful in reducing the manifestations of illness that there is no need to explore deeper-lying problems, whose harmfulness may remain undisclosed by virtue only of 'a kind fate which has spared [the patient] ordeals that are too severe' (**220**). The question of prevention, of 'inoculat[ing]' patients is present throughout the essay, though it needs sometimes to be disclaimed: 'Perhaps it may not be possible at present to give any certain answer... at all' (**223**). There are 'limits' (**231**), Freud repeatedly writes, invoking as he does elsewhere a technological figure of theory: 'the power of the instruments with which analysis operates is not unlimited but restricted' (**230**). Another favoured analogy – the military one – is also reprised: 'analysis can only draw upon definite and limited amounts of energy which have to be measured against the hostile forces. And it seems as if victory is in fact as a rule on the side of the big battalions' (**240**). Faced during therapy with evidence of trouble that seems to come out of some basic biological recalcitrance, Freud concedes, temporarily at least, 'we must bow to the superiority of the forces against which we see our efforts come to nothing' (**243**). This note of resignation is to be heard also at the end of the essay, with its avowal that, in relation to gender, 'all one's repeated efforts have been in vain' (**252**).

In Chapter 4, I discussed the complexity of Freud's topological ideas, emphasizing how much more elaborate they are than comparable ideas in Breuer's writing. In 'Analysis Terminable and Interminable', there are comparable conceptualizations – ideas of interpretative crisis, transgression, impairment, obstruction – that may be treated as figures of theory. There is, for example, the striking idea not of 'absolute psychical normality' (**220**) or 'schematic "normality"' (**250**), but of an 'ideal fiction' (**235**) of normality. That idea is strikingly hypothetical. A purely heuristic notion it may be, but it is a concept of makeshift meaning, to do with nonviability of generalizing explanation as much as it is to do with effective classification or understanding. In the third section of the essay, in which Freud is also to be found bemoaning his own 'ponderous exposition' of his theory of mental life, there are more such concepts of provisional or partial meaning. Freud refers to 'intermediate stages', 'partial alterations' and 'residual phenomena, a partial hanging-back' (**228**). These ideas are conceptual counterparts to the disclaimers that are to be found elsewhere in the essay.

'Analysis Terminable and Interminable' sets out concepts of intermediary stages, interruption, stalling, even as it pauses, digresses and reflects on the limitations to its own progress. It therefore resembles 'Mourning and Melancholia', among other texts. In that essay, it seems that Freud's writing is prone to the same disorders that are attributed to mourning that is not yet finished. Thus the concepts that are named in the essay may be read as being figures of theory. Something similar may be said about the descriptions of the truly disconcerting work of the hypothetical death instinct as it is described by Freud in the fifth and sixth sections of the essay in terms of a force of 'resistance' so deep-lying that it is protected by 'a resistance against the uncovering of resistances' (**238**). Freud writes about the possibility of conclusive treatment, successful disclosure, accomplished understanding and he notes intermediate or interrupting variants of such culminations. He also imagines the most absolute undoing of thought and meaning, 'a force which is defending itself by every possible means against recovery' (**242**).

Absent friends

'Analysis Terminable and Interminable' is an essay on technique, therapy, theorizing, the nature of understanding in psychoanalysis. But it is moreover both highly personal and repetitively retrospective. The essay is about Freud and it is about the past. In the most contained manner, this is to say that Freud reviews those who formed or still presently occupy his intimate circle: his family, his collaborators, certain patients, the writers who shaped his views (even perhaps without his knowledge of the influence): Rank, Adler, the Wolf Man, Ferenczi, Anna Freud, Goethe, Empedocles, Fliess. Like *Beyond the Pleasure Principle*, 'Analysis Terminable and Interminable' is substantially autobiographical. It provides a litany of names that metonymically describes the bonds and rifts between persons, the often disturbed conjugations of the personal. But there is always an uncertainty implicit in these invocations; the first readers of the published edition of the text would, notably, not for the most part have been able to identify a 'certain man' as Ferenczi at one point in Freud's text, a fact that is pointed up by editorial interpolations in the *Standard Edition* (**221n**). I mention this in passing for now because it suggests the countersense-smuggling that I have claimed goes on in Freud's writing: there is something that is not named. There can be more conceptual trouble in a statement than there at first seems; there may be 'false friends' here.

Ferenczi and Fliess were dead by the time Freud, near the end of life, wrote his essay. Rank and Adler were estranged and repudiated; the friends were mostly gone. There is then a poignancy if not a mournfulness inherent in Freud's namings and non-namings. For the most part the convocation of intimates is retrospective. It must be so; 'Analysis Terminable and Interminable' is in part an act of recollection and one that quite precisely goes further and further into the past. In the forward movement of the essay there is increasing retrospection; as it goes on, it goes back. The last-named friends are the oldest. Freud comes finally to Empedocles and Fliess, the one a figure from antiquity, the other the closest colleague in Freud's own life. Antiquarian and autobiographical, the recollections in the essay thus stage in miniature the complex methodological intertwining of anthropology and psychology that I have been concerned to discuss throughout this book. The retrospection of Freud's work is enacted here as a chorus of remembrances, the work of Empedocles being rather directly analogous to the supposed facts of Egyptian monotheism that Freud discusses in the contemporary *Moses and Monotheism* in that, as Freud puts it, the theory of love and strife competing has remained dormant until 'its re-emergence after two and a half millennia' (**246**). But it was, like the inherited knowledge of the primal murder in Freud's psycho-Lamarckian theory, preserved: 'I can never be certain, in view of the wide extent of my reading in early years, whether I took for a new creation might not be an effect of cryptomnesia' (**245**). Freud's account of Empedocles is a version of the inherited-memory theory.[8]

Throughout this book I have argued that Freud's psycho-Lamarckism cannot be marginalized. I have, in summary, claimed that the inherited-memory theory encapsulates a countersense of ruined identity and conceptual crisis, a countersense that becomes more not less significant in Freud's work. This transgressive idea furthermore frequently steals in like contraband, masked rather than hidden as it makes its way across the verge of Freud's theorizing. A concept of radical transgression is transgressive in its entering as when, in my presentation of the matter, its incursion takes the form of a figure of quasi-arithmetical explanation. Without having attention drawn to it, the inherited-memory theory is more often to be found in his work than is often conceded. In particular the defining Freudian formulation of the superego is psycho-Lamarckian. But there are all sorts of persuasions to the contrary which disarmingly license commentators to overlook the incursion; to stress in particular that psycho-Lamarckism is a *sui generis* aberration that is not relevant to Freud's work – being rather an odd personal quirk of an idea. We may watch the disingenuous persuasion again in 'Analysis Terminable and Interminable'. Freud notes, in order rather to dismiss it, that Empedocles had a belief in metempsychosis. He does not dwell on this, zeroing in instead on the prototype of instinct theory, so close to Freud's own as to be identical but for the fact that 'the Greek philosopher's theory is a cosmic phantasy while ours is content to claim biological validity' (**245**). This is the sort of remark – Freud did it a little earlier in the essay when he defended the idea of an 'archaic heritage' by asserting that its postulation should imply 'no mystical overvaluation of heredity' (**240**) – that allows commentators to assert that psycho-Lamarckism is to be distinguished, despite any evidence to the contrary, from the twin legitimate pillars of Freudian theorizing: the 'talking cure' and, above all, the so-called metapsychology. But, I have argued, no such distinction should be made on the basis of Freud's own remarks. Metapsychology is, in rather specific ways, indistinguishable from psycho-Lamarckism. I offer a last piece of evidence for this contention in the form of an allusion – one might follow Freud's lead and call it an instance of secret remembering – lodged within another allusion.

In the third section of 'Analysis Terminable and Interminable', Freud alludes to Goethe, in addressing the question he has posed as to how instincts are, as he puts it, brought into a harmony with consciousness, going on: 'We can only say: "So muss denn doch die Hexe dran!" – the Witch Metapsychology' (**225**). The allusion echoes a letter to Marie Bonaparte of 29 May 1918: 'Here we must have recourse to the witch Prehistory or Phylogenesis.'[9]

Leonardo's ghost

The shadows of other texts fall upon this one, making phantom shapes. These shapes are figures of Freud's own theorizing, its sense, in some way surreptitious and recondite but all the same evident, of itself. It is, in my reading, perhaps a little like what Freud describes in relation to certain ideas about sexuality that children may mistakenly infer and which persist as cherished theories in spite of subsequent, more accurate knowledge. In this prolonged attachment to favourite ideas, children, Freud writes, 'behave like primitive races who have had Christianity thrust upon them and who continue to worship their old idols in secret' (**234**). But in the case of Freud's writing, what persists is rather, or so I argue, ideas about transgression and a crisis of identity that pertain above all to Freud's own argument and theorizing. It is perhaps something analogous to a metaphysical superstition but is emphatically non-metaphysical, having to do with forms of argument. There is even a sort of inversion of the schema whereby obstinate superstition is hidden by the semblance of reason. Instead, behind the chimera of superstition the contraband is a concept of identity in crisis. The witchcraft is, paradoxically, out in the open in 'Analysis Terminable and Interminable'; it is the inherited-memory theory – and so, in my account, the idea of ruined identity – that is, demonstrably, under cover. Rather than the other way around, the metaphysical language smuggles in a figure of theory.

There is perhaps another 'idol' outlined in the shadows of Freud's essay. It is clear to what extent Freud admires Empedocles; his tribute is fond and enthusiastic. I, however, discern another admiration, an implicit parallel – with Leonardo da Vinci, who is in fact nowhere named or apparently alluded to in 'Analysis Terminable and Interminable.' The substantiation I offer for this claim is a pair of remarks. The first comes in the sixth section, when Freud is once more reflecting on what he hesitantly calls 'adhesiveness of the libido': some love obstinately, others promiscuously, Freud observes and he refers the matter of the difference between the two modes of desire to 'the one felt by a sculptor, according to whether he works in hard stone or soft clay' (**241**). This observation put me in mind of a remark in 'On Psychotherapy' (1905 [1904]), one incidentally that also quotes Goethe's *Faust*:

> There is, actually, the greatest possible antithesis between suggestive and analytic technique – the same antithesis which, in regard to the fine arts, the great Leonardo da Vinci summed up in the formulas: *per via di porre* and *per via di levare*. Painting, says Leonardo, works *per via di porre*, for it applies a substance – particles of colour – where there was nothing before, on the colourless canvas; sculpture, however, proceeds *per via di levare*, since it takes away from the block of stone all that hides the surface of the statue contained in it. In a similar way, the technique of suggestion aims at proceeding *per via di porre*; it is not concerned with the origin, strength and meaning of the morbid symptoms, but instead, it superimposes something – a suggestion – in the expectation that it will be strong enough to restrain the pathogenic idea from coming to expression. Analytic therapy, on the other hand, does not seek to add or to introduce anything new, but to take away something, to bring out something; and to this end concerns itself with the genesis of the morbid symptoms and the psychical context of the pathogenic idea which it seeks to remove. (**7: 260–1**)

The linkage between the two passages is to an extent vague, relying simply on the analogy with sculpture (and yet, after all, it is not so necessary an analogy). Nevertheless, this is a major figure of Freudian theory; the comparison with hypnosis is recurrently used by Freud to get at the modality of psychoanalytic understanding and this taking-away – quasi-surgical as it is – is a fundamental figure of theory, like elucidation or mystery-solving. Yet as I discussed in the previous chapter, this figure has its troubled counterpart: the alien substance that will not shift or come away no matter that its continuing transgressive lodgement is harmful and painful. The counterpart figure has to do therefore with a crisis of identity.

I have emphasized how this crisis is in particular ways formulated as agonizing, but I also in Chapter 1 adduced the formalism of a passage in *Totem and Taboo* that formulated inexplicability in less harrowing terms. That citation is relevant to my reading here because the second, more substantive return of Leonardo has to do with the emphasis Freud places at the end of his essay on 'the distinction between the sexes' (**250**). Rather like the culmination of 'Mourning and Melancholia', Freud, having 'penetrated through all the psychological strata', closes with 'bedrock…the great riddle of sex' (**252**), a principle at least for the present of inexplicability. These lasts remarks recall for me *Leonardo da Vinci and a Memory of His Childhood*:

> These pictures [Leda, John the Baptist, Bacchus] breathe a mystical air into whose secret one dares not penetrate; at the very most one can attempt to establish their connection with Leonardo's earlier creations. The figures are still androgynous, but no longer in the sense of the vulture phantasy. They are beautiful youths of feminine delicacy and with effeminate forms: they do not cast their eyes down, but gaze in mysterious triumph, as if they knew of a great achievement of happiness, about which silence must be kept. The familiar smile of fascination leads one to guess that it is a secret of love. It is possible that in these figures Leonardo has denied the unhappiness of his erotic life and has triumphed over it in his art, by representing the wishes of the boy, infatuated with his mother, as fulfilled in this blissful union of the male and female natures. (**11: 117–8**, 14: 210–11)

Once more, I take Freud at his word in his repudiation of mysticism. What is at stake in this figure of theory is the recurrent but insufficiently acknowledged emphasis on unintelligibility in his work.

X-ray analysis

There is also, in my reading of the essay, a shadow-play *inside* 'Analysis Terminable and Interminable'; it too is suggestive not of mystical rapture or gender indeterminacy, but of hurt. As noted, there are various concepts of provisionality and inconclusiveness throughout 'Analysis Terminable and Interminable'. Not the least of these is the idea of an ending itself. Patient and analyst may 'cease to meet' (**219**) but this is not the same as completion of their work together, upon which 'there is no need to fear a repetition of the pathological processes concerned' (**219**). A course of treatment may finish, but not be completed; be over, but not be settled. The ending may not be conclusive or final. Such a failure to conclude, a halt that is not a finish, occurs in the last paragraph of the essay with 'bedrock... the great riddle of sex' that is irreducible. (And then, with one pragmatic final sentence, Freud breaks off.)

In this way the essay draws to a close. But this is not the end of my reading, which proposes that the termination of the essay is like a dead end in a labyrinth and it is necessary not to stop at it, but to go back, ricocheting as it were along a backward path that may be said to have opened up in the essay: a path that returns – as Freud endlessly does – to the beginning.

That path, as I trace it, begins at perhaps the gravest remark in 'Analysis Terminable and Interminable.' 'It seems,' Freud writes, 'that a number of analysts learn to make use of defensive mechanisms which allow them to divert the implications and demands of analysis from themselves'; and he goes on that 'when we try to understand this, we are driven into drawing a disagreeable analogy with the effect of X-rays on people who handle them without taking special precautions' (**249**).

In *Beyond the Pleasure Principle,* as I mentioned in Chapter 3, Freud writes about the primal organism as being subject to brutalization. Such is the pressure in its environment that it must undergo a liminal death. That process is described specifically as an exposure to extreme heat: 'A crust would thus be formed which would at last have been so thoroughly "baked through" by stimulation that it would present the most favourable possible conditions for the reception of stimuli and become incapable of any further modification' (**18: 26**, 11: 297). So the organism acquires a foreign burnt surface, which is its integral injury.

Where else may we find this idea of extreme heat? It is in fact implicit in the idea of over-exposure to X-rays and so that idea in turn links back to something Freud mentioned earlier about the Wolf Man:

> Some of these attacks were still concerned with residual portions of the transference; and, where this was so, short-lived though they

> were, they showed a distinctly paranoid character. In other attacks, however, the pathogenic material consisted of pieces of the patient's childhood history, which had not come to light while I was analysing him and which now came away – the comparison is unavoidable – like sutures after an operation, or small fragments of necrotic bone. I have found the history of this patient's recovery scarcely less interesting than that of his illness. (**23: 218**)

It is the very condition of necrosis, of tissue killed off inside a living body (the *OED* adds the sense of 'inward mortification'), that may ensue as a result of the mishandling of X-rays, according to the *American Medical Association Encyclopedia of Medicine*: 'The death of tissue cells. Necrosis can occur as a result of *ischemia* (inadequate blood supply), which may lead to *gangrene*; infection (such as *tuberculosis*); or damage by extreme heat or cold, noxious chemicals, or excessive exposure to X-rays or other forms of radiation.' I find this passage in 'Analysis Terminable and Interminable' to be profoundly strange. The penultimate figure that I will discuss, it is however not untypical in some respects. It is a variant on the 'foreign body' image, a figure of injury. As with the description of the embattled primitive organism, Freud dwells on a body that is burnt and so once more there is a basic incongruity about it. That incongruity is finessed, however. Yet once more, Freud couches a transgressive idea – that hurtful memories may be like dead substance lodged inside one – in terms of successful explanation: 'the comparison is unavoidable,' Freud insists, and after all the image is being used (as 'foreign body' had been at the beginning) in the context of the therapeutic work of removal ('the pathogenic material…now came away'). There is smuggling taking place in this passage. And the passage figures Freud's theorizing. The whole of the complex movement between concepts of therapeutic and explanatory success, on the one hand, and inconclusiveness and resistance, on the other, that goes on in the essay is evident here. The unavoidable comparison and the sutures healthily detached suggest efficacy and a state of culmination that the very idea of necrotic bone, of a foreign body, refuses.

We have seen already that the image of the foreign body is linked in Freud's writing with medical negligence, with the harm doctors may do to patients, with the ethical breaches that Freud often addresses. The reference to analysts who are irresponsible, like scientists recklessly unleashing radiation, inflects the passage about the Wolf Man. This passage seems to imply some larger trouble in psychoanalysis. I mean here, once more, that the trouble is theoretical, to do with Freud's writing, with the way the explanatory ambition of his work is shadowed by ideas of impediment, transgression, injury; the way concepts of identity are ruined; the way the promise of meaning in the past becomes a sadness of loss. I offer one final passage in support, which is even nearer to the beginning of 'Analysis Terminable and Interminable', on its first page, and which is also ostensibly concerned with the recklessness of a renegade psychoanalyst. Freud mocks Rank's claim that therapy may be hastened by confining itself to the after-effects of the 'primal trauma' of birth:

> We have not heard much about what the implementation of Rank's plan has done for cases of sickness. Probably not more than if the fire-brigade, called to deal with a house that had been set on fire by an overturned oil-lamp, contented themselves with removing the lamp from the room in which the blaze has started. (**216–7**)

Yet Freudian psychoanalysis is like that lamp too, its ideas of elucidation and understanding yielding to the idea of burned and harmed bodies that Freud recurrently imagines.

Conclusion: Freud's Secret

Vladimir Nabokov was exuberantly contemptuous of Freud's work. 'Let the credulous and the vulgar continue to believe,' he said in an interview, 'that all mental woes can be cured by a daily application of old Greek myths to their private parts.'[1] In *Lolita* (1955), he has Humbert Humbert delight in recalling a stay in a psychiatric hospital:

> The reader will regret to learn that soon after my return to civilization I had another bout with insanity (if to melancholia and a sense of insufferable oppression that cruel term must be applied). I owe my complete restoration to a discovery I made while being treated at that particular very expensive sanatorium. I discovered there was an endless source of robust enjoyment in trifling with psychiatrists: cunningly leading them on; never letting them see that you know all the tricks of the trade; inventing for them elaborate dreams, pure classics in style (which make *them*, the dream-extortionists, dream and wake up shrieking); teasing them with fake 'primal scenes'; and never allowing them the slightest glimpse of one's real sexual predicament. By bribing a nurse I won access to some files and discovered, with glee, cards calling me 'potentially homosexual' and 'totally impotent.' The sport was so excellent, its results – in *my* case – so ruddy that I stayed on a whole month after I was quite well (sleeping admirably and eating like a schoolgirl).[2]

Nothing is more characteristic in psychoanalysis than the retrospective search for shock and hurt and confusion. The child is hurt; the child is overwhelmed by sexuality; the adult is burdened by the child's hurt; the psychoanalyst seeks to name, find and perhaps salve the hurt. Many commentators have objected to many aspects of this narrative. Gilles

Deleuze and Félix Guattari, following D. H. Lawrence, for example, rebut the whole business:

> Let us keep D.H. Lawrence's reaction to psychoanalysis in mind, and never forget it. In Lawrence's case, at least, his reservations with regard to psychoanalysis did not stem from terror at having discovered what real sexuality was. But he had the impression – the purely instinctive impression – that psychoanalysis was shutting sexuality up in a bizarre sort of box painted with bourgeois motifs, in a kind of rather repugnant artificial triangle, thereby stifling the whole of sexuality as production of desire so as to recast it along entirely different lines, making of it a 'dirty little secret,' the dirty little family secret, a private theater rather than the fantastic factory of Nature and Production. Lawrence had the impression that sexuality possessed more power or more potentiality than that. And though psychoanalysis may perhaps have managed to 'disinfect the dirty little secret,' the dreary, dirty little secret of Oedipus-the-modern-tyrant benefited very little from having been thus disinfected.[3]

'Primal scene' and sexual secret are fundamental units of privileged historical meaning in psychoanalysis, the meaning hidden in a person's past. But those units are not so coherent or untransgressed in Freud's work as is often supposed, as I have endeavoured to show in my readings and especially in the emphasis I have placed on Freud's psycho-Lamarckism.

However, I have touched upon certain recorded incidents in Freud's life, and especially his involvement with the injury inflicted upon Fliess's patient, which in another account of this material might have provided the basis for a so-called psychobiographical argument.

For Freud's sake

Nabokov's interest in the 'primal scene' and Deleuze and Guattari's idea of a confined space where psychoanalysis claims to discover its meanings and causes converge interestingly in Wittgenstein's deceptively moderate response to Freud. Freud's ideas are, Wittgenstein says, charming: 'The picture of people having subconscious thoughts has a charm. The idea of an underworld, a secret cellar. Something hidden, uncanny. … A lot of things one is ready to believe because they are uncanny.'[4] It is an oddly temperate sketch of psychoanalysis. For Wittgenstein, some of the frankly gloomier elements of Freud's work give comfort: it is a genially engaging affair to consider a gothic, subterranean dimension to everyday life. There is a certain carefree romance involved in which the mundane reality of life takes on a dank air of mysteriousness; this is claimed to be appealing – it may convince or be conveniently believable to someone who is susceptible to such ideas.

Wittgenstein's comments are arguably much more effectively demystifying than the more outraged polemical comments that often arise. Neither doctrine nor lie, the charming theory may be persuasive or credible or diverting,[5] but it is not apparently very dangerous. Yet Wittgenstein is not really quite so lenient as that, as can be seen from comparatively sustained remarks from a conversation with Rush Rhees:

> Freud refers to various ancient myths ... and claims that his researches have now explained how it came about that anybody should think or propound a myth of that sort.
>
> Whereas in fact Freud has done something different. He has not given a scientific explanation of the ancient myth. What he has done is to propound a new myth. The attractiveness of the suggestion, for instance, that all anxiety is a repetition of the anxiety of birth trauma, is just the attractiveness of a mythology. 'It is all the outcome of something that happened long ago.' Almost like referring to a totem.
>
> Much the same can be said of the notion of the 'Urszene'. This often has the attractiveness of giving a sort of tragic pattern to one's life. It is all the repetition of the same pattern which was settled long ago. Like a tragic figure carrying out the decrees under which the fates had placed him at birth. Many people have, at some period, serious trouble in their lives – so serious as to lead to thoughts of suicide. This is likely to appear to one as something nasty, as a situation which is too foul to be a subject of a tragedy. And it may then be an immense relief if it can be shown that one's life has the pattern of a tragedy – the tragic working out and repetition of a pattern which was determined by the primal scene.[6]

It needs to be stressed that Wittgenstein's published remarks on Freud are few, casual and scattered and at certain points they are inaccurate. Here there is a misdescription of Freud's views in the reference to 'the anxiety of birth trauma', a theory which is to be attributed to Otto Rank not Freud, who dismissed the hypothesis in no uncertain terms in 'Analysis Terminable and Interminable': 'Rank's argument was bold and ingenious; but it did not stand the test of critical examination' (**23: 216**) and moreover, Freud adds, has been of no therapeutic value. Leaving that aside, I would emphasize again the perhaps counter-intuitive emphasis that is given to the notionally soothing effect psychoanalytic ideas may have: the 'immense relief' that may ensue if one can replace the 'nasty' reality of a situation with a narrative of inescapable tragic destiny. With the aid of psychoanalytic ideas of a connecting 'pattern', the true 'foul' facts of the matter may be perceived differently even if they are not ameliorated as such. There is consolation to be found, according to Wittgenstein, of a certain kind: the 'serious trouble' of life may be clothed in lighter garb.

Because of the sparseness of Wittgenstein's comments in this area, a lot remains unelaborated and there is some incongruity. I am struck especially by the way the words 'foul' and 'nasty' recur in a 1945 letter:

> I, too, was greatly impressed when I first read Freud. He's extraordinary. – Of course he is full of fishy thinking and his charm and the charm of the subject is so great that you may easily be fooled. He always stresses what great forces in the in the mind, what strong prejudices work against the idea of psycho-analysis. But he never says what an enormous charm that idea has for people, just as it has for Freud himself. There may be strong prejudices against uncovering something nasty, but sometimes it is infinitely more *attractive* than it is repulsive. Unless you think *very* clearly psycho-analysis is a dangerous and a foul practice, & it's done no end of harm &, comparatively, very little good. (If you think I'm an old spinster – think again!) – All this, of course, doesn't detract from Freud's extraordinary scientific achievement. Only, extraordinary scientific achievements have a way these days, of being used for the destruction of human beings (I mean their bodies, or their souls, *or their intelligence*). *So hold on to your brains.*[7]

In the conversation with Rhees, Wittgenstein suggests that Freudian ideas may allow for nasty facts to be glossed over. Their very nastiness is too much and so it is welcome to be able to make reference to a pattern established long ago. Here, though, the statement is that it is the very nastiness that is appealing to uncover. Whereas in the Rhees passage, the idea of tragic fate was a 'relief' from a nasty situation, a comfort, in this one Wittgenstein claims that it is the nastiness that is cheering. What is more, the three-times-identified 'charm' of psychoanalysis seems here much less polite; it is the charm of a charming demon. Whereas with Rhees, Wittgenstein reserved his stark 'foul' for the nearly intolerable crises of life – the situations that may even drive people to suicide – which psychoanalytic theories may alleviate, here it is those very theories that are so dangerous and overwhelming.

Conviction and consolation seem to me to be the key issues here. It is conviction that is crucially involved in the idea of myth that is recurrent in the remarks I have so far quoted. When Wittgenstein refers to a 'new myth' and 'the attractiveness of a mythology', he means, according to Jacques Bouveresse that Freud has managed to propound theories that accommodate a pre-existing appetite for ideas that will satisfyingly explain certain affairs in certain ways:

> the mythological character of an explanation depends much less on its crude, naive, or overly speculative character than on its capacity to impress people as being the universally valid explanation, convincing a priori because of the desire, and not the thought, that it should be able to account for every case.

Therefore:

> It is not really very important whether Freud's reconstructions are true or false if, as Wittgenstein believes, they are basically accepted because of their charm, received spontaneously as explanations that *must* be true and not as hypotheses whose truth or falseness is important. The events they relate, like those in myths, are events that *had to* happen, and not events whose actual occurrence is at issue.[8]

Wittgenstein's remarks are not explicitly concerned with Freud's psycho-Lamarckism at all, but they are pertinent. As I have tried to show, it is often the case that an explanatory proficiency is attributed to Freud's arguments that is not justified by the way these arguments are developed; often one in fact finds hesitation, paradox, a criss-crossing of alternatives rather than the unified explanation that Freud's detractors so often claim to demystify. Then and now, psycho-Lamarckism was an unpopular, unconvincing theory: its persistence in Freud's work needs to be explained in terms other than intellectual bullying. In my reading, moreover, the theory's work is a work of transgression and crisis – it is not conducive to consolation, or at any rate to the consolation provided by certainty or the appearance of certainty.

The comments about consolation are echoed in the biography of Freud by his personal physician, Max Schur:

> We must suspect that in this book, as in *Beyond the Pleasure Principle*, some of Freud's formulations arose out of inner conflicts, the existence of which he continually referred to throughout the period during which he was writing the *Moses* book. We can only speculate here as to why these particular formations were chosen and, following Freud's example, ask *'Cui bono?'* – what psychic agency profits thereby? The only answer would seem to be that if man's guilt feelings about parricide were a response to an archaic heritage dating back to primeval times when parricide was still frequent, this would mean that a great distance existed between the feelings and the deed. We would be able to say: 'It is those long-gone ancestors who did the deed. We are merely repeating some fantasies in an attenuated way.' This would be a different method of coming to terms with the 'primal sin' from the one attributed by Freud to the Apostle Paul. It would be another aspect of Freud's struggle to come to terms with his own 'primal sin.'[9]

To what extent can the crisis of understanding that I have discussed in this book be referred to what Paul Roazen also calls 'certain inner conflicts in Freud'?[10] I have quoted several instances of the habit that some vehement critics of psychoanalysis have of using terms from psychiatry or psychoanalysis in order to censure Freud. There was, for example, John Farrell's quasi-diagnosis (quoted in Chapter 3) of 'narcissistic projections' on Freud's part, and Farrell entitles his book *Freud's Paranoid Quest*. Todd Dufresne concurs: 'Freud… reserves for himself the only position outside the structure of mind that he devised: the impossible position of a super-man-child of absolute narcissism.'[11] Again there is the assertion that psychoanalysis is a kind of coercion, its rigid ideas ruthlessly forced onto any set of facts. But this assertion is undermined in a number of ways. There is the volubility of all the commentators, including when it comes to psycho-Lamarckism, who patently have suffered no such coercion; there is the disintegration of explanation to be found in Freud's texts; and there is the problem that in order to denounce psychoanalysis in these terms, the detractors are effectively conceding the psychological premises that they might otherwise repudiate.[12]

Champions of Freud are no less inclined to make Freud the object of psychobiography, even of psychoanalysis *in absentia*. This sympathetic exercise seems to me to be capable of being even more bewildering than its sceptical counterpart.[13] Nicholas Rand and Maria Torok's recent effort is especially notable, since it claims to have found the source trouble responsible for the fragmentariness of Freud's theorizing, 'the root of his contradictory psychoanalytic investigations':

> Freud conducted his psychological investigations of himself and others against the backdrop of a permanent blackout about his own traumatic history.
>
> The situation is all the more significant because Freud's clinical and theoretical ambitions focused on the possibility of gaining access to even the most obscure regions of the psyche. Yet the darkness he met with in his own family placed him at odds with his psychological inquiries. The silence surrounding the familial drama has led to the paradoxical status of psychoanalysis. The most far-reaching attempt to understand the human psyche constantly collided with an absence and sometimes even a refusal of understanding. Our goal then is to bring to light, for Freud's sake and ours, the nature and intensity of his family's trauma – in order to free psychoanalysis from the contradictions that have plagued it since its inception and that continue to threaten it to this day despite countless attempts at improvement and renewal.[14]

(The scandal, according to the authors, involved the arrest and prosecution on counterfeiting charges of Freud's uncle Josef. I find the claim unpersuasive.) Rand and Torok argue that 'Freudian psychoanalysis [is] beset by the mute pain of its creator'[15] This account of the pathos of a suppressed secret is consistent with a view expressed by Derrida:

> Beyond every possible and necessary inquiry, we will always wonder what Freud (for example), what every 'careful concealer' may have wanted to keep secret. We will wonder what he may have kept of his unconditional right to secrecy, while burning with the desire to know, to make known, and to archive the very thing he concealed forever. What was concealed? What did he conceal even beyond the intention to conceal, to lie, to perjure?
>
> We will always wonder what, in this *mal d'archive*, he may have burned. We will always wonder, sharing with compassion in this archive fever, what may have burned of his secret passions, of his correspondence, or of his 'life.' Burned without him, without remains and without knowledge. With no possible response, be it spectral or

> not, short of or beyond a suppression, on the other edge of repression, originary or secondary, without a name, without the least symptom, and without even an ash.[16]

For all that Derrida's language is carefully non-psychoanalytic, he nevertheless proposes the same scheme of secrets and personal paths. As with mourning-as-safekeeping, this is elaborated with reference to 'compassion', though there is some kind of tugging going on between that claim to kindness or care and the quasi-forensic language of perjury and lying: an accusatoriness, perhaps lessened by the idea of an 'unconditional right to secrecy', is in play even as Derrida invokes altruistic concern. And, as with the personalized remarks quoted in the introduction, there is a fundamentally quasi-psychoanalytic psychology at stake. Derrida may be said to avoid a simplistic kind of psychoanalytic explanation by invoking a general problem of secrecy rather than supposing (as Schur does) that a specific incident or experience is in the background, but he does all the same concur with the principle that Freud's writing might be explicable in terms of his biography. There is something here of Freud's own confidence in the possibility of tracing sickness back to experience, one's own or others'. And yet, if the readings in this book are considered to have merit, it is precisely this tracing-back that proves to be impossible or self-perpetuating in Freud's work.

'We will wonder...while burning with the desire to know,' Derrida claims, generalizing the notional desire. But we may not; we may believe that exercise has no merit, even if there were something to find. We may come to think that such passionate retrospective theorizing is the difficulty – one repeatedly exemplified in Freud's work – not the proper response to it, let alone its solution. Is not Freud's work, as I have presented it, a kind of unendingly impossible retrospection? Does one not begin to suspect that the trap of Freudian explanation is that it is, precisely, retrospective and moreover radically internally so – an introspective retrospection or a retrospection which can only go by way of an unfulfillable introspection. The sense I finally get from Freud's work is not that he failed to come upon truth in the past that was there, but rather that he was impelled always to give accounts of how truth could not be found there. This is, to use Derrida's phrase, his 'archive sickness'. But the constantly evoked and affirmed paradoxes of deconstruction have no equivalent in Freud's writing although, as I tried to show in my account of the use of 'foreign body' there, we may have to entertain versions of them in order to account for the theory of inherited memory and its prefiguring and consolidation in the countersense of some of Freud's tropes and images. That countersense is, I have argued, the transgression of a concept of experience-based identity; the countersense is tormented retrospection, unfinishable thinking, embattled and diminished subjectivity encroached upon by others' experience. This transgression is figured in the image of the garrison that is also a foreign body, an image of crisis and anguish. There is thus a difficulty in following the lead of deconstruction in affirming, perhaps in some playful or ironic way, the paradox of the 'healed-over' or otherwise inextirpable foreign body.

My premise in Chapter 2 was that it might be important not to disregard Freud's psycho-Lamarckism – that it might be revealing to explore the ways in which the theory of inherited memory is neither a successful form of causal explanation nor some disposable supplement to Freud's work. I claim that the psycho-Lamarckian ideas are in fact in a certain way central, the strangers at the heart or in the home of psychoanalysis, the foreign bodies that have not been broken down. It is the inherited-memory theory that most explicitly requires that one begin to conceptualize Freud's work in terms of unfinishability. As regards its dispossession of one's own experience, there is the sense of an impossible introspection, thinking deprived of its way back to the identity of experience – and so thinking forever unreconciled (as Gillian Rose suggests) to the past, forever taking an inconclusive retrospective path. And Freud's psycho-Lamarckism is his own most extensive and far-reaching attitude to the past – but one that, like the remorseful or grieving such attitudes that he asserts to configure language and religion and thinking as such, has a doleful inadequacy, seemingly ever more overburdened by the weight of the past. Or rather of downwardly and endlessly spiralling and entwining alternative versions of the past. It is no good, in my view, to try to refer the kind of theorizing that we may begin to think defines Freud's writing to the causal explanation it ruins – the attribution of thought processes to experienced or imagined incidents (no matter how belatedly impactful) or to secrets (no matter how compassionately undisturbed).

When I discussed the superego in Chapter 5, my argument was that we may read this most fundamental of Freudian psychological concepts not in terms of the supposed explanatory anatomization of mental functioning but rather as the final consolidation or, as I put it, centralization of a figural countersense of non-assimilation and breaching – and so of pain, melancholy, guilt, understood here not as personal emotions but as problems of conceptualization, paradox and self-regenerating retrospective theorizing. In my reading of Freud, we are dealing neither with myths that have the power to destroy souls (as Wittgenstein puts it) nor with a theory that amounts to what Rand and Torok call the 'most far-reaching attempt to understand the human psyche'; we are moreover not dealing with the heroism of intellectual discovery or the pathos of personal suffering. Notwithstanding the astonishing power that is attributed to psychoanalysis by its detractors and proponents alike, we are rather dealing with complex writings that disclose a fascinatingly self-reflexive crisis of argument.

It is after all not so confining a labyrinth. If there is a secret of Freud's work it is in plain sight: its theorizing has always been in ruins.[17]

Notes

Introduction

The deconstructionist reading of Freud, with which this book has a partial affinity, claims that there is a certain inescapability in the practice: it is not possible to stand apart from what one studies, to escape the labyrinth of Freudian theory. Here and elsewhere (I mention work by Yosef Hayim Yerushalmi and Patrick Mahony), this may be seen to lead to 'conceits of intimacy' with Freud, in which a writer claims some special familiarity with him. By contrast, I state that I attempt to stay at a distance from Freud's work, notably by avoiding psychoanalytic terminology. I give some examples of how this avoidance is achieved and also note in particular why I have not used the term 'trauma'.

1. Leo Bersani, *The Freudian Body: Psychoanalysis and Art* (New York: Columbia University Press, 1986).
2. Michel de Certeau, 'Translator's Introduction: For a *Literary* Historiography', in *The Writing of History* (1975), trans. Tom Conley (New York: Columbia University Press, 1988), p. xiv.
3. Samuel Weber, *The Legend of Freud* (1979), expanded edn (Stanford, CA: Stanford University Press, 2000), p. xiv.
4. Derrida Jacques, *Archive Fever: A Freudian Impression* (1995), trans. Eric Prenowitz (Chicago, IL: University of Chicago Press, 1996), p. 36.
5. It should be added, however, that Derrida is consistent in being sceptical about Freudian terminology. He repeatedly refuses that intimacy in a rigorous way. See Derrida and Elisabeth Roudinesco, *For What Tomorrow…: A Dialogue* (2001), trans. Jeff Fort (Stanford, CA: Stanford University Press, 2004), p. 172:

   > I may be mistaken, but the id, the ego, the superego, the ideal ego, the ego ideal, the secondary process and the primary process of repression, etc. – in a word, the large Freudian machines (including the concept and the word 'unconscious') – are in my opinion only provisional weapons, or even rhetorical tools cobbled together to be used against a philosophy of consciousness, of transparent and fully responsible intentionality. I have little faith in their future. I do not think that a metapsychology can hold up for long under scrutiny. Already, it is hardly being talked about anymore.

6. Derrida Jacques, 'Telepathy' (1980), trans. Nicholas Royle, *Oxford Literary Review* 10 (1988), nos 1–2, p. 22.
7. Yosef Hayim Yerushalmi, *Freud's Moses: Judaism Terminable and Interminable* (New Haven, CT: Yale University Press, 1991), p. 100. See Rob White, 'Archive Power', *Oxford Literary Review* 21 (1999), pp. 161–80.
8. *Archive Fever*, p. 89.
9. Patrick Mahony, *Freud and the Rat Man* (New Haven, CT: Yale University Press, 1987), p. 221.

10. I have used the following editions and translations of Freud's work: *The Standard Edition of the Complete Psychological Works*, trans. under the general editorship of James Strachey in collaboration with Anna Freud, Alan Tyson and Alix Strachey, 24 vols (London: Hogarth Press and the Institute of Psycho-Analysis, 1953–74). Where possible, I have also cited *The Penguin Freud Library* (formerly *The Pelican Freud Library*), which modifies the *Standard Edition* translations in minor ways, individual volumes edited by Strachey and others, 14 vols (Harmondsworth: Penguin, 1973–86). When reproducing Freud's German, I have consulted the *Gesammelte Werke*, edited by Anna Freud and others, 18 vols (London: Imago, 1940–52 [vols 1–17]; Frankfurt am Main: Fischer Verlag, 1968 [vol. 18]). I have included references to Freud's texts in the main body of my own, referring first – in bold – to the *Standard Edition*, then (where possible) – in roman – to the *Penguin Freud Library*, and finally (if I have quoted from it) – in italic – to the *Gesammelte Werke*. A reference to the *New Introductory Lectures on Psycho-Analysis* might read, therefore: (**22: 160**, 2: 195, *15: 172–3*).
11. See Henri F. Ellenberger, *The Discovery of the Unconscious: The History and Evolution of Dynamic Psychiatry* (London: Fontana, 1970), p. 550:

    > Almost from the beginning Freud made psychoanalysis a movement, with its own organization and publishing house, its strict rules of membership, and its official doctrine, namely the psychoanalytic theory. The similarity between the psychoanalytic and the Greco-Roman philosophical schools was reinforced after the imposition of an initiation in the form of the training analysis. Not only does the training analysis demand a heavy financial sacrifice, but also a surrender of privacy and of the whole self.

    Jeffrey Masson, *Final Analysis: The Making and Unmaking of a Psychoanalyst* (London: HarperCollins, 1991); Malcolm Janet, *In the Freud Archives* (London: Jonathan Cape, 1984); Philip Rieff, *The Triumph of the Therapeutic: Uses of Faith after Freud* (London: Chatto and Windus, 1966), p. 102–3:

    > even in their research, analysts have developed a false empiricism, in which their highest intellectual achievement is often nothing more than yet another report to their colleagues of a case history, complete with pious cross-references in the footnotes to show that they remember the great, who are dead, and the mediocre, who are alive. Paper-reading has begun to bore even the psychoanalysts themselves. In some cities it is difficult to collect even these inferior specimens of intellectual vitality. The movement is softened, its mind lulled by feather-beds of dead data, collected in the ritual act of having been published. While worrying too much about whether they are scientists in any sense of the word acceptable to their most bigoted opponents, the psychoanalysts have become at worst technicians of therapy, and at best erudites, writing up data without any sense of responsibility for their more general import. The curse of erudition in the eighteenth and early nineteenth century was that it collected trivia, and cluttered the humanist culture of the time with ornamental knowledge. Psychoanalytic work is becoming ornamental to the scientific culture of our own time. False empiricism can have its own pathology; from papers with manifest titles such as 'On a Theme Suggested by One of

My Patients' it is an easy move to the latent title 'On a Patient Suggested by One of My Themes.'

12. Prefatory methodological remarks in a recent book indicate well the kind of difficulties that arise when commentators co-opt psychoanalytic terms in the enterprise of scrutinizing psychoanalysis. In *A Compulsion for Antiquity: Freud and the Ancient World* (Ithaca, NY: Cornell University Press, 2005), pp. 6–7, Richard H. Armstrong writes:

    > my need to explicate Freud's compulsion for antiquity obviously shows the trace elements of transference which one might expect in any sustained treatment of a controversial figure, a 'great man of history.' Any immanent critique of Freud must by definition use the tools he forged or at least popularized (such as the concept of ambivalence) in order to pick away at the edifice of his work. ... If such an operation inevitably stinks of intellectual patricide, we can at least assert that to kill Freud as the Father is to free him to return to the position of being the father, the historical individual who founded this discourse with all its blindness and insight, and not the impossible colossus he often balloons into under the storm and stress of cultural debate.

13. For a summary of recent work in this area, see Nerea Arruti, 'Trauma, Therapy and Representation: Theory and Critical Reflection', *Paragraph* 30: 1 (March 2007), pp. 1–8.

1 Figures of Freudian Theory

The chapter begins with an apparent inconsistency. A militant rationalist, scornful of any superstition, Freud nevertheless from time to time invokes preternatural phenomena, especially ghosts and 'evil spirits'. This inconsistency takes its place alongside other somewhat anomalous aspects of Freud's writing, and notably his fondness for self-dramatizing autobiographical digressions. These unconventional habits are significant in themselves, evidence of the ingenuity and distinctiveness of Freud's writing; but they additionally often deal with distressing themes or situations, or they are direct statements of personal sadness or alarm. There is a melancholic vein in Freud's writing, which I seek to make visible. In so doing, I invoke a passage from Rilke's *Duino Elegies* to suggest the extent to which Freud's habit of retrospection is anguished.

These features of Freud's work are puzzling. They are at odds not only with the rationalism but also with repeated statements of explanatory accomplishment to be found elsewhere: Freud often confidently trumpets psychoanalytic achievements in understanding (which he describes in terms of elucidation, riddle-solving, defining, and so on).

How, if at all, to reconcile these different elements? In exploring their manifestations and nuances, I propose two ideas. The first is the concept of a 'figure of theory', a figural passage that more or less explicitly describes Freud's theorizing, as with analogies between psychoanalysis and archaeology. The second is the idea of 'countersense': the idea that apparently discordant or anomalous or extraneous passages in Freud's writing may, instead of being dismissed as incidental, be shown to make sense – and in particular to constitute a sort of unofficial commentary on Freudian theory. I argue that this is so, indeed, with the references to ghosts and spirits. I interpret these references as indications of a burdened, preoccupied sense of understanding that is in crisis, as if haunted by the past.

1. Lionel Trilling, 'Freud and Literature' (1940), in *The Liberal Imagination* (Oxford: Oxford University Press, 1981), p. 54.
2. Malcolm Bowie, *Freud, Proust and Lacan: Theory as Fiction* (Cambridge: Cambridge University Press, 1987), p. 44.
3. Ibid., p. 17.
4. Ibid., pp. 43–4.
5. Ibid., p. 25.
6. Ibid., p. 26.
7. Rainer Maria Rilke, *'Duino Elegies' and 'The Sonnets to Orpheus'* (1923/1922), trans. A. Poulin, Jr. (Boston, MA: Mariner Books, 2005) pp. 58–9, lines 43–60. On the relationship of Freud and Rilke, who met (though Rilke broke off the association abruptly), see a curious study by Matthew von Unwerth, *Freud's Requiem: Mourning, Memory and the Invisible History of a Summer Walk* (London: Continuum, 2005).
8. See, among innumerable such comments about distortion, Sigmund Freud, 'Psycho-Analytic Notes on an Autobiographical Account of a Case of Paranoia (Dementia Paranoides)' (1911 [1910]): 'The psycho-analytic investigation of paranoia would be altogether impossible if the patients themselves did not possess the peculiarity of betraying (in a distorted form [*entstellter*], it is true) precisely those things which other neurotics keep hidden as a secret' (**12: 9**, 9: 138, *8: 240*).
9. See Harold Bloom, *A Map of Misreading* (Oxford: Oxford University Press, 1975), p. 91:

   > If death ultimately represents the earlier state of things, then it also represents the earlier state of meaning, or pure anteriority; that is to say, repetition of the literal, or literal meaning. Death is therefore a kind of literal meaning, or from the standpoint of poetry, *literal meaning is a kind of death. Defenses can be said to trope against death, rather in the same sense that tropes can be said to defend against literal meaning.*

10. See François Roustang, *Dire Mastery: Discipleship from Freud to Lacan* (1976), trans. Ned Lukacher (Baltimore, MD: Johns Hopkins University Press, 1982), p. 95:

    > Freud preserved within himself a fund of superstition that resisted his courageous attempts at criticism and the strength of his reason … If Freud had really been the rationalizing scientist Jones would have liked him to be, he would hardly have taken an interest in the dreams and stories of midwives.

    Roustang is referring to Freud's psycho-Lamarckism, which I will discuss in detail in the next chapter.
11. See Roland Barthes, *A Lover's Discourse: Fragments* (1977), trans. Richard Howard (London: Jonathan Cape, 1979), pp. 114–5:

    > Freud, apparently, did not like the telephone, however much he may have liked *listening*. Perhaps he felt, perhaps he foresaw that the telephone

> is always a *cacophony*, and that what it transmits is the *wrong voice*, the false communication ... the telephone is not a good transitional object, it is not an inert string; it is charged with meaning, which is not that of junction but that of distance: the loved, exhausted voice heard over the telephone is the fade-out in all its anxiety. First of all, this voice, when it reaches me, when it is here, while it (with great difficulty) survives, is a voice which I never entirely recognize; as if it emerged from under a mask (thus we are told that the masks used in Greek tragedy had a magical function: to give the voice a chthonic origin, to distort, to alienate the voice, to make it come from somewhere under the earth). Then, too, on the telephone the other is always in a situation of departure; the other departs twice over, by voice and by silence: whose turn is it to speak? We fall silent in unison: crowding of two voids. *I'm going to leave you*, the voice on the telephone says with each second.

Quoted in Nicholas Royle, *Telepathy and Literature: Essays on the Reading Mind* (Oxford: Basil Blakwell, 1991), p. 178; Ned Lukacher, *Primal Scenes: Literature, Philosophy, Psychoanalysis* (Ithaca, NY: Cornell University Press, 1986), p. 69. See also Derrida, 'Telepathy', p. 19, with regard to 'a terrifying telephone (and he, the old man, is frightened, me too)'.

2 Others' Memories

By way of references to *Angels in America* and *Moby-Dick*, this chapter explores in detail Freud's persistent adherence, in the face of derisive opinion to the contrary, to the psycho-Lamarckian theory of the inheritance of 'memory-traces of the experience of earlier generations.' This theory is very counterintuitive and it substantially alters the premises of Freud's theory of individual psychology. In Freud's early work, it was always assumed that memory related to 'an experience of one's own' – even if that experience were an act of imagination rather than a perception or sensation. But with the consolidation in *Totem and Taboo* and the *Introductory Lectures* of the inherited-memory theory, there is a fundamental change. An individual, it is argued, may remember something that was experienced (though not communicated) by an ancestor. There is therefore a transition from a theory concerned with memory deficit to one concerned with memory surplus.

Having followed the development of the theory, I discuss a number of notable commentaries upon it (by Richard J. Bernstein, Yosef Hayim Yerushalmi, Paul Robinson and Frank Sulloway). I argue that each of these commentaries tends to marginalize Freud's theory, or to minimize its transgressive force. What is especially troubling about the theory, especially as it is elaborated in the Wolf Man case history (the reading of which by Peter Brooks is adduced), is that it leads Freud to propose multiple alternative explanations of the origins of his patient's illness. I therefore term Freud's theorizing in this context 'genetigenic'.

But Freud does not bring this multiplication or the associated mutilation of identity to the fore. Indeed what he frequently does instead is to refer to the inherited-memory theory as if it were a mere natural supplement to his psychological theory. In this way, I argue, it is as if Freud smuggles transgressive ideas, and ideas of transgression, into psychoanalysis; and the upshot is that Freud's account of individual minds and those minds themselves (in Freud's description of them) seem increasingly weighed down and invaded by a troubling past.

1. Tony Kushner, *Angels in America: A Gay Fantasia on National Themes. Part One: Millennium Approaches* (London: Royal National Theatre / Nick Hern Books, 1992), p. 21.
2. Ibid., p. 19.
3. *Angels in America* was directed for HBO television by Mike Nichols in 2004. Mary-Louise Parker played Harper, Justin Kirk played Prior.
4. *Moby-Dick or The Whale* (New York: Penguin, 1992), p. 211.
5. Ibid.
6. The German text is to be found in Sigmund Freud, *Aus den Anfängen der Psychoanalyse: Briefe an Wilhelm Fliess, Abhandlungen und Notzien aus den Jahren 1887–1902* (ed.), Anna Freud and Ernest Kris (London: Imago, 1950), p. 416.
7. See *Moses and Monotheism: Three Essays* (1939 [1937–39]). 'We find that in a number of important relations our children react, not in a manner corresponding to their own experience, but instinctively, like the animals, in a manner that is only explicable as phylogenetic acquisition' (**23: 132–3**, 13: 381–2).
8. See Ritchie Robertson, 'Freud's Testament: Moses and Monotheism', in Edward Timms and Naomi Segal (eds), *Freud in Exile: Psychoanalysis and its Vicissitudes* (New Haven, CT: Yale University Press, 1990), p. 87: '[Freud] is arguing that ethical and intellectual doctrines are transmitted by irrational means. We no longer have the Enlightenment assumption that truth is discovered by a rational process of enquiry in which the more reasonable side eventually wins.'
9. Cathy Caruth, *Empirical Truths and Critical Fictions: Locke, Wordsworth, Kant, Freud* (London: Johns Hopkins University Press, 1991), pp. vii–viii.
10. Mikkel Borch-Jacobsen *The Freudian Subject* (1988), trans. Catherine Porter (London: Macmillan, 1989), p. 20.
11. See Christopher Badcock, *PsychoDarwinism: The New Synthesis of Darwin and Freud* (London: HarperCollins, 1994), p. 15:

    > to dismiss Freud merely because he is stigmatized as 'Lamarckian' in certain respects is no more fair to him that [*sic*] it would be to dismiss Darwin's *Expression of Emotions in Man and Animals* just because it is similarly Lamarckian in presentation. If we are prepared to make allowances for Darwin in this respect I see no reason why we should not make similar ones for Freud.

    See also Lucille B. Ritvo, *Darwin's Influence on Freud: A Tale of Two Sciences* (New Haven, CT: Yale University Press, 1990).
12. Frank J. Sulloway, *Freud, Biologist of the Mind. Beyond the Psychoanalytic Legend* (1979) (Cambridge, MA: Harvard University Press, 1992), pp. 497, 498.
13. Stephen Jay Gould, 'Freud's Phylogenetic Fantasy', *Natural History* 96: 12 (December 1987), p. 19. Gould explains, p. 18:

    > Freud's theory requires the passage to heredity of events that occurred tens of thousands of years ago at most. But such events – anxiety at

> approaching ice sheets, castration of sons, and murder of fathers – have no hereditary impact. However traumatic, they do not affect the eggs and sperm of parents and therefore cannot pass into heredity under Mendelian and Darwinian rules.

See also Gould's earlier substantial work (which is especially concerned with the 'recapitulation theory' propounded by Ernst Haeckel), *Ontogeny and Phylogeny* (Cambridge, MA: Belknap Press of Harvard University Press, 1977), pp. 96–7:

> But what is the physical ground of memory, indeed of all inheritance, if thoughts and things follow the same laws of transmission? What is impressed upon the germ cells to allow them to reproduce a sequence of acquired characters in the proper order? The question divided adherents to the general view: some spoke of vibrations and wave motions... others of electrical potentials... still others of chemical changes.

14. See Yosef Hayim Yerushalmi, *Freud's Moses: Judaism Terminable and Interminable* (New Haven, CT: Yale University Press, 1991), p. 31: 'even the most ardent and loyal admirer of Freud can only whisper to himself "Certum, quia absurdum est"'.
15. The most vehement of anti-Freudians are especially sharp-eyed here. See Malcolm Macmillan, *Freud Evaluated: The Completed Arc* (1991) (Cambridge, MA: MIT Press, 1997), p. 650: 'Alluding to some of Freud's phrases in which he expresses caution in drawing on phylogenesis simply overlooks the central part it played in the explanations of the Wolf Man and the Rat Man, to say nothing of the development of morality and human society'; Frederick Crews, 'Beyond Sulloway's *Freud*: Psychoanalysis minus the Myth of the Hero', in Peter Clark and Crispin Wright (eds), *Mind, Psychoanalysis and Science* (Oxford: Basil Blackwell, 1988), p. 251:

> when contemporary Freudians pride themselves on doing without the phylogenetic line of reasoning, as if the rest of the system were adequately determinate in its specifying of claims and consequences, they appear to be doing their best to illustrate the Freudian mechanism of denial. Apparently they feel that psychoanalysis can now survive by gradually dismantling some of its excrescent theoretical knobs and pulleys, just as it formerly survived by superadding them. Both stratagems are reprehensible dodges against long-standing and unanswerable doubts about Freud's original scientific romance.

Frank Cioffi, 'Freud – New Myths to Replace the Old', *New Society* 50: 895 (29 November 1979), p. 503: '[phylogenesis] tends to loom larger in Freud's later than in his earlier career'.

For a near-contemporary example of this selectiveness at work, see Otto Rank, *The Trauma of Birth* (1929) (New York: Dover Publications, 1993), p. 191:

> Since the development of the analytic technique has enabled us in the course of our experience to trace this infantile stage of development ever further back, till finally we reach the pre-natal stage, it follows – especially from a more thoroughgoing study of dream symbolism – that

we may dispense with the phylogenetic point of view of an inherited *psychical* endowment or can limit it, in Haeckel's sense, to the biogenetic fundamental law. Hence all problems of symbolism are explained in a simpler and more satisfying manner than by Jung's untimely introduction of the phylogenetic point of view into analysis, for, being purely a psychiatrist and using mythological material as a comparison, he lacked the real experience of the analysis of neuroses which would have allowed him to go beyond mere description and the speculation connected with it. Freud likewise recognized the unproductiveness of Jung's attempt to explain the phenomena of individual psychology by means of uninterpreted ethnological material, and he pursued the only correct way, which we now pursue still further and thus place the phylogenetic point of view considerably further in the background.

16. Ernest Jones, *Sigmund Freud: Life and Work. The Last Phase 1919–1939* (London: Hogarth Press, 1957), p. 336.
17. Richard Wollheim, *Freud*, 2nd edn (London: Fontana, 1991).
18. *Freud's Moses*, pp. 87–8.
19. Jan Assmann, *Moses the Egyptian: The Memory of Egypt in Western Monotheism* (Cambridge, MA: Harvard University Press, 1997), p. 216.
20. *Freud: Biologist of the Mind*, p. 365.
21. Ibid., p. 367.
22. Sulloway's views have developed in an increasingly sceptical direction. See a published conversation with Mikkel Borch-Jacobsen, 'Psychoanalysis and Pseudoscience: Frank J. Sulloway Revisits Freud and His Legacy', in Todd Dufresne, *Against Freud: Critics Talk Back* (Stanford, CA: Stanford University Press, 2007).
23. Paul Robinson, *Freud and His Critics* (Berkeley: University of California Press, 1993), pp. 85–6.
24. Richard J. Bernstein, *Freud and the Legacy of Moses* (Cambridge: Cambridge University Press, 1998), p. 73.
25. *A Phylogenetic Fantasy: Overview of the Transference Neuroses* (ed.), Ilse Grubrich-Simitis, trans. Alex Hoffer and Peter T. Hoffer (Cambridge, MA: Belknap Press of Harvard University Press, 1987), p. 10. For Freud's description of the paper as being in part 'fantasy', see p. 20.
26. *Reading for the Plot: Design and Intention in Narrative* (1984; Cambridge, MA: Harvard University Press, 1992), p. 277.
27. The Writing of History, p. 327.
28. René Girard, *Violence and the Sacred* (1972), trans. Patrick Gregory (Baltimore, MD: Johns Hopkins University Press, 1979), p. 217.
29. Philip Rieff, *Freud: The Mind of the Moralist* (1959), 3rd edn (Chicago, IL: Chicago University Press, 1979), pp. 207–8.
30. Ibid., p. 210.
31. *Empirical Truths and Critical Fictions*, pp. 86–7.
32. Jean Laplanche, *New Foundations for Psychoanalysis* (1987), trans. David Macey (Oxford: Basil Blackwell, 1989), p. 31.
33. Jean Laplanche and J.-B. Pontalis, 'Fantasy and the Origins of Sexuality', *International Journal of Psycho-Analysis* 49: 1 (1968), pp. 8, 9.

34. See also some remarks by Sarah Kofman, *The Childhood of Art: an Interpretation of Freud's Aesthetics* (3rd edn, 1985), trans. Winifred Woodhull (New York: Columbia University Press, 1988), pp. 99–100:

> Freud, who sees this [oedipal] structure repeated everywhere in its very differences, tries to ground its historical truth in a material truth, the murder of the primal father. But this grounding rests on a myth, the myth of the primal horde. If the structure can be explained by genesis, the latter is still mythic, and its meaning is still structural. Which means that there is no simple origin, that the origin is both plural and conflictual. The psychic apparatus with its three agencies always already exists ... in order for the brothers to have repented of the primal murder, the superego had to have been already in existence. But the psychic apparatus is itself a model for understanding the psyche. The oedipal structure is a construction of science, an anhypothetical hypothesis.

3 Mourning as Ethics and Argument

If it does not simply exasperate commentators, Freud's psycho-Lamarckism prompts denunciations of demagoguery. I begin this chapter by arguing, especially with references to some remarks made by Jonathan Lear, that Freud's theorizing in this area is not so much a grandiose self-deception as a quasi-fictive sort of theorizing, gyrant rather than focused on a unitary point. Its attitude to the past, in particular, is undecided and troubled.

There is a widespread dismay in Freud's work. It is evidenced by pessimism and especially repeated descriptions of anguished origins: spoken language, writing, philosophy and religion are all claimed by Freud to begin in a state of distress, guilt, terror, grief. The element of grief brings me to Derrida's writing on mourning, which I read closely. Dense and demanding, this work proposes an ethical theory of mourning to do with 'safekeeping of the other *as other*': to finish mourning, Derrida asserts, is to abandon a dead loved one. It is a theory of loyalty. I refer also to Gillian Rose's compelling objections to Derrida's work in this area. She conversely argues that there is a powerful ethical imperative to conclude mourning and so be free of 'devastating inner grief'.

These contrasting accounts of mourning bring me to Freud's essay, 'Mourning and Melancholia'. I look in detail at the essay, paying special attention to the interplay between statements of explanatory confidence or normative generalization and statements of disclaimer, uncertainty or metaphor (especially the idea of bereavement as wounding). I propose that although the essay sketches out an idea of functional mourning, the way it dwells on obstacles to the process is suggestive of failed mourning, melancholy.

1. *Freud Evaluated*, p. 480.
2. Frank Cioffi, 'Wittgenstein's Freud' (1969), in *Freud and the Question of Pseudoscience* (Chicago: Open Court, 1998), p. 108.
3. John Farrell, *Freud's Paranoid Quest: Psychoanalysis and Modern Suspicion* (New York: New York University Press, 1996), p. 28.

4. It is worth quoting an example of Jung's writing in this area and specifically a remark aimed at discrediting Freud (and Adler) in 'Sigmund Freud in His Historical Setting' (1932), in C.G. Jung, *The Spirit in Man, Art and Literature* (1967), trans. R.E.C. Hull (London: ARK, 1984), p. 40:

    The human psyche... is not simply a product of the *Zeitgeist*, but is a thing of far greater constancy and immutability. The nineteenth century is a merely local and passing phenomenon, which has deposited but a thin layer of dust on the age-old psyche of mankind.... Freud has not penetrated into that deeper layer which is common to all men.

5. *Freud's Requiem*, p. 110.
6. *Freud: The Mind of the Moralist*, p. 202.
7. Ibid., pp. 198–9.
8. Jonathan Lear, *Freud* (New York: Routledge, 2005), pp. 215–6.
9. Jacques Derrida, 'Before the Law' (1985), trans. Avital Ronell and Christine Roulston, collected in Derrida, *Acts of Literature*, ed. Derek Attridge (London: Routledge, 1992), p. 199. See also Mikkel Borch-Jacobsen, *The Emotional Tie: Psychoanalysis, Mimesis, and Affect*, trans. Douglas Brick and others (Stanford: Stanford University Press, 1992), p. 30: 'The "Father," then, in this strange Freudian myth, emerges only as myth – the myth of his own power, and the power of his own myth'.
10. *Archive Fever*, p. 91.
11. Nicolas Abraham and Maria Torok, *The Shell and the Kernel: Renewals of Psychoanalysis*, trans. Nicholas T. Rand (Chicago, IL: University of Chicago Press, 1994), p. 171.
12. Jacques Derrida, '*Fors*: The Anglish Words of Nicolas Abraham and Maria Torok' (1976), trans. Barbara Johnson, in Abraham and Torok, *The Wolf Man's Magic Word: A Cryptonymy*, trans. Nicholas Rand (Minneapolis: University of Minnesota Press, 1986), pp. xxvi–vii.
13. *The Emotional Tie*, p. 20.
14. Jacques Derrida, *Mémoires for Paul de Man*, revised edn. trans. Cecile Lindsay, Jonathan Culler, Eduardo Cadava, and Peggy Kamuf (New York: Columbia University Press, 1989), p. 34; see Geoffrey Bennington, *Derridabase*, in Bennington and Derrida, *Jacques Derrida*, trans. Bennington (London: University of Chicago Press, 1993), pp. 146–8.
15. *Mémoires*, p. 6. Derrida's subsequent writing about mourning continues in the paradoxical mode. See Jacques Derrida, *Of Hospitality. Anne Dufourmantelle Invites Jacques Derrida to Respond* (1997), trans. Rachel Bowlby (Stanford, CA: Stanford University Press, 2000), pp. 111/13, in relation to Antigone:

    How can a mourning be wept for? How can one weep at not being able to go through one's mourning? How can one go through the mourning of mourning? But how can one do otherwise, when the mourning has to be finished? And the mourning of mourning has to be infinite? Impossible in its very possibility?

16. Gillian Rose, *Mourning Becomes the Law: Philosophy and Representation* (Cambridge: Cambridge University Press, 1996), pp. 69–70. See also p. 103: 'to incorporate the dead one into one's own body and soul is to refuse the work of mourning, to refuse, in melancholy, to let go'.
17. Jean Laplanche and J.-B. Pontalis, *The Language of Psychoanalysis*, trans. Donald Nicholson-Smith (London: Hogarth Press, 1973), p. 485.

18. *Mémoires*, pp. 56–7; p. 38.
19. Jacques Derrida, *Specters of Marx: The State of the Debt, the work of Mourning, and the New International* (1993), trans. Peggy Kamuf (London: Routledge, 1994), p. 52.
20. See 'On Transience': mourning is 'a great riddle' (**14: 306**, 14: 288).

4 Across Limits

The chapter begins with a reading of two passages from Rilke, which describe an uncanny happening whereby a strange thing passes over a threshold into the heart. This happening is correlated with statements about strangeness made by Freud, notably his use of the term 'foreign body'.

Freud often discusses mental phenomena in topological terms and I explore this feature of his writing in terms of three categories. First is the category of subdivided identities. Freud does not, like Breuer, have a binary idea of mental interiority (but Freud's idea is still recognizably to do with a coherent arrangement of spaces, even though the arrangement is multiform). Second is the category of boundaries and I emphasize the way in which psychoanalysis is a 'frontier concept' (to use a phrase of Harold Bloom's). Third is the category of breaching, which is to say the process by which boundaries are crossed, spaces penetrated; Freud's concepts in this category are forcible and I refer them to his account of pain.

Having itemized the main elements of Freud's topological theorizing, I attempt to correlate them with some of my earlier readings, arguing in particular that the well-known account (involving a 'little fragment of living substance... suspended in the middle of an external world charged with the most powerful energies') in *Beyond the Pleasure Principle* of the origin of consciousness in brutalization. To conclude, I discuss Freud's interest in telepathy. That interest involves an idea of a foreign body, which is to say in this case a piece of knowledge that passes from one person to another by means other than 'communication' – a transition that is thus comparable to the idea of transmission involved in Freud's psycho-Lamarckism.

1. Rainer Maria Rilke, *Letters to a Young Poet* (1929), trans. M.D. Herter Norton (New York: W.W. Norton, 2004), p. 53. Rilke, *Briefe an einen jungen Dichter* (Leipzig: Im Insel-Verlag, nd.), p. 48.
2. *Letters*, p. 49. *Briefe*, p. 44.
3. *'Duino Elegies' and 'The Sonnets to Orpheus'*, trans. A. Poulin, Jr., pp. 64, 65, lines 60–7.
4. Jacqueline Rose, *Why War? Psychoanalysis, Politics and the Return to Melanie Klein* (Oxford: Blackwell, 1993), p. 19.
5. *The Correspondence of Sigmund Freud and Sándor Ferenczi. Volume 2, 1914–1919*, ed. Ernest Falzeder and Eva Brabant, trans. Peter T. Hoffer (Cambridge, MA: Belknap Press of Harvard University Press, 1996), p. 74.
6. *Why War?*, pp. 19–20.
7. *Specters of Marx*, p. 9.
8. Harold Bloom, 'Freud: Frontier Concepts, Jewishness, and Interpretation', in Cathy Caruth (ed.), *Trauma: Explorations in Memory* (Baltimore, MD: Johns Hopkins University Press, 1995).
9. *A Phylogenetic Fantasy*, p. 10.

10. *The Correspondence of Sigmund Freud and Sándor Ferenczi*, p. 179.
11. Paul-Laurent Assoun, *Introduction à l'épistémologie freudienne* (Paris: Payot, 1981), p. 190.
12. *Freud to Fliess*, p. 146.
13. Jacques Derrida, *The Post Card: From Socrates to Freud and Beyond*, trans. Alan Bass (Chicago, IL: University of Chicago Press, 1987), pp. 347–8.
14. Harold Bloom, 'Freud's Concepts of Defense and the Poetic Will', in *Agon: Towards a Theory of Revisionism* (Oxford: Oxford University Press, 1982), p. 120.

5 The Foreign Bodies of Psychoanalysis

Reviewing the elements in Freud's theories that undermine the selfsame identity of experience, I begin with reference to the novelist Richard Hughes, whose remarks about selfhood being 'no tight little stockade' are compelling conceptualizations that reverberate with Freud's own.

I move on to an extended discussion of the history of 'foreign body' in Freud's work, beginning with its dual early use in the *Studies on Hysteria* and also in a letter to Fliess in which Freud reveals to his friend how he had botched an operation, causing the patient severe harm. I trace the way the term recedes and then returns to prominence. I read a number of late passages in major texts – *The Ego and the Id*, *Inhibitions, Symptoms and Anxiety* and the *New Introductory Lectures* – and make the claim that there is a linkage between the figure of a 'garrison' and that of the foreign body which permits the latter to be read as a description of the superego, which is also, according to Freud, the part of the mind responsible for the inheritance of memory. Because of the other associations of 'foreign body', I claim that the theory of the superego brings the countersense of transgressed identity to the centre of Freud's work.

The chapter ends with an extended reading of 'Analysis Terminable and Interminable', concerned to show how Freud's late essay exemplifies the textual features that have been the subject of the book.

1. Richard Hughes, *The Fox in the Attic* (Harmondsworth, Middlesex: Penguin Books, 1964), pp. 98–9.
2. *The Complete Correspondence of Sigmund Freud and Ernest Jones, 1908–1939*, (ed.), R. Andrew Paskauskas (Cambridge, MA: Belknap Press of Harvard University Press, 1993), p. 597.
3. *The Fox in the Attic*, p. 104; the ellipses are Hughes's.
4. See Jeffrey Masson, *The Assault on Truth: Freud and Child Sexual Abuse* (1984; London: Fontana, 1992), pp. 55–106.
5. *The Complete Letters of Sigmund Freud to Wilhelm Fliess, 1887–1904*, trans. and ed. Jeffrey Moussaief Masson (Cambridge, MA: Harvard University Press, 1985), pp. 116–7.
6. See Paul Ricoeur, *Freud and Philosophy: An Essay on Interpretation*, trans. Dennis Savage (New Haven, CT: Yale University Press, 1970), p. 181: 'The agencies of the second topography are not so much places as roles in a personology. Ego, id and super-ego are variations on the personal pronoun or grammatical subject; what is involved is the relation of the personal to the anonymous and the superpersonal in the individual's coming-to-be';

see also Cynthia Chase's remark in 'Oedipal Textuality: Reading Freud's Reading of *Oedipus*', *Diacritics* 9: 1 (Spring 1979), p. 65, concerning 'the "*fantomes*" of parental fantasies that fix the nuclear oedipal triangle in a network of endless interlocking triangles'.

7. For a gloss on 'foreign body' that emphasizes a more ludic approach to the idea, see Nicholas Royle, *After Derrida* (Manchester: Manchester University Press, 1995), p. 147:

   > As Derrida puts it in 'Limited Inc': 'the parasite is by definition never simply *external*, never simply something that can be excluded from or kept outside of the body "proper", shut out from the "familial" table or house'... As foreign body, the parasite both belongs and does not belong to what it inhabits, its 'own' identity is of a different order, being at once *para-* ('beside') and *non-para-*, inside and outside, coming to figure what is the same as and different from itself.

8. It can also be argued that the theory of the death instinct is yet another version of the inherited-memory theory by virtue not only of its concern with death-in-life, but also its status as a controversial, marginal element in Freud's work.
9. *Sigmund Freud and Lou Andreas-Salomé: Letters*, ed. Ernst Pfeiffer (London: Hogarth Press / Institute of Psycho-Analysis, 1972), p. 80. The letter is quoted (in a slightly different wording) in *Freud's Requiem*, p. 111.

Conclusion: Freud's Secret

1. *The Annotated Lolita*, ed. Alfred Appel, Jr. (1955/71; London: Penguin, 1995), p. 325.
2. Ibid., p. 34.
3. Gilles Deleuze and Félix Guattari, *Anti-Oedipus: Capitalism and Schizophrenia* (1972), trans. Robert Hurley, Mark Seem and Helen R. Lane (London: Athlone Press, 1984), pp. 50–1. See also Leo Bersani, *The Freudian Body*, p. 83:

   > The mythologization of the human as a readable organization is a fundamental political strategy, and the eagerness with which both literature and psychoanalysis have contributed to that mythology may be the surest sign of their willingness to serve various types of orders interested in the shaping of the human as a precondition for predicting and controlling it.

4. Ludwig Wittgenstein, *Lectures and Conversations on Aesthetics, Psychology and Religious Belief*, ed. Cyril Barrett (Oxford: Blackwell, 1966), p. 25.
5. Wittgenstein emphasizes the element of persuasion: 'If you are led by psycho-analysis to say that really you thought so and so or that really your motive was so and so, this is not a matter of discovery, but of persuasion' (Ibid., p. 27).
6. Ludwig Wittgenstein, 'Conversations on Freud' (1970 [1946]), noted by Rush Rhees, in *Sigmund Freud: Critical Assessments*, ed. Laurence Spurling, vol. 4 (London: Routledge, 1989), p. 253.
7. Norman Malcolm, *Ludwig Wittgenstein: A Memoir* (London: Oxford University Press, 1958), p. 44.
8. Jacques Bouveresse, *Wittgenstein Reads Freud: The Myth of the Unconscious* (1992), trans. Carol Cosman (Princeton, NJ: Princeton University Press, 1995), pp. 52, 68.

9. Max Schur, *Freud: Living and Dying* (London: Hogarth Press, 1972), p. 474. See also Henry Edelheit, 'On the Biology of Language: Darwinian/ Lamarckian Homology in Human Inheritance (with Some Thoughts about the Lamarckism of Freud)', in *Psychoanalysis and Language*, ed. Joseph H. Smith (New Haven, NJ: Yale University Press, 1978), p. 64:

    paradoxically and on an unconscious level, he [Freud] would seem to have shared a biblical time scale with the anti-Darwinian religious fundamentalists of the second half of the nineteenth century. These unconscious remnants of a biblical perspective seemed to grow more pronounced as Freud grew older and are most clearly represented in *Moses and Monotheism*, precisely the work where, in relation to Oedipal guilt and the fear of castration, he most explicitly and stubbornly took a Lamarckian position on the inheritance of acquired characteristics.

10. Paul Roazen, *Freud and His Followers* (Harmondsworth: Penguin, 1979), p. 251:

    It should be at least possible to recognize how certain inner conflicts in Freud, even if they can be only partially understood, may have been obscure to Freud himself, and at the time played havoc with some of his key human relationships. It was Freud's mystical yearnings, and his uneasy interest in the occult, which, in addition to objective scientific differences, contributed to the falling out between him and his chosen successor.

11. Todd Dufresne, *Tales from the Freudian Crypt: The Death Drive in Text and Context* (Stanford, CA: Stanford University Press, 2000), pp. 181–2.
12. See *Dire Mastery*: 'it was through his own psychosis that he believed in telepathy' p. 95.
13. See, for example, Patrick J. Mahony, *Freud as a Writer*, expanded edn (New Haven, CT: Yale University Press, 1987), chapter 7.
14. Nicholas Rand and Maria Torok, *Questions for Freud: The Secret History of Psychoanalysis* (Cambridge, MA: Harvard University Press, 1997), pp. 142–3.
15. Ibid., p. 139.
16. *Archive Fever*, p. 101. For some fascinating pragmatic remarks on secrecy and psychoanalysis, see Henri F. Ellenberger, 'The Pathogenic Secret and Its Therapeutics' (1966), in *Beyond the Unconscious: Essays of Henri F. Ellenberger in the History of Psychiatry*, ed. Mark S. Micale, trans. Françoise Dubor and Micale (Princeton, NJ: Princeton University Press, 1993).
17. If I were to move on from here, the main starting points would be: the large-scale historiography of Jean-Joseph Goux, *Oedipus, Philosopher*, trans. Catherine Porter (Stanford, CA: Stanford University Press, 1993), and, above all, the critique of psychoanalysis that is being elaborated by Leo Bersani. See, for an indication of the terms of this critique, 'Against Monogamy', *Oxford Literary Review* 20 (1998), p. 21:

    Freud initiated the systematic study of all the ways in which we remain faithful, the strategies by which we manage to go on loving and fearing our first fantasmatic objects. Psychoanalysis, with its obsessive concern with the difference between the self and the world, necessarily sees the latter as the repository of everything hostile to the self. It is a place to which, at best, we adapt and from which we retreat and regress to the imagined familial securities nourished by such privileged institutions as monogamy and marriage. The family is the psychoanalytic haven to which we regress, a regression that might be unnecessary if we had left it in the first place. If psychoanalysis, in its account of the extraordinary mobility of childhood and, more specifically, even Oedipal desires, has itself described for us the original inconceivability of a monogamous fixity of desire, and therefore of a stable sexual identity, monogamy nonetheless is the relational figure most congenial to what we might call the psychoanalytic fidelity of the self to the self, its indifference to signs of self that are not signs of interpretation, and, finally, its profoundly immoral rejection of our promiscuous humanity.

Bibliography

Freud

The Standard Edition of the Complete Psychological Works of Sigmund Freud, trans. under the general editorship of James Strachey in collaboration with Anna Freud, Alan Tyson and Alix Strachey, 24 vols (London: Hogarth Press and the Institute of Psycho-Analysis, 1953–74).

'Psychical (or Mental) Treatment' (1890).
Studies on Hysteria (1895 [1893–95]).
The Interpretation of Dreams (1900).
'Fragment of an Analysis of a Case of Hysteria' (1905 [1901]).
Jokes and their Relation to the Unconscious (1905).
'On Psychotherapy' (1905 [1904]).
Three Essays on the Theory of Sexuality (1905).
Delusions and Dreams in Jensen's Gradiva (1907 [1906]).
'Analysis of a Phobia in a Five-Year-Old Boy' (1909).
'Notes upon a Case of Obsessional Neurosis' (1909).
Five Lectures on Psycho-Analysis (1910 [1909]).
'The Future Prospects of Psycho-Analytic Therapy' (1910).
Leonardo da Vinci and a Memory of His Childhood (1910).
'Psycho-Analytic Notes on an Autobiographical Account of a Case of Paranoia (Dementia Paranoides)' (1911).
'Recommendations to Physicians Practising Psycho-Analysis' (1912).
Totem and Taboo: Some Points of Agreement between the Mental Lives of Savages and Neurotics (1912–13).
'On Narcissism: An Introduction' (1914).
'Thoughts for the Times on War and Death' (1915).
'The Unconscious' (1915).
'Some Character-Types Met with in Psycho-Analytic Work' (1916).
'On Transience' (1916 [1915]).
Introductory Lectures on Psycho-Analysis (1916–1917 [1915–1917]).
'A Difficulty in the Path of Psycho-Analysis' (1917).
'Mourning and Melancholia' (1917 [1915]).
'From the History of an Infantile Neurosis' (1918 [1914]).
'"A Child is Being Beaten": A Contribution to the Study of the Origin of the Sexual Perversions' (1919).
'The "Uncanny"' (1919).
Beyond the Pleasure Principle (1920).
Group Psychology and the Analysis of the Ego (1921).
The Ego and the Id (1923).
'The Dissolution of the Oedipus Complex' (1924).
'A Short Account of Psycho-Analysis' (1924 [1923]).
An Autobiographical Study (1925 [1924]).

'The Resistances to Psycho-Analysis' (1925 [1924]).
Inhibitions, Symptoms and Anxiety (1926 [1925]).
The Question of Lay Analysis: Conversations with an Impartial Person (1926).
The Future of an Illusion (1927).
'Dostoevsky and Parricide' (1928 [1927]).
Civilization and its Discontents (1930 [1929]).
New Introductory Lectures on Psycho-Analysis (1933 [1932]).
'A Disturbance of Memory on the Acropolis' (1936).
'Analysis Terminable and Interminable' (1937).
Moses and Monotheism: Three Essays (1939 [1937–39]).
An Outline of Psycho-Analysis (1940 [1938]).
'Psychopathic Characters on the Stage' (1942 [1905–6]).
'Project for a Scientific Psychology' (1950 [1887–1902]).
'Memorandum on the Electrical Treatment of War Neurotics' (1955 [1920])
Aus den Anfängen der Psychoanalyse: Briefe an Wilhelm Fliess, Abhandlungen und Notzien aus den Jahren 1887–1902, ed. Anna Freud and Ernest Kris (London: Imago, 1950).
Sigmund Freud and Lou Andreas-Salomé: Letters, ed. Ernst Pfeiffer (London: Hogarth Press / Institute of Psycho-Analysis, 1972).
The Complete Letters of Sigmund Freud to Wilhelm Fliess, 1887–1904, trans. and ed. Jeffrey Moussaief Masson (Cambridge, MA: Belknap Press of Harvard University Press, 1985).
A Phylogenetic Fantasy: Overview of the Transference Neuroses, ed. Ilse Grubrich-Simitis, trans. Alex Hoffer and Peter T. Hoffer (Cambridge, MA: Belknap Press of Harvard University Press, 1987).
The Complete Correspondence of Sigmund Freud and Ernest Jones, 1908–1939, ed. R. Andrew Paskauskas (Cambridge, MA: Belknap Press of Harvard University Press, 1993).
The Correspondence of Sigmund Freud and Sándor Ferenczi. Volume 2, 1914–1919, ed. Ernst Falzeder and Eva Brabant, trans. Peter T. Hoffer (Cambridge, MA: Belknap Press of Harvard University Press, 1996).

General commentary on psychoanalysis

Armstrong, Richard H., *A Compulsion for Antiquity: Freud and the Ancient World* (Ithaca, NY: Cornell University Press, 2005).
Arruti, Nerea, 'Trauma, Therapy and Representation: Theory and Critical Reflection', *Paragraph* 30: 1 (March 2007), 1–8.
Bernheimer, Charles and Claire Kahane (eds), *In Dora's Case: Freud–Hysteria–Feminism* (London: Virago, 1985).
Bouveresse, Jacques, *Wittgenstein Reads Freud: The Myth of the Unconscious* (1992), trans. Carol Cosman (Princeton, NJ: Princeton University Press, 1995).
Buck, Claire, *H.D. and Freud: Bisexuality and a Feminine Discourse* (Hemel Hempstead: Harvester Wheatsheaf, 1991).
Butler, Judith, *Gender Trouble: Feminism and the Subversion of Identity* (London: Routledge, 1990).
Caruth, Cathy (ed.), *Trauma: Explorations in Memory* (Baltimore, MD: Johns Hopkins University Press, 1995).

Davidson, Arnold I., 'How to Do the History of Psychoanalysis: a Reading of Freud's *Three Essays on the Theory of Sexuality*', *Critical Inquiry* 13: 2 (Winter 1987), 252–77.

Ellenberger, Henri F., *The Discovery of the Unconscious: The History and Evolution of Dynamic Psychiatry* (London: Fontana, 1970).

——, *Beyond the Unconscious: Essays of Henri F. Ellenberger in the History of Psychiatry*, ed. Mark S. Micale, trans. Françoise Dubor and Micale (Princeton, NJ: Princeton University Press, 1993).

Forrester, John, *The Seductions of Psychoanalysis: Freud, Lacan and Derrida* (Cambridge: Cambridge University Press, 1990).

——, *Dispatches from the Freud Wars: Psychoanalysis and Its Passions* (Cambridge, MA: Harvard University Press, 1997).

Gardiner, Muriel, *The Wolf-Man and Sigmund Freud* (London: Hogarth Press/ Institute of Psycho-Analysis, 1972).

Jones, Ernest, *Sigmund Freud: Life and Work. The Last Phase 1919–1939* (London: Hogarth Press, 1957).

Jung, C.G., *The Spirit in Man, Art and Literature* (1967), trans. R.E.C. Hull (London: ARK, 1984).

Laplanche, Jean, *Life and Death in Psychoanalysis* (1970), trans. Jeffrey Mehlman (Baltimore, MD: Johns Hopkins University Press, 1976).

——, *New Foundations for Psychoanalysis* (1987), trans. David Macey (Oxford: Basil Blackwell, 1989).

Laplanche, Jean and J.-B. Pontalis, 'Fantasy and the Origins of Sexuality', *International Journal of Psycho-Analysis* 49: 1 (1968), 1–18.

——, *The Language of Psychoanalysis*, trans. Donald Nicholson-Smith (London: Hogarth Press, 1973).

Lear, Jonathan, *Freud* (New York: Routledge, 2005).

Mahony, Patrick, *Freud and the Rat Man* (New Haven, CT: Yale University Press, 1986).

——, *Freud as a Writer*, expanded edn (New Haven, CT: Yale University Press, 1987).

Malcolm, Janet, *In the Freud Archives* (London: Jonathan Cape, 1984).

Marcuse, Herbert, *Eros and Civilization: A Philosophical Enquiry into Freud* (1955), 2nd edn (Boston: Beacon Press, 1966).

Rand, Nicholas and Maria Torok, 'The Secret of Psychoanalysis: History Reads Theory', trans. Nicholas Rand, *Critical Inquiry* 13: 2 (Winter 1987), 278–86.

——, 'Questions to Freudian Psychoanalysis: Dream Interpretation, Reality, Fantasy', trans. Nicholas Rand, *Critical Inquiry* 19: 3 (Spring 1993), 567–94.

——, *Questions for Freud: The Secret History of Psychoanalysis* (Cambridge, MA: Harvard University Press, 1997).

Rank, Otto, *The Trauma of Birth* (1929) (New York: Dover Publications, 1993).

Ricoeur, Paul, *Freud and Philosophy: An Essay on Interpretation*, trans. Dennis Savage (New Haven, CT: Yale University Press, 1970).

Rieff, Philip, *Freud: The Mind of the Moralist* (1959), 3rd edn with a new epilogue (Chicago, IL: University of Chicago Press, 1979).

——, *The Triumph of the Therapeutic: Uses of Faith After Freud* (London: Chatto and Windus, 1966).

——, *Fellow Teachers* (London: Faber and Faber, 1975).

——, *The Feeling Intellect: Selected Writings*, ed. Jonathan B. Imber (Chicago, IL: University of Chicago Press, 1990).

Roazen, Paul, *Freud and His Followers* (1975) (Harmondsworth: Penguin, 1979).
Robinson, Paul, *Freud and His Critics* (Berkeley: University of California Press, 1993).
Rose, Jacqueline, *Why War? – Psychoanalysis, Politics and the Return to Melanie Klein* (Oxford: Blackwell, 1993).
Roth, Michael S., *Psycho-Analysis as History: Negation and Freedom in Freud*, with a new postscript (Ithaca, NY: Cornell University Press, 1995).
Schorske, Carl E., *Fin-de-siècle Vienna: Politics and Culture* (Cambridge: Cambridge University Press, 1981).
Schur, Max, *Freud: Living and Dying* (London: Hogarth Press, 1972).
Spector, Jack, *The Aesthetics of Freud: A Study in Psychoanalysis and Art* (London: Allen Lane/Penguin, 1972).
von Unwerth, Matthew, *Freud's Requiem: Mourning, Memory and the Invisible History of a Summer Walk* (London: Continuum, 2005)
Wollheim, Richard, *Freud* (1971), 2nd edn (London: Fontana, 1991).
——, *On Art and the Mind* (Cambridge, MA: Harvard University Press, 1974).
Wright, Elizabeth (ed.), *Feminism and Psychoanalysis: A Critical Dictionary* (Oxford: Blackwell, 1992).
Yerushalmi, Yosef Hayim, *Freud's Moses: Judaism Terminable and Interminable* (New Haven, CT: Yale University Press, 1991).

The 'Literary Freud'

Barthes, Roland, *A Lover's Discourse: Fragments* (1977), trans. Richard Howard (London: Jonathan Cape, 1979).
Bersani, Leo, *The Freudian Body: Psychoanalysis and Art* (New York: Columbia University Press, 1986).
Bloom, Harold, *The Anxiety of Influence: A Theory of Poetry* (Oxford: Oxford University Press, 1973).
——, *A Map of Misreading* (Oxford: Oxford University Press, 1975).
——, *Poetry and Repression: Revisionism from Blake to Stevens* (New Haven, CT: Yale University Press, 1976).
——, *Agon: Towards a Theory of Revisionism* (Oxford: Oxford University Press, 1982).
——, *The Breaking of the Vessels* (Chicago, IL: University of Chicago Press, 1982).
——, *The Western Canon: The Books and School of the Ages* (London: Macmillan, 1995).
Bowie, Malcolm, *Freud, Proust and Lacan: Theory as Fiction* (Cambridge: Cambridge University Press, 1987).
——, *Lacan* (London: Fontana, 1991).
——, *Psychoanalysis and the Future of Theory* (Oxford: Blackwell, 1993).
Brooks, Peter, *Reading for the Plot: Design and Intention in Narrative* (1984) (Cambridge, MA: Harvard University Press, 1992).
——, *Psychoanalysis and Storytelling* (Oxford: Blackwell, 1994).
Edmundson, Mark, *Towards Reading Freud: Self-Creation in Milton, Wordsworth, Emerson, and Sigmund Freud* (Princeton, NJ: Princeton University Press, 1990).
——, *Literature against Philosophy: A Defence of Poetry* (Cambridge: Cambridge University Press, 1995).

Kofman, Sarah, *The Childhood of Art: An Interpretation of Freud's Aesthetics* (3rd edn, 1985), trans. Winifred Woodhull (New York: Columbia University Press, 1988).

Lukacher, Ned, *Primal Scenes: Literature, Philosophy, Psychoanalysis* (Ithaca, NY: Cornell University Press, 1986).

Marcus, Steven, *Freud and the Culture of Psychoanalysis: Studies in the Transition from Victorian Humanism to Modernity* (London: George Allen and Unwin, 1984).

McGrath, William J., *Freud's Discovery of Psychoanalysis: The Politics of Hysteria* (Ithaca, NY: Cornell University Press, 1986).

Obholzer, Karin, *The Wolf-Man: Conversations with Freud's Patient – Sixty Years Later* (1980), trans. Michael Shaw (London: Routledge and Kegan Paul, 1982).

Rashkin, Esther, *Family Secrets and the Psychoanalysis of Narrative* (Princeton, NJ: Princeton University Press, 1992).

Rimmon-Kenan, Shlomith (ed.), *Discourse in Psychoanalysis and Literature* (London: Methuen, 1987).

Trilling, Lionel, 'Freud and Literature' (1940), in *The Liberal Imagination* (Oxford: Oxford University Press, 1981).

Wright, Elizabeth, *Psychoanalytic Criticism: Theory in Practice*, with a new appendix (London: Routledge, 1987).

Post-structuralist approaches

Abraham, Nicolas, 'Notes on the Phantom: A Complement to Freud's Metapsychology' (1975), in Abraham and Maria Torok, *The Shell and the Kernel: Renewals of Psychoanalysis* (1987), ed. and trans. Nicholas T. Rand (Chicago, IL: University of Chicago, 1994).

Abraham, Nicolas and Maria Torok, *The Wolf Man's Magic Word: A Cryptonymy* (1976), trans. Nicholas Rand (Minneapolis: University of Minnesota Press, 1986).

Borch-Jacobsen, Mikkel, *The Freudian Subject* (1988), trans. Catherine Porter (London: Macmillan, 1989).

——, *The Emotional Tie* (1991), trans. Douglas Brick and others (Stanford, CA: Stanford University Press, 1993).

——, *Remembering Anna O.: A Century of Mystification*, trans. Kirby Olson in collaboration with Xavier Callahan and the author (New York: Routledge, 1996).

Caruth, Cathy, *Empirical Truths and Critical Fictions: Locke, Wordsworth, Kant, Freud* (Baltimore, MD: Johns Hopkins University Press, 1991).

——, *Unclaimed Experience: Trauma, Narrative and History* (Baltimore, MD: Johns Hopkins University Press, 1996).

Certeau, Michel de, *The Writing of History* (1975), trans. Tom Conley (New York: Columbia University Press, 1988).

Chase, Cynthia, 'Oedipal Textuality: Reading Freud's Reading of *Oedipus*', *Diacritics* 9: 1 (Spring 1979), 54–68.

——, 'The Witty Butcher's Wife: Freud, Lacan, and the Conversion of Resistance to Theory', *MLN* 102: 5 (December 1987), 989–1013.

Girard, René, *Violence and the Sacred* (1972), trans. Patrick Gregory (Baltimore, MD: Johns Hopkins University Press, 1979).

Hartman, Geoffrey (ed.), *Psychoanalysis and the Question of the Text* (Baltimore, MD: Johns Hopkins University Press, 1978).

Johnson, Barbara, *The Critical Difference: Essays in the Contemporary Rhetoric of Reading* (London: Johns Hopkins University Press, 1980).

Muller, John P., and William J. Richardson (eds), *The Purloined Poe: Lacan, Derrida and Psychoanalytic Reading* (Baltimore, MD: Johns Hopkins University Press, 1988).

Royle, Nicholas, *Telepathy and Literature: Essays on the Reading Mind* (Oxford: Basil Blackwell, 1991).

——, *After Derrida* (Manchester: Manchester University Press, 1995).

Smith, Robert, *Derrida and Autobiography* (Cambridge: Cambridge University Press, 1995).

——, 'The Death Drive Does Not Think', *Common Knowledge* 5: 1 (Spring 1996).

Weber, Samuel, *The Legend of Freud* (1979), expanded edn (Stanford, CA: Stanford University Press, 2000).

White, Rob, 'Archive Power', *Oxford Literary Review* 21 (1999), 161–80.

Derrida on Freud, mourning

Derrida, Jacques, *Writing and Difference* (1967), trans. Alan Bass (London: Routledge and Kegan Paul, 1978).

——, 'My Chances/*Mes Chances*: A Rendezvous with Some Epicurean Stereophonies' (1984), trans. Irene Harvey and Avital Ronell, in Joseph H. Smith and William Kerrigan (eds), *Taking Chances: Derrida, Psychoanalysis, and Literature* (Baltimore, MD: Johns Hopkins University Press, 1984).

——, '*Fors*: The Anglish Words of Nicolas Abraham and Maria Torok' (1977), trans. Barbara Johnson, in Abraham and Torok, *The Wolf Man's Magic Word: A Cryptonymy*, trans. Nicholas Rand (Minneapolis: University of Minnesota Press, 1986).

——, *The Post Card: from Socrates to Freud and Beyond* (1980), trans. Alan Bass (Chicago, IL: University of Chicago Press, 1987).

——, 'Telepathy' (1980), trans. Nicholas Royle, *Oxford Literary Review* 10 (1988), 3–41.

——, *Mémoires: for Paul de Man*, rev. edn, trans. Cecile Lindsay, Jonathan Culler, Eduardo Cadava and Peggy Kamuf (Oxford: Columbia University Press, 1989).

——, 'Before the Law' (1985), trans. Avital Ronell and Christine Roulston, in Derek Attridge (ed.), *Acts of Literature* (London: Routledge, 1992).

——, *Specters of Marx: The State of the Debt, the Work of Mourning, and the New International* (1993), trans. Peggy Kamuf (London: Routledge, 1994).

——, *Archive Fever: A Freudian Impression* (1995), trans. Eric Prenowitz (Chicago, IL: University of Chicago Press, 1996).

——, *Resistances of Psychoanalysis* (1996), trans. Peggy Kamuf, Pascale-Anne Brault and Michael Naas (Stanford, CA: Stanford University Press).

——, *Of Hospitality. Anne Dufourmantelle Invites Jacques Derrida to Respond* (1997), trans. Rachel Bowlby (Stanford, CA: Stanford University Press, 2000).

——, 'Psychoanalysis Searches the States of Its Soul: The Impossible Beyond of a Sovereign Cruelty' (2000), in Derrida, *Without Alibi*, ed. and trans. Peggy Kamuf (Stanford, CA: Stanford University Press, 2002).

—— and Elisabeth Roudinesco, *For What Tomorrow … : A Dialogue* (2001), trans. Jeff Fort (Stanford, CA: Stanford University Press, 2004)

Psycho-Lamarckism, science

Assoun, Paul-Laurent, *Introduction à l'épistémologie Freudienne* (Paris: Payot, 1981).

Badcock, Charles [C.R.], *The Psychoanalysis of Culture* (Oxford: Blackwell, 1980).

——, *PsychoDarwinism: The New Synthesis of Darwin and Freud* (London: HarperCollins, 1994).

Edelheit, Henry, 'On the Biology of Language: Darwinian/Lamarckian Homology in Human Inheritance (with Some Thoughts about the Lamarckism of Freud)', in *Psychoanalysis and Language*, ed. Joseph H. Smith (New Haven, NJ: Yale University Press, 1978).

Gould, Stephen Jay, *Ontogeny and Phylogeny* (Cambridge, MA: Belknap Press of Harvard University Press, 1977).

——, 'Freud's Phylogenetic Fantasy', *Natural History* 96: 12 (December 1987), 10–19.

Ritvo, Lucille B., *Darwin's Influence on Freud: A Tale of Two Sciences* (New Haven, CT: Yale University Press, 1990).

Sulloway, Frank J., *Freud, Biologist of the Mind. Beyond the Psychoanalytic Legend* (1979), with a new preface (Cambridge, MA: Harvard University Press, 1992).

Sceptical views

Cioffi, Frank, 'Freud – New Myths to Replace the Old', *New Society* 50: 895 (29 November 1979), 503–4.

——, *Freud and the Question of Pseudoscience* (Chicago: Open Court, 1998).

Clark, Peter, and Crispin Wright (eds), *Mind, Psychoanalysis and Science* (Oxford: Basil Blackwell, 1988).

Crews, Frederick et al., *The Memory Wars: Freud's Legacy in Dispute* (London: Granta, 1997).

Dufresne, Todd, *Against Freud: Critics Talk Back* (Stanford, CA: Stanford University Press, 2007).

——, *Tales from the Freudian Crypt: The Death Drive in Text and Context* (Stanford, CA: Stanford University Press, 2000)

Farrell, John, *Freud's Paranoid Quest: Psychoanalysis and Modern Suspicion* (New York: New York University Press, 1996).

Fish, Stanley, *Doing What Comes Naturally: Change, Rhetoric, and the Practice of Theory in Literary and Legal Studies* (Oxford: Oxford University Press, 1989).

Macmillan, Malcolm, *Freud Evaluated: The Completed Arc* (1991) (Cambridge, MA: MIT Press, 1997).

Masson, Jeffrey Moussaieff, *The Assault on Truth: Freud's Suppression of the Seduction Theory* (London: Faber and Faber, 1984); retitled *The Assault on Truth; Freud and Child Sexual Abuse*, with a revised preface and afterword (London: Fontana, 1992).

Masson, Jeffrey Moussaieff, *Final Analysis: The Making and Unmaking of a Psychoanalyst* (London: HarperCollins, 1991).

——, *Against Therapy*, new edn (London: Fontana, 1993).

Roustang, François, *Dire Mastery: Discipleship from Freud to Lacan* (1976), trans. Ned Lukacher (Baltimore, MD: Johns Hopkins University Press, 1982).

——, *Psychoanalysis Never Lets Go* (1980), trans. Ned Lukacher (Baltimore, MD: Johns Hopkins University Press, 1983).

——, *How to Make a Paranoid Laugh, or, What Is Psychoanalysis?*, trans. Anne C. Vila (Philadelphia: University of Pennsylvania Press, 2000).

Webster, Richard, *Why Freud Was Wrong: Sin, Science and Psychoanalysis* (London: HarperCollins, 1995).

Beyond psychoanalysis

Bersani, Leo, 'Is the Rectum a Grave?, in Douglas Crimp (ed.), *AIDS: Cultural Analysis, Cultural Activism* (Cambridge, MA: MIT Press, 1988).

——, *Homos* (Cambridge, MA: Harvard University Press, 1995).

——, 'Against Monogamy', *Oxford Literary Review* 20 (1998), 3–22.

Bersani, Leo and Ulysse Dutoit, *Caravaggio's Secrets* (Cambridge, MA: MIT Press, 1998).

——, *Caravaggio* (London: BFI Publishing, 1999).

——, *Forms of Being: Cinema, Aesthetics, Subjectivity* (London: BFI Publishing, 2004).

Deleuze, Gilles, 'Coldness and Cruelty' (1967), trans. Jean McNeil, in Deleuze and Leopold von Sacher-Masoch, *Masochism* (New York: Zone, 1989).

—— and Félix Guattari, *Anti-Oedipus: Capitalism and Schizophrenia* (1972), trans. Robert Hurley, Mark Seem and Helen R. Lane (London: Athlone, 1984).

Foucault, Michel, *Madness and Civilization: A History of Insanity in the Age of Reason* (1961), trans. Richard Howard (London: Tavistock Publications, 1967).

——, 'My Body, this Paper, this Fire' (1971), trans. Geoff Bennington, *Oxford Literary Review* 4: 1 (Autumn 1979), 5–28.

——, *Discipline and Punish: The Birth of the Prison* (1975), trans. Alan Sheridan (London: Peregrine, 1979).

——, *Language, Counter-Memory, Practice: Selected Essays and Interviews*, ed. Donald F. Bouchard, trans. Bouchard and Sherry Simon (Ithaca, NY: Cornell University Press, 1977).

——, *The History of Sexuality, vol. 1: An Introduction* (1976), trans. Robert Hurley (London: Pelican, 1981).

Goux, Jean-Joseph, *Oedipus, Philosopher*, trans. Catherine Porter (Stanford, CA: Stanford University Press, 1993).

Other works

Assmann, Jan, *Moses the Egyptian: The Memory of Egypt in Western Monotheism* (Cambridge, MA: Harvard University Press, 1997).

Malcolm, Norman, *Ludwig Wittgenstein: A Memoir* (London: Oxford University Press, 1958)
Rose, Gillian, *Mourning Becomes the Law: Philosophy and Representation* (Cambridge: Cambridge University Press, 1996).
The American Medical Association Encyclopedia of Medicine, ed. Charles B. Clayman (New York: Random House, 1989).
Wittgenstein, Ludwig, *Lectures and Conversations on Aesthetics, Psychology and Religious Belief*, ed. Cyril Barrett (Oxford: Blackwell, 1966).
——, 'Conversations on Freud' (1970 [1946]), noted by Rush Rhees, in *Sigmund Freud: Critical Assessments*, ed. Laurence Spurling, vol. 4 (London: Routledge, 1989).

Index